Doing Optimality Theory

Applying Theory to Data

John J. McCarthy

D1157343

Blackwell
Publishing

BLACKWELL PUBLISHING
350 Main Street, Malden, MA 02148-5020, USA
9600 Garsington Road, Oxford OX4 2DQ, UK
550 Swanston Street, Carlton, Victoria 3053, Australia

The right of John McCarthy to be identified as the author of this work has been
asserted in accordance with the UK Copyright, Designs, and Patents Act 1988.

First published 2008 by Blackwell Publishing Ltd

1   2008

Library of Congress Cataloging-in-Publication Data

McCarthy, John J., 1953-
    Doing optimality theory : applying theory to data / John J. McCarthy.
        p. cm.
    Includes bibliographical references and index.
    ISBN 978-1-4051-5135-1 (hardcover : alk. paper) — ISBN 978-1-4051-5136-8
(pbk. : alk. paper)   1. Optimality theory (Linguistics)   2. Constraints (Linguistics)
I. Title.

    P158.42.M429 2008
    415'.018—dc22

                                                                2007051238

A catalogue record for this title is available from the British Library.

Set in 10/12.5pt Palatino
by Graphicraft Limited, Hong Kong

The publisher's policy is to use permanent paper from mills that operate a sustainable
forestry policy, and which has been manufactured from pulp processed using acid-
free and elementary chlorine-free practices. Furthermore, the publisher ensures that
the text paper and cover board used have met acceptable environmental accreditation
standards.

For further information on
Blackwell Publishing, visit our website at
www.blackwellpublishing.com

Contents

Acknowledgments

This book is the product of 15 years of teaching Optimality Theory to undergraduate and graduate students at the University of Massachusetts Amherst and at two Linguistic Institutes (Cornell in 1997 and MIT in 2005). Some of it was first circulated on CD-ROM as a collection of handouts for teaching OT (McCarthy 1999). The many students I have taught over the years have shaped this work profoundly.

My colleague Joe Pater, who shares responsibility for teaching introductory phonology at the University of Massachusetts, has been an important influence, as have John Kingston and Lisa Selkirk. Alan Prince and I have talked many times about the challenges of teaching and doing OT, and I have learned much from him. His comments on portions of chapter 2 were valuable and led to significant changes in the presentation.

I am very grateful for help from the members of our weekly phonology group, who devoted a meeting to helping me brainstorm about what should go in this book and another meeting to going over the results: Leah Bateman, Michael Becker, Tim Beechey, Ioana Chitoran (Dartmouth College), Emily Elfner, Kathryn Flack, Elena Innes, Gaja Jarosz, Karen Jesney, Mike Key, Wendell Kimper, Kathryn Pruitt, Ma Qiuwu (Nankai University), Nathan Sanders (Williams College), Ellen Simon (Ghent University), and Matt Wolf. In addition, I received useful written comments from Ubiratã Kickhöfel Alves, Ioana Chitoran, Gaja Jarosz, and Shigeto Kawahara. The students in a course I taught at the III Seminário Internacional de Fonologia in Porto Alegre, Brazil, gave me lots of good feedback through their comments and questions.

Kathryn Flack read the entire book and gave me literally hundreds of useful and insightful comments. I've used as many of them as I could. I'm also grateful to Anna Oxbury for her superb work copy-editing the manuscript.

This book is dedicated to my nephews and niece Michael, Jack, and Kennedy McCarthy.

Read This First!

The goal of this book is to explain how to do analysis and research in Optimality Theory. Many of OT's basic premises are very different from other linguistic theories. This means that OT requires new and often unfamiliar ways of developing analyses, arguing for them, and even writing them up. Furthermore, the research frontier in OT isn't too distant from the core of basic knowledge. For this reason, any analyst, even a novice, may soon find herself or himself in the position of making proposals about universal grammar.

Throughout this book, there is plenty of practical advice – do this, but don't do that! This advice is presented in a maximally general way, but it's also illustrated with specific examples. The examples require minimal previous background, and explanatory notes (printed in a box) are included wherever necessary. The intended audience includes readers who are encountering OT for the first time as well as those who are more advanced. Because of its focus on practical matters, this book is a good companion to my *Thematic Guide to Optimality Theory* (McCarthy 2002), which has a more theoretical and polemical orientation.

Chapter 1 provides a succinct summary of the core concepts of OT. Readers who are new to OT will want to read this chapter closely. Chapter 2 explains how to construct, justify, and test an analysis. Chapter 3 is the expositional counterpart to chapter 2: it provides suggestions and a model for writing up OT analyses in a way that is clear and persuasive. A lot of chapter 3's advice about writing in linguistics is independent of OT, so even readers who aren't interested in OT might find it useful.

In OT, it's sometimes necessary to posit new universal constraints or modify old ones. This special responsibility is the topic of chapter 4.

Positing a new constraint changes the typological predictions, and so chapter 5 addresses that topic. Finally, chapter 6 introduces some of the areas of recent research.

Every few pages, there are sections labeled "Exercises" or "Questions." The primarily theoretical chapters (1 and 6) have more questions than exercises, and the primarily practical chapters (2–5) have more exercises than questions. The exercises call for pencil and paper (or computer and keyboard); they are good practice and suitable as homework assignments. A few of the questions could also be assigned as homework, but most of them are more open-ended; they are intended to stimulate thought and discussion. By dispersing the exercises and questions throughout the book rather than leaving them for the ends of chapters, I hope to encourage readers to master each concept or technique before going on and to engage in a continuing dialogue with the text and with their classmates and teachers.

Abbreviations

Abbreviations of constraint names can be found in the index of constraints.

C	Any consonant
CON	Constraint component of Optimality Theory
EVAL	Evaluator component of Optimality Theory
GB	Government Binding Theory (Chomsky 1981)
GEN	Generator component of Optimality Theory
OT	Optimality Theory
ROA	Rutgers Optimality Archive, http://roa.rutgers.edu
SPE	*The Sound Pattern of English* (Chomsky and Halle 1968)
t	A syntactic trace
UG	Universal grammar
V	Any vowel
XP	Any phrasal category

1

An Introduction to Optimality Theory

1.1 How OT Began

Around 1990, Alan Prince and Paul Smolensky began collaborating on a new theory of human language. This collaboration led in fairly short order to a book-length manuscript, *Optimality Theory: Constraint Interaction in Generative Grammar*. Photocopies of the manuscript were widely distributed and had a terrific impact on the field of linguistics, even though it wasn't formally published until more than a decade later (as Prince and Smolensky 1993/2004). OT had and continues to have its greatest effect on phonology, but it has also led to important work in syntax, semantics, sociolinguistics, historical linguistics, and other areas. OT belongs on anyone's list of the top three developments in the history of generative grammar.

One of Prince and Smolensky's goals for OT was to solve a long-standing problem in phonology. Phonological theory in the tradition of Chomsky and Halle's (1968) *The Sound Pattern of English* (*SPE*) was based on rewrite rules. The rewrite rule $A \rightarrow B/C\_\_D$ describes an input configuration CAD and an $A \rightarrow B$ transformation that applies to it. Rewrite rules can describe lots of phenomena, but they do a poor job of explaining how phonological systems fit together. (For a brief explanation of *SPE*'s main assumptions, see the boxed text at the end of this section.)

To illustrate, we'll look at some data from Yawelmani, a nearly extinct dialect of the California Penutian language Yokuts (Newman 1944).[1] In this language, syllables cannot be bigger than CVC (consonant-vowel-consonant). Various phonological processes are involved with this limit on syllable size. For instance, Yawelmani has a process that deletes a vowel at the end of a word, as the data in (a) of (1) show. (The "." marks the boundary between two syllables.) But the data in (b) show that final vowels do not delete when they are preceded by a consonant cluster. The explanation for the difference between (a) and (b) is that deletion after a cluster would require a syllable that is too big or leave a consonant that cannot be syllabified: *[xatk$^?$].[2]

(1) Yawelmani final vowel deletion

	Underlying	Surface	
a.	/taxaː-k$^?$a/	[ta.xak$^?$]	'bring!'
	/taxaː-mi/	[ta.xam]	'having brought'
b.	/xat-k$^?$a/	[xat.k$^?$a]	'eat!'
	/xat-mi/	[xat.mi]	'having eaten'

Yawelmani also has a process of vowel epenthesis that applies to a cluster of three consonants in the middle of a word. (See (2). The data in (a) show epenthesis into triconsonantal clusters, and the data in (b) show that there is no epenthesis in smaller clusters.) If there were no epenthesis process, then the result would again be a syllable that is too big or a consonant that cannot be syllabified: *[?ilk.hin].

(2) Yawelmani vowel epenthesis

	Underlying	Surface	
a.	/?ilk-hin/	[?i.lik.hin]	'sing (nonfuture)'
	/lihm-hin/	[li.him.hin]	'run (nonfuture)'
b.	/?ilk-al/	[?il.kal]	'sing (dubitative)'
	/lihm-al/	[lih.mal]	'run (dubitative)'

It is certainly possible to state *SPE*-style rewrite rules to account for these two processes in Yawelmani – V → Ø/VC___# and Ø → i/C___CC will do the job nicely. But, as Kisseberth (1970) first argued, those rewrite rules are missing an important generalization about the special role of surface-structure constraints in both rules. Final vowel deletion cannot create bad syllables in surface forms, and epenthesis exists to eliminate them. Adopting a suggestion from Haj Ross, Kisseberth called this situation a *conspiracy*.

When two or more rewrite rules are involved in a conspiracy, they directly or indirectly support some constraint on surface forms. In Yawelmani, the relevant constraints are a CVC limit on syllable size and a prohibition on unsyllabified consonants. Final vowel deletion is *blocked* from applying when it would produce a surface form like *[xatkʔ], which cannot be fully parsed into maximally CVC syllables. Epenthesis is *triggered* to apply by the need to fix sequences that cannot be parsed into CVC syllables. In every conspiracy there is a constraint on surface forms, which we can refer to more succinctly as an output constraint, since it evaluates the output of the grammar. There is also some mixture of processes that are blocked by that output constraint and/or processes that are triggered by it.

Conspiracies are common in the languages of the world, and so it was a matter of some concern that the *SPE* theory of rewrite rules couldn't explain them. A rewrite rule, by its very nature, describes an input configuration and an operation that applies to it. A conspiracy is completely different: it refers to an output configuration, it involves several different operations, and those operations may participate in the conspiracy by applying or failing to apply, depending on the circumstances. When analysts try to describe conspiratorial behavior in terms of rewrite rules, they have to start using counterfactuals, as I did in the preceding paragraph: "blocked from applying when it *would* produce," "to fix sequences that *could* not be parsed." Statements like these show that the analyst understands what's really going on in the language, but counterfactual conditions have no place in *SPE*'s theory of how to apply rules. When a phonologist says something like "The epenthesis rule ensures that the language has only unmarked syllables," he or she is describing an intuition about how the system works. But that intuition has to be expressed formally, in the theory itself. Otherwise, we are just telling ourselves stories.

At around the same time that phonologists were beginning to grasp the importance of output constraints, syntacticians were having a similar revelation. For example, clitic movement in Spanish is triggered by an output constraint requiring that second person clitics precede first person clitics (Perlmutter 1971). That is why the direct and indirect objects appear in different orders in *Te$_{IO}$ me$_{DO}$ presento* 'I introduce myself to you' versus *Te$_{DO}$ me$_{IO}$ presentas* 'You introduce yourself to me.' Another example: in English, movement of *wh*-question words is blocked when it would leave the trace of *wh* immediately after the complementizer *that* (Chomsky and Lasnik 1977): **Who did you say that t left?* (cf. *Who did you say t left?*). These syntactic examples have parallels in Yawelmani phonology. The triggering of clitic movement by an output constraint in Spanish is like the triggering of epenthesis in Yawelmani. And the blocking of *wh*-movement in English is like the blocking of final vowel deletion in Yawelmani.

Chomsky and Lasnik (1977) proposed a theory of output constraints and their function that had (and continues to have) a great deal of influence in syntax. Their main idea is that all of the rewrite rules – that is, the syntactic transformations – are technically optional. An input to the grammar freely undergoes any, all, or none of the transformations. The result of freely applying transformations is a set of candidate surface structures. These candidate surface structures are checked by the output constraints, which are called filters, and some of them are marked as ungrammatical by the filters. For instance, the *wh*-movement transformation applies optionally, producing both *Who did you say that t left?* and *You said that who left?* as candidate surface structures. The *that*-trace filter marks the first of these as ungrammatical, so only the second is well-formed. Henceforth, I'll refer to Chomsky and Lasnik's proposal as the *filters model*.

The filters model does a good job of explaining how output constraints can seem to trigger or block transformations. Because the transformations are strictly optional, if there is a candidate surface structure that has undergone a transformation T, there is also a candidate derived from the same deep structure that has not undergone T. If a filter marks the result of applying T as ungrammatical, then the filter has in effect blocked T, since the derivation in which T has applied does not lead to a well-formed output. If a filter marks the result of *not* applying T as ungrammatical, then the filter has in effect triggered T, since the derivation in which T has failed to apply does not lead to a well-formed output. The filter isn't literally triggering or blocking T – it cannot, since the filter doesn't even apply in the same grammatical component as T – but the filter appears to be blocking or triggering T by ruling out the surface structure where T has or has not applied.

A goal of the filters model was to shift most of the burden of explaining syntactic patterns from the theory of transformations to the theory of filters. Transformations could be made much simpler and more general. In Government-Binding Theory (GB) (Chomsky 1981), the theory of transformations withered away almost entirely, leaving just the transformation Move α.

Although the filters model in syntax emerged not long after the discovery of the conspiracy problem in phonology, the filters model had surprisingly little influence on the field of phonology at that time. There are two main reasons for this, in my opinion. One of them, which I will explain in the next section, is that the filters model fails as an explanation for phonological conspiracies like Yawelmani's if output constraints are inviolable, and constraints of that era were always assumed to be inviolable.

The other reason is that the field of phonology was so strongly influenced by *SPE*. *SPE*'s central hypothesis is that rules with simpler formulations are more natural, in the sense that they are more likely to occur in languages and to express linguistically significant generalizations. In accordance with this hypothesis, the *SPE* theory supplies abbreviatory devices that allow putatively natural rules to be formulated more simply. In a conspiracy, the output constraint is what makes the rules natural – the output constraint is the generalization that unites the disparate rules. Therefore, a theory of conspiracies embedded in the overall *SPE* research program would have to use the output constraint to simplify the statement of the rules that participate in the conspiracy.

Kisseberth (1970) proposed a theory of blocking effects along exactly these lines. He assumed for yawelmani an output constraint *CC{C, #} that is violated by medial clusters of three consonants or final clusters of two consonants. By assumption, a rule is blocked from applying if its immediate output violates this constraint. That assumption allows the formulation of the final vowel deletion rule to be simplified from $V \rightarrow \emptyset / VC\_\_\#$ to $V \rightarrow \emptyset / \_\_\#$. And since simpler rules are more natural under *SPE*'s assumptions, the existence of the output constraint has in some sense explained why final vowel deletion is blocked after consonant clusters.

Kiparsky (1973b: 77–78) presents several criticisms of this proposal. One problem is that the rule $V \rightarrow \emptyset / \_\_\#$ is just as as simple, and therefore should be just as natural, in a language without the *CC{C, #} output constraint. But a language without the output constraint is a language without the conspiracy, and if conspiracies contribute to naturalness, then the language without one should be *less* natural. Another problem with this proposal is that it only works for blocking effects. Rules that are triggered by the output constraint won't receive simpler formulations. For instance, there is no way of using the output constraint to simplify the statement of the epenthesis rule, replacing $\emptyset \rightarrow i / C\_\_CC$ with, say, $\emptyset \rightarrow i / \_\_C$. The problem with $\emptyset \rightarrow i / \_\_C$ is that it would epenthesize [i] before every single consonant. The theory at that time lacked any sort of economy mechanism to ensure that epenthesis applies only when it's needed and not otherwise.

Starting in the mid-1970s, phonological research moved toward richer theories of representation that included syllables and other structures. As phonological representations became more elaborated, it became possible to imagine an almost ruleless phonology in which automatic satisfaction of universal constraints on representations was all that mattered. Goldsmith (1976a, 1976b) and Prince (1983) worked on proposals along these lines for autosegmental and metrical phonology, respectively. This work ran headlong into another problem, however: the proposed universal constraints did not hold in every language all of the time. That is why the subsequent literature on autosegmental and metrical phonology, such as Pulleyblank (1986) and Hayes (1995), returned to language-particular rewrite rules as the central analytic mechanism.

By the end of the 1980s, there was certainly a consensus about the importance of output constraints, but there were also major unresolved questions about the nature and activity of these constraints. That "conceptual crisis at the center of phonological thought," as Prince and Smolensky (1993/2004: 2) refer to it, was not very widely acknowledged at the time, but in hindsight it's hard to miss. It's a major feature of the intellectual context in which OT was developed.

Explanation: The *SPE* theory and its relation to OT phonology

In *SPE*, every morpheme is assumed to have a unique underlying representation that is stored in the lexicon. The underlying representation includes all of the unpredictable phonological properties of a morpheme. For example, the Yawelmani imperative suffix has surface alternants [-kʼa] and [-kʼ], and the nonfuture suffix has alternants [-mi] and [-m] (see (1)). Their underlying representations are /-kʼa/ and /-mi/. (The underlying representations couldn't be /-kʼ/ and /-m/, because there would be no good way of explaining why [a] is epenthesized in one suffix and [i] in the other.)

The mapping from underlying to surface representations is accomplished by applying a series of ordered rewrite rules. For instance, the path from /taxaː-kʼa/ to [ta.xakʼ] requires two rules: first, the final vowel is deleted, yielding [ta.xaːkʼ], and then the vowel is shortened to produce the surface form [ta.xakʼ]. As the text mentions, a rewrite rule is an expression A → B/C___D that changes any CAD sequence into a CBD sequence. OT does not have rewrite rules or anything that resembles them.

SPE also includes a theory of representations. Every speech sound consists of a bundle of values for certain universal, binary distinctive features: [nasal], [round], and so on. In the 1970s and 1980s, *SPE*'s rather simple representational theory was greatly enhanced. For instance, *SPE* does not include syllables in its representations, but later work would analyze the [ta.xaːkʔ] → [ta.xakʔ] mapping as a process of vowel shortening in a syllable that is closed by a consonant.

Most work in OT phonology presupposes *SPE*'s view of underlying representations, its theory of distinctive features, and many of the subsequent representational enhancements. It's important to realize, however, that OT itself does not require a commitment to any of these ideas.

QUESTIONS

1 How will the filters model work when several different transformations are applicable? What about when a transformation is applicable at several different places in a sentence? What about when a transformation is applicable to its own output?

2 The text promises that the next section will give an argument that the filters model cannot explain phonological conspiracies if constraints are inviolable. Try to figure out the argument before reading the section. (Hint: An output constraint is needed to ensure that final vowel deletion occurs in /taxaː-kʔa/ → [ta.xakʔ].)

EXERCISE

3 Yawelmani has output constraints that limit syllables to a CVC maximum and require exhaustive syllabification. In Yawelmani, these constraints trigger epenthesis and block final vowel deletion. Can you imagine a different language that has the same output constraints but which block and/or trigger other processes? Hypothetical examples are fine; it isn't necessary to identify actual languages.

1.2 Why Must Constraints Be Violable?

In the previous section, I alluded to a second reason why phonology did not develop an optional-rules-plus-output-constraints theory, similar to the filters model in syntax. The main impediment was the assumption, standard at the time, that output constraints are never violated.

Suppose we try to apply the filters model to Yawelmani. (It may be helpful to follow the chart in (3) as you read the rest of this paragraph.) Since there is epenthesis in the language, the transformational component must contain an optional epenthesis rule. Given /ʔilk-hin/ as the input to the transformational component, the output of that component will include [ʔi.lik.hin], with epenthesis, and various ways of syllabifying the word without epenthesis, such as *[ʔilk.hin] and *[ʔil.k.hin]. (I will use the notation ".k." to indicate that the [k] is outside the syllable on its left and right. It's unsyllabified.) These three forms are then checked by the filters. One filter, which I'll call *C^unsyll, prohibits unsyllabified consonants. It marks *[ʔil.k.hin] as ungrammatical. Another filter marks *[ʔilk.hin] as ungrammatical because it contains a syllable that exceeds the CVC limit. (I'll call this filter *COMPLEX-SYLLABLE.) Since *[ʔil.k.hin] and *[ʔilk.hin] are ruled out by the two filters, [ʔi.lik.hin] is the only grammatical output from this input. From the perspective of someone looking at the output of the grammar, it looks as if the filters *C^unsyll and *COMPLEX-SYLLABLE are triggering the epenthesis process. (For a brief explanation of the role of syllable structure in phonological processes, see the boxed text at the end of this section.)

(3) Filters model applied to Yawelmani – input /ʔilk-hin/ → [ʔi.lik.hin]

Input	Transformational component (all optional)	Output of transformational component	Filter component	Output of filter component
/ʔilk-hin/	syllabification epenthesis	[ʔi.lik.hin] [ʔil.k.hin] [ʔilk.hin]	*C^unsyll *COMPLEX-SYLLABLE	[ʔi.lik.hin] vs. *[ʔil.k.hin] *[ʔilk.hin]

Since Yawelmani also has final vowel deletion, the transformational component would also have to contain an optional rule that deletes final vowels. As a result of this rule, the output of the transformational component will include both [ta.xakʔ] and *[ta.xaː.kʔa]. Since *[ta.xaː.kʔa] is ungrammatical, some filter must rule it out. What filter? The obvious move is to posit a filter that forbids word-final vowels. We can call this filter *V#.

When we try to extend this analysis to the input /xat-kʔa/, however, we run into trouble. (Follow along in (4).) Among the outputs of the transformational component are [xat.kʔa] (which is correct), *[xat.kʔ] (with an unsyllabified consonant), and *[xatkʔ] (with a syllable that is too big). Unfortunately, all of these forms, including the correct one, violate some filter. The forms *[xat.kʔ] and *[xatkʔ] are marked as ungrammatical because they violate the filters *C^{unsyll} and *Complex-Syllable, respectively. The form that we want, [xat.kʔa], is marked as ungrammatical by the filter *V#, which was needed to make final vowel deletion obligatory in [ta.xakʔ]. The only form that isn't marked as ungrammatical is *[xa.tikʔ], which is wrong.

(4) Filters model applied to Yawelmani – input /xat-kʔa/ → wrong output

Input	Transformational component (all optional)	Output of transformational component	Filter component	Output of filter component
/xat-kʔa/	syllabification epenthesis final vowel deletion	[xat.kʔa] [xat.kʔ] [xatkʔ] [xa.tikʔ]	*C^{unsyll} *Complex-Syllable *V#	[xa.tikʔ] *vs.* *[xat.kʔa] *[xat.kʔ] *[xatkʔ]

This analysis fails because it's based on a wrong assumption, the assumption that filters are never violated. If filters are inviolable constraints on outputs, Yawelmani cannot possibly have a filter *V# – obviously, since it has vowel-final words like [xat.kʔa]! We could get around this problem by replacing *V# with a more specific filter, *VCV#, but this would be admitting defeat. The filter *VCV# stipulates something that our analysis really should explain: final vowel deletion is blocked in [xat.kʔa] because letting it apply would produce an unsyllabified consonant or a syllable that is too big. If we haven't explained that, then we haven't really accounted for Yawelmani's conspiracy.

A real explanation needs to derive the failure of final vowel deletion in [xat.kʔa] from the independently necessary filters *C^{unsyll} and *Complex-Syllable. The idea goes something like this. Even though [xat.kʔa] violates *V#, the alternative *[xat.kʔ] is even worse, since it violates *C^{unsyll}, and *C^{unsyll} *has a higher priority than* *V#. To say the same thing in a different way, *V# triggers final vowel deletion, but the constraint *C^{unsyll} sometimes blocks satisfaction of *V#. The same goes for *Complex-Syllable: it too has higher priority than *V#, so it too can block satisfaction of *V#. (You will be dealing with the *[xa.tik$^?$] problem in exercise 17 in chapter 2.)

Although constraint priority relationships were occasionally mentioned in the pre-OT literature (e.g., Burzio 1994), the standard assumption was that all output constraints are inviolable and therefore unprioritized. The central thesis of OT, on the other hand, is that constraints are ranked and violable. Constraint prioritization is fundamental to the theory (Prince and Smolensky 1993/2004). The comparison between [xat.k$^?$a] and *[xat.k$^?$] reveals a type of *constraint conflict* between *V# and *C^{unsyll}: a form that obeys one violates the other (see (5)). If *V# takes precedence, then the result is *[xat.k$^?$], which obeys *V# at the expense of violating *C^{unsyll}. If *C^{unsyll} takes precedence, then the result is [xat.k$^?$a], which obeys *C^{unsyll} but violates *V#. Since [xat.k$^?$a] is what we want, priority goes to *C^{unsyll}.

(5) Constraint conflict with /xat-k$^?$a/

	*C^{unsyll}	*V#
[xat.k$^?$a]	*obeyed*	*violated*
*[xat.k$^?$]	*violated*	*obeyed*

In OT terms, the higher-priority constraint *dominates* the lower-priority constraint. *C^{unsyll} must dominate *V# in the grammar of Yawelmani. We write this as *C^{unsyll} >> *V#. *Complex-Syllable also dominates *V#. This means that *V# will be satisfied only when this doesn't require an output with an unsyllabified consonant or a too-big syllable. With the input /xat-k$^?$a/, these constraints impose conflicting demands and the higher-ranking ones are decisive, blocking vowel deletion. With the input /taxaː-k$^?$a/, however, the final vowel can be deleted with no danger of leaving a consonant unsyllabified or creating a syllable that is too big (see (6)). In this case, there is no conflict between *C^{unsyll} and *V#, so both of them can and must be satisfied. Constraints are violable in OT, but violation is never gratuitous; it must always be compelled by some higher-ranking, conflicting constraint.

(6) No constraint conflict with /taxaː-kʼa/

	*Cᵘⁿˢʸˡˡ	*V#
[ta.xakʼ]	obeyed	obeyed
*[ta.xaː.kʼa]	obeyed	violated

The goal in this discussion of Yawelmani was to explain away a conspiracy by deriving the failure of final vowel deletion in VCCV# words from independently necessary constraints on syllabification. The OT analysis that I've just sketched does exactly that: there is no final vowel deletion in [xat.kʼa] because the alternatives, *[xat.kʼ] and *[xatkʼ], leave a consonant unsyllabified or require a syllable that exceeds the language's limit on size. The most important and novel elements of this explanation are constraint ranking and violability, which allow *V# to be active in Yawelmani but not always satisfied.

This seemingly modest change in how to think about output constraints is in reality quite profound, with important implications that are still being explored more than a decade later. In the rest of this chapter we will see some of those implications.

Syllable structure and phonological processes

One of the most important developments in phonology during the 1970s and 1980s was the realization that syllable structure affects many phonological processes. Vowel epenthesis, for example, is often motivated by the need to fit consonants into restrictive syllable templates. Yawelmani /ʔilk-hin/ → [ʔi.lik.hin] is an example of this; because of epenthetic [i], the [k] can fit into Yawelmani's maximally CVC syllables, whereas without the [i] it couldn't (*[ʔil.k.hin] or *[ʔilk.hin]). Syllable structure requirements can also block processes, such as final vowel deletion in Yawelmani /xat-kʼa/ → [xat.kʼa].

Syllable structure offered some help with the conspiracy problem, but not enough. Selkirk (1981) proposed to solve the problem of how epenthesis is triggered by assuming that the initial pass of syllabification is able to create "degenerate" syllables that lack a vowel nucleus: [ʔi.lΔk.hin], with Δ standing for an empty nucleus constituent in the second syllable. In this way, the language's syllable structure template determines where and when epenthetic vowels are required.

The epenthesis process itself is just a matter of spelling out the empty nucleus as [i].

There were intractable problems in trying to extend this sort of approach to blocking effects, however. The /xat-k$^{\text?}$a/ → [xat.k$^{\text?}$a] mapping tells us that final vowel deletion is blocked because its output cannot be exhaustively syllabified. But when final vowel deletion is applied to /ta.xaː.k$^{\text?}$a/, the immediate output is [ta.xaː.k$^{\text?}$], which also cannot be exhaustively syllabified. Presumably the difference is that Yawelmani also has a process of closed syllable shortening that changes [ta.xaː.k$^{\text?}$] into the final output [ta.xak$^{\text?}$], which can be exhaustively syllabified. The derivation, then, is /ta.xaː.k$^{\text?}$a/ → [ta.xaː.k$^{\text?}$] → [ta.xak$^{\text?}$]. By the same logic, then, what's wrong with the derivation /xat-k$^{\text?}$a/ → [xat.k$^{\text?}$] → *[xa.tik$^{\text?}$], since Yawelmani also has a process of vowel epenthesis? Clearly, there were difficult problems in sorting out when languages block processes and when they allow them to apply but fix up the results. (See Goldsmith (1990: 319ff.), Myers (1991), Paradis (1988a, 1988b), and Prince and Smolensky (1993/2004: 238–257) for discussion of this and related issues.)

The importance of syllable structure in phonology continues to be recognized in most OT work. There is nothing in OT *per se*, however, that requires a commitment to any particular theory of syllable structure or even to the existence of syllables.

QUESTIONS

4 "[T]he standard assumption was that all output constraints are inviolable and therefore unprioritized." Why "therefore"? Explain the connection between constraint violability and constraint prioritization.

5 "*C^{unsyll} must dominate the constraint *V# in the grammar of Yawelmani. . . . Likewise *COMPLEX-SYLLABLE dominates *V#. This means that *V# will be satisfied only when this doesn't require an output with an unsyllabified consonant or a too-big syllable." Why does it mean that?

EXERCISE

6 The following Three Laws of Robotics are cited by Asimov (1950) from the *Handbook of Robotics* (56th edition, published 2058). Restate the laws as ranked constraints.

1 A robot may not injure a human being, or, through inaction, allow a human being to come to harm.
2 A robot must obey the orders given to it by human beings except where such orders would conflict with the First Law.
3 A robot must protect its own existence as long as such protection does not conflict with the First or Second Law.

1.3   The Nature of Constraints in OT

In OT, constraints on output forms are called *markedness constraints* to distinguish them from constraints of a very different sort, *faithfulness constraints*. Faithfulness constraints prohibit differences between input and output. When underlying /taxaː-kʼa/ maps to surface [ta.xakʔ], faithfulness constraints against vowel deletion and vowel shortening are violated. When underlying /ʔilk-hin/ maps to surface [ʔi.lik.hin], there is a violation of a different faithfulness constraint, one that prohibits vowel epenthesis.

Faithfulness constraints are one of Prince and Smolensky's cleverest and least obvious ideas. No other theory of language has anything like OT's faithfulness constraints. Faithfulness constraints only make sense in a theory like OT that allows constraints to be violated. The reason: phonology and syntax are full of examples of unfaithful mappings like /taxaː-kʼa/ → [ta.xakʔ] and /ʔilk-hin/ → [ʔi.lik.hin], so faithfulness constraints have to be violable if they are going to be at all useful.

The job of a constraint is to assign *violation marks* to candidates. (Violation marks are conventionally written as asterisks.) Depending on how the constraint is defined and what the candidate is, a constraint can assign any number of marks from zero upwards. For example, *V# assigns no marks to [ta.xakʔ], since [ta.xakʔ] ends in a consonant. It assigns one mark to *[ta.xaː.kʼa], however, since *[ta.xaː.kʼa] ends in a vowel. The anti-epenthesis faithfulness constraint assigns one violation mark for every epenthesized segment. This constraint is called DEP, because it requires the output to DEPend on the input as the source of all its segments.[3] As (7) shows, DEP assigns no violation marks to *[ʔil.k.hin], one mark to [ʔi.lik.hin], two marks to *[ʔi.li.ki.hin], three to *[ʔi.li.ki.hi.ni], and so on. Each constraint's definition tells us how to determine the number of violation marks that it assigns to a given candidate.

(7) Violation marks assigned by DEP

	DEP
a. ʔil.k.hin	
b. ʔi.lik.hin	*
c. ʔi.li.ki.hin	**
d. ʔi.li.ki.hi.ni	***

DEP *favors* *[ʔil.k.hin] over [ʔi.lik.hin], *[ʔi.li.ki.hin], *[ʔi.li.ki.hi.ni], and so on (Samek-Lodovici and Prince 1999). Furthermore, DEP favors [ʔi.lik.hin] over *[ʔi.li.ki.hin], *[ʔi.li.ki.hi.ni], and so on. Likewise, DEP favors *[ʔi.li.ki.hin] over *[ʔi.li.ki.hi.ni], and so on. These preferences are DEP's *favoring relation* over this set of candidates. If a constraint assigns *n* violation marks to some candidate, then it favors that candidate over all of the candidates to which it assigns more than *n* marks. The candidates that totally obey a constraint are just one aspect of the constraint's favoring relation. Because constraints are violable in OT, it often happens that all viable candidates violate some constraint. In that case, it's important to know which candidates the constraint favors among those that violate it. For example, *[ʔil.k.hin] is ruled out because of its unsyllabified [k], so violation of DEP is unavoidable. The form [ʔi.lik.hin] is optimal because it is most favored among the DEP-violating candidates, as we can see from (7).

In general, the candidates that are most favored by some constraint C have two things in common: they receive the same number of violation marks from C, and no other candidate receives fewer violation marks from C. There is always at least one candidate that is most favored by C. At the other extreme, it's possible for all of the candidates to be most favored by C, if all candidates violate C equally.

Constraints are a major focus of research effort in OT, and that is why this book devotes an entire chapter (chapter 4) just to the problems of discovering, defining, and improving constraints. Furthermore, as we will see in chapter 5, most explanations and predictions in OT derive from specific assumptions about which constraints exist. The activities of modifying or rejecting old constraints and positing new ones are important research tools and important responsibilities of researchers working in OT.

Although research on constraints is central to OT, OT itself does not say much about the nature of constraints, beyond distinguishing between markedness and faithfulness. OT is a theory of how constraints interact with one another; it isn't a theory of what the constraints are, nor is it a theory of representations. For example, OT does not commit the analyst to any particular approach to syllable structure or phrase structure. Instead, OT supplies a framework for applying the constraints and evaluating the representations that are a necessary part of any theory of syllable structure or phrase structure. This is the reason why it has been possible to apply OT to phonology, syntax, and semantics, despite their different subject matter.

Prince and Smolensky put forward two very strong hypotheses about the universality of constraints. First, the constraints themselves are universal. Universal Grammar (UG) includes a constraint component CON that contains the entire repertoire of constraints. (There are separate CONs for phonology and syntax, with some overlap in their formal properties.) Second, all constraints are present in the grammars of all languages. These hypotheses follow from the more general assumption that constraint ranking is the *only* systematic difference between languages. (More about this in the next section.)

In actual practice, the hypothesis of absolute constraint universality is usually somewhat weakened. It may be necessary to admit language-particular limitations on the domains of constraints in the lexicon to deal with exceptions, loan words, and the like. There may also be formal schemas for constructing language-particular constraints, such as alignment or constraint conjunction. I will say more about these issues in chapter 4.

QUESTIONS

7   Chomsky (1995: 380) says this: "In Prince and Smolensky 1993, there seems to be no barrier to the conclusion that all lexical inputs yield a single phonetic output, namely, whatever the optimal syllable might be (perhaps /ba/)." This is sometimes known as the "*ba* objection" to OT. Respond to it.

8   Chomsky (1995: 380) criticizes faithfulness constraints on the grounds that identity between input and output is "a principle that is virtually never satisfied." Respond to this criticism.

9   "Because constraints are violable in OT, it often happens that all viable candidates violate some constraint. In that case, it's important to know which candidates the constraint favors among those that violate it." In light of this

statement, would you describe the presentation of constraint conflict in (5) as somewhat misleading? How would you correct this?

1.4 Candidate Sets: OT's Gᴇɴ Component

In Chomsky and Lasnik's filters model, the transformations are all optional, so the transformational component produces a variety of possible outputs in which transformations have and have not applied. The filter component marks some of these possible outputs as ungrammatical. In OT, the equivalent of the transformational component is called the *Generator*, or Gᴇɴ for short. The list of possible outputs supplied by Gᴇɴ for a given input is called the *candidate set* for that input. The relationship among the input, Gᴇɴ, and the candidate set is diagrammed in (8).

(8) Partial flowchart for OT
  /input/ → Gᴇɴ → {*cand₁, cand₂,* ... }

Details of the input and of Gᴇɴ, like details of the constraints, depend on our theory of representations and whether we are analyzing phonology, syntax, or semantics.

In phonology, where there is the widest agreement on such matters, the input is usually taken to be identical with the underlying representation of generative phonology. This is a level of representation in which every morpheme that alternates regularly has a unique form, such as plural /-z/ in /bæg-z/, /bʊk-z/, and /noːz-z/ (*bags, books,* and *noses*). The phonological Gᴇɴ performs various operations on the input, deleting segments, epenthesizing them, and changing their feature values. These operations apply freely, optionally, and repeatedly to derive the members of the candidate set. For example, the candidate set from input /bʊk-z/ will include the results of rightward and leftward voice assimilation ([bʊks], [bʊgz]), epenthesis ([bʊkəz]), deletion ([bʊk]), and various combinations of these processes (e.g., [bʊkəs]). It will also include a faithful candidate, where nothing has happened: [bʊkz]. These diverse candidates, nearly all of which are ungrammatical, aren't the final output of the grammar; the final output is determined by how the constraint component filters the candidate set.

Candidates *compete* to be realizations of some input. For example, [bʊks], [bʊgz], [bʊkəz], [bʊk], [bʊkəs], [bʊkz], etc. all compete to be the surface realization of the input /bʊk-z/. Candidates from different inputs do not compete; there is no comparison of the mapping /bʊk-z/ → [bʊks] with the mapping /noːz-z/ → [noːzəz]. Therefore, GEN defines the range of competitors for a given input. This range must include at least all of the ways that the input could be realized in any possible human language. In phonology, the candidate set typically contains much more than that – perhaps even every possible sequence of segments. In syntax, the nature of the candidate set is more of an open question, though see §2.9 and Legendre, Smolensky, and Wilson (1998) for discussion of how to go about answering this question, starting from OT's basic premises about competition.

It makes sense to assume that the operations in GEN are extremely general. The epenthesis operation, for example, does not specify certain contexts for epenthesis or certain segments to be epenthesized. Instead, it can insert any segment in any context. Of course, there are all sorts of limits on what can be epenthesized and where epenthesis can happen in actual output forms. But GEN isn't the place to impose these limits. Instead, an important goal of research in OT is to derive the language-particular and universal properties of linguistic processes from a specific theory of CON and the assumption that grammars are rankings of CON. A similar goal was articulated for the filters model: to show "that the consequences of ordering, obligatoriness, and contextual dependency can be captured in terms of surface filters . . . and further, that these properties can be expressed in a natural way at this level" (Chomsky and Lasnik 1977: 433). Government-Binding theory (Chomsky 1981) was an attempt to follow through on this goal by reducing the transformational component of the grammar to a single optional context-free operation, Move α. This highly general transformation is in the same spirit as OT's GEN.

If GEN is so unrestricted in its effects, then the candidate set is infinite. There are infinitely many candidates if GEN includes context-free structure-building operations like epenthesis in phonology or phrase-structure projection in syntax. These operations are allowed to apply indefinitely many times in candidate formation. For example, the candidates based on the input /noːz-z/ will include not only [noːzəz] but also [noːzəəz], [noːzəəəz], and so on.

The diversity and infinity of candidates is a source of worry to many people when they first encounter OT, and I will try to lay these worries to rest now.

The diversity of candidates can be troubling because it means that any candidate set will include forms that couldn't possibly be the output in any language. Presumably, no human language could possibly map underlying /noːz-z/ to surface [noːzəəəz]. But if [noːzəəəz] is never optimal, what is it doing in /noːz-z/'s candidate set? The answer to this worry is that the output of GEN isn't the final output of the grammar. The grammar as a whole does not overgenerate because the constraints filter the contents of the candidate set. Any decent theory of CON will explain why mappings like /noːz-z/ → [noːzəəəz] are impossible. That is where such explanations belong, in accordance with the overall goals of OT research that were discussed a couple of paragraphs above. This matter is the topic of chapter 5.

Another source of worry is mental or electronic computation: GEN will require infinite time to produce a candidate set, and the constraint component will require infinite time to evaluate the candidates. This worry starts from a wrong assumption: the formal definition of a theory of language is also its computational implementation. Since the very beginning, generative grammar has made a distinction between models of language competence and models of language processing or use. "If these simple distinctions are overlooked, great confusion must result," according to Chomsky (1968: 117). There is a lot of good work on computational modeling of OT, and none of this work stumbles over the infinity of candidates because all of it recognizes the distinction between theory and implementation. See the suggestions for further reading at the end of the chapter.

QUESTIONS

10 "Any decent theory of CON will explain why mappings like /noːz-z/ → [noːzəəəz] are impossible." How? [Hint: Think about markedness, since for [noːzəəəz] to win it must be less marked than its more faithful competitors [noːzz], [noːzəz], and [noːzəəz].]

11 Why not put a limit on the number of epenthesis operations that GEN can perform? Would this ensure that the phonological candidate set is finite, or does the phonological GEN include other potential sources of an infinity of candidates?

12 What are some hypotheses about the input in syntactic theory? How would we go about determining which hypothesis is best?

1.5   Candidate Evaluation: OT's EVAL Component

GEN produces a candidate set from an input, and that candidate set is submitted to OT's other main component, the *Evaluator*, or EVAL for short. The complete OT flowchart is given in (9). EVAL's job is to find the *optimal* candidate. EVAL does this by applying a language-particular constraint hierarchy to the set of candidates.

(9)   Flowchart for OT
      /input/ → GEN → {$cand_1$, $cand_2$, ... } → EVAL → [output]

Since EVAL is so important in OT, I will describe it in a couple of different ways, first in formal terms and then in a more procedural fashion. (The procedural description is just an alternative way of thinking about the formalization. As I noted at the end of the previous section, this isn't a claim about some actual process of mental or electronic computation.)

The formal description of EVAL starts from the observation that any constraint can be defined as a function from a set of candidates {*cands*} to some subset of {*cands*} – specifically, to the subset consisting of those candidates that the constraint most favors. Then EVAL is the function defined by composing all of the constraints in the order in which they are ranked (Karttunen 1998, Samek-Lodovici and Prince 1999). For instance, the constraint hierarchy *C^{unsyll} >> DEP in functional form looks like DEP(*C^{unsyll}({*cands*})) or, in the other notation for function composition, DEP ∘ *C^{unsyll}({*cands*}).

In more procedural terms, EVAL starts with the constraint that is ranked highest, CONST1, and extracts the subset of {*cands*} that is most favored by CONST1. This subset is passed along to the next constraint in the ranking, CONST2, which does the same thing: it locates the subset of candidates that it most favors and discards the rest. This process continues until the set has been reduced to just one candidate. This is the optimal candidate. It does better on the constraints as ranked than any other candidate in the original candidate set.

The workings of EVAL are illustrated in (10). To keep things simple, we start with the assumptions in (a) about the candidate set and the constraints that evaluate it. In (b), the top-ranked constraint *C^{unsyll} is applied. It favors three of the candidates over the fourth. Those favored candidates are kept, and the disfavored one is discarded. In (c), this set of three candidates is submitted to the next constraint in the ranking, DEP. It favors one of the candidates over the other two.

Since we have now reduced the candidate set to just one candidate, we have found the optimal candidate. This is the output of the grammar.

(10) EVAL at work
    a. Assume:
        Candidate set = {[ʔil.k.hin], [ʔi.lik.hin], [ʔi.li.ki.hin], [ʔi.li.ki.hi.ni]}
        Constraint hierarchy = *C^{unsyll} >> DEP
    b. Apply *C^{unsyll}
        Favors {[ʔi.lik.hin], [ʔi.li.ki.hin], [ʔi.li.ki.hi.ni]} (no marks) over {[ʔil.k.hin]} (one mark).
    c. Apply DEP
        Favors {[ʔi.lik.hin]} (one mark) over {[ʔi.li.ki.hin]} (two marks) and {[ʔi.li.ki.hi.ni]} (three marks).
    d. Output = [ʔi.lik.hin]

In theory, EVAL could run out of constraints before the candidate set has been reduced to a single member. This can only happen if two or more candidates receive exactly the same number of violation marks from all of the constraints. In other words, there is a tie. This kind of tie has occasionally been used to account for language variation or optionality, but often it's unwelcome and requires an additional constraint. (See §2.4 on the resolution of ties and §6.2 on analyzing variation in OT.)

To return to a point made earlier, EVAL never looks for candidates that *obey* a constraint; it only asks for candidates that *are most favored by* a constraint. Being favored by a constraint isn't the same as obeying it. One or more candidates are always favored, but it will sometimes happen that no candidate obeys a given constraint. As a result, there is always some optimal candidate (unless, absurdly, the initial candidate set is empty).

From the perspective of other linguistic theories, this is probably the most surprising thing about EVAL. EVAL maps every input to some output. In other theories, some inputs have no well-formed output because of inviolable constraints. In those other theories, for example, inviolable constraints mark *[bnæg] and *Who did he say that left? as ungrammatical in English. Since OT has only violable constraints, how can it account for ungrammaticality?

In OT, a candidate's ungrammaticality is a consequence of its inferiority to other candidates rather than violating an inviolable constraint.

For instance, *[bnæg] isn't a possible word of English because the phonological grammar of English does not select *[bnæg] as the optimal candidate for any input. To show this, we naturally want to look at the input /bnæg/. Since every faithfulness constraint favors the mapping /bnæg/ → *[bnæg], some higher-ranking markedness constraint must rule it out. This constraint is perhaps a prohibition on onset clusters containing two (nasal or oral) stops. If this constraint dominates Dep, then Eval will select [bənæg] rather than *[bnæg] as the output for the input /bnæg/. ([bənæg] isn't a real word of English, but unlike *[bnæg] it's pronounceable, and that is the point of the example.) This isn't quite enough to guarantee *[bnæg]'s ungrammaticality, however; that requires showing that *[bnæg] isn't optimal for *any* input. It's similar to studying language typology (see chapter 5).

This discussion of ungrammaticality in OT emphasizes a key point about this theory: it's *inherently comparative*. No candidate is good or bad in itself; it's only good or bad in relation to other candidates from the same input. A candidate set defines the limits of the comparison. Every member of a candidate set is in competition with every other member to be the output realization of that candidate set's input. For this reason, when we construct analyses we need to be sure to consider candidates that might give the desired winner some serious competition. For instance, it would be wrong to neglect candidates with final consonant epenthesis (*[ta.xaː.k$^{\prime}$aʔ], *[xat.k$^{\prime}$aʔ]) as competing ways of satisfying *V# in Yawelmani. I will have more to say about this important point in §2.5.

Some final remarks on terminology. Sometimes, we will need to say that one candidate is better than another without necessarily asserting that the better candidate is optimal. The phrase "*cand1* is more optimal than *cand2*" is very awkward; it's better to say that *cand1* is *more harmonic* than *cand2*. Harmony is the property that Eval selects for. If *cand1* is more harmonic than *cand2*, then the highest ranking constraint that distinguishes between *cand1* and *cand2* is a constraint that favors *cand1*. The expressions *optimal* and *most harmonic* mean exactly the same thing when the full candidate set is under discussion.

QUESTION

13 "In theory, Eval could run out of constraints before the candidate set has been reduced to a single member. This can only happen if two or more candidates receive exactly the same number of violation marks from all of the constraints. In other words, there is a tie. This kind of tie has occasionally been

used to account for language variation or optionality . . ." This approach to variation in OT is almost never used because it almost never produces multiple winning candidates. Why is that? (Hint: Think about the potential effects of low-ranking constraints.)

1.6   Constraint Activity

A constraint is *active* on some candidate set if it's the highest-ranking constraint that favors the winner over some loser. In other words, an active constraint knocks some loser out of the competition, accomplishing something that no higher-ranking constraint has managed to do.

For example, the constraint *C^{unsyll} is active in the /xat-k$^{?}$a/ → [xat.k$^{?}$a] mapping because it favors the winner [xat.k$^{?}$a] over the loser *[xat.k$^{?}$], and no higher-ranking constraint does the same thing. (In fact, there is no constraint ranked higher than *C^{unsyll}.) In (11), the active role of *C^{unsyll} is signaled by adding "!" next to the violation mark that it assigns to *[xat.k$^{?}$]. This is sometimes referred to as a *fatal violation*, since it knocks a candidate out of the competition for optimality.

(11)   Active *C^{unsyll}

	*C^{unsyll}
a. → xat.k$^{?}$a	
b. xat.k$^{?}$	*!

The constraint *V# is active in the /taxaː-k$^{?}$a/ → [ta.xak$^{?}$] mapping because it favors the winner [ta.xak$^{?}$] over the loser *[ta.xaː.k$^{?}$a] (see (12)). There is a higher-ranking constraint, *C^{unsyll}, but it isn't active on this pair of candidates.

(12)   Active *V#

	*C^{unsyll}	*V#
a. → ta.xak$^{?}$		
b. ta.xaː.k$^{?}$a		*!

On the other hand, *V# isn't active in the choice between [xat.kʔa] and *[xat.kʔ], since higher-ranking *C^{unsyll} does deprive *V# of the chance to be active in this evaluation (see (13)). Lower-ranking constraints are potentially active only when the winner and one or more losers tie on all of the higher-ranking constraints.

(13) Active *C^{unsyll}, but inactive*V#

	*C^{unsyll}	*V#
a. → xat.kʔa		*
b. xat.kʔ	*!	

A constraint can still be active even when the winner violates it. In Yawelmani, *C^{unsyll} has to dominate Dep to account for epenthesis in /ʔilk-hin/ → [ʔi.lik.hin] (vs. *[ʔil.k.hin]). As (14) shows, the optimal candidate violates Dep once, but losers like *[ʔi.li.ki.hin] and *[ʔi.li.ki.hi.ni] violate it even more. When candidates violate a constraint by different amounts, the severity of the violation matters, and the constraint favors the candidate that violates it the least.

(14) Active but violated Dep

	*C^{unsyll}	Dep
a. → ʔi.lik.hin		*
b. ʔil.k.hin	*!	
c. ʔi.li.ki.hin		**!
d. ʔi.li.ki.hi.ni		***!

Example (14) illustrates a property of Eval called *minimal violation*. Although the winner violates Dep, it violates Dep less than any other candidate except the one ruled out by higher-ranking *C^{unsyll}. Constraints are violable in OT, but violation is minimal.

Example (14) also shows that minimal violation of faithfulness constraints produces a kind of economy of derivation, in something like Chomsky's (1991) sense. Because faithfulness constraints are violated minimally, the winning output candidate can differ from the input only as much as necessary to do better on any higher-ranking constraints. With the input /ʔilk-hin/, DEP must be violated in order to satisfy *C^{unsyll}, so some discrepancy between input and output is unavoidable. But the discrepancy is still minimal because DEP is violated minimally.

Markedness constraints can also be active when they are dominated. Some observations about syllable structure illustrate this. The markedness constraint ONSET is violated by onsetless (i.e., vowel-initial) syllables (Ito 1989: 222 and others). In the Malaysian Austronesian language Timugon Murut, ONSET must be crucially dominated because onsetless syllables occur in surface forms, such as [am.bi.lu.o] 'soul'. (The [u] and [o] are in "two distinct phonetic syllables," according to Prentice (1971: 24).) Onsetless syllables could be avoided by epenthesizing a consonant, as in *[ʔam.bi.lu.ʔo], so DEP has to be ranked above ONSET to prevent this from happening (see (15)). And since onsetless syllable could also be avoided by deleting the problematic segments ((c) in (15)), ONSET has to be dominated by the anti-deletion faithfulness constraint MAX. (It is called MAX because it requires the input segments to be MAximally expressed in the output.[4])

(15)   Active but violated ONSET

	DEP	MAX	ONSET
a. → am.bi.lu.o			**
b. ʔam.bi.lu.ʔo	**!		
c. bi.lu		***!	
d. am.bil.u.o			***!

Now look at candidate (d) in (15). Because of how [l] is syllabified, this candidate has one more onsetless syllable than the winner has, and so it's disfavored by ONSET. Even though the winner violates ONSET, this constraint still actively eliminates candidate (d). When a markedness constraint is active in a language but also violated by some winners in that language, the situation is known as *the emergence of the unmarked*, sometimes abbreviated TETU (McCarthy and Prince 1994a). The idea is that a preference for some universally unmarked structure, such as syllables with onsets, can emerge under the right circumstances even if the language as a whole permits the corresponding marked structure. Candidate (d) loses because ONSET emerges to disfavor it, even though ONSET is violated elsewhere in the language (and even in this very word). Emergence of the unmarked is an important difference between OT and parametric theories of language, as we will see in §1.7.

The idea that markedness constraints can be active but violated is hard to absorb and exploit fully. When I first learned about OT, I brought with me the belief that legitimate linguistic constraints had to state absolute truths about surface forms. I was uncomfortable with saying that ONSET actively favors [am.bi.lu.o] over *[am.bil.u.o]. I would have been happier with a specific constraint against, say, *[VC.V] syllabification, where a syllable-final consonant is followed by syllable-initial vowel. This constraint is categorically true in Timugon Murut, but only because it stipulates additional conditions that allow it to be categorically true. (In that respect, it's like the rejected constraint *VCV# in Yawelmani.)

It requires some effort to get past these prejudices inherited from other theories. The best practice in OT is to state constraints in very general ways and then try to limit their activity through interaction with higher-ranking constraints. Formulating constraints that refer to highly specific surface configurations, such as *[VC.V], isn't a very successful analytic strategy in OT.

QUESTIONS

14   Explain how the minimal violation property follows from the definition of EVAL in §1.5.

15   The emergence of the unmarked is relevant to the choice of *which* segment to epenthesize when other constraints have determined that *some* segment must be epenthesized. Can you figure out why?

EXERCISES

16   From the information given in this section, can you determine the relative ranking of MAX and DEP in Timugon Murut? If so, what is the ranking? If not, what sort of additional evidence would you need?

17   Imagine you have joined an internet dating site. To find your compatible mate, you are required to rank five desirable qualities in a mate according to the importance you place on them. The qualities are physical attractiveness,

intelligence, sense of humor, good hygiene, and wealth. How would you go about figuring out your personal priority system for these attributes using OT style ranking methods? Could you have a problem determining the relative priority of good hygiene and wealth if all of the wealthy people you know also practice good hygiene?

1.7 Differences between Languages

Different languages have different rankings of CON. In Timugon Murut, DEP and MAX dominate ONSET, so there are onsetless syllables. In Arabic, ONSET dominates DEP, so a consonant is epenthesized: /al-walad/ → [ʔal.wa.lad], *[al.wa.lad] 'the boy'.

The strongest hypothesis is that constraint ranking is the *only* way that languages differ. In other words, all systematic differences between languages should be accounted for by permuting the ranking of a set of universal constraints. This hypothesis means, among other things, that every constraint in CON is in the grammar of every language. Even when a language seems to completely ignore some constraint C, C remains in the language's constraint hierarchy. In this situation, C is inactive because of other constraints that dominate it and not because it has been removed from the grammar.

In other linguistic theories, differences between languages are often attributed to *parameters*. A parameter is a constraint that can be turned off. For instance, the [Onset] parameter would be turned off in Timugon Murut, which allows onsetless syllables, and turned on in Arabic, which forbids them. Parametric theories have problems with emergence of the unmarked effects. If [Onset] is off in Timugon Murut, then why is [am.bi.lu.o] preferred to *[am.bil.u.o] and *[amb.il.u.o]? In pre-OT days, Ito (1989: 223) addressed this problem by parameterizing [Onset] as strong/weak rather than on/off. [Strong Onset] says "Onsetless syllables are forbidden." [Weak Onset] says "Avoid onsetless syllables." The word "avoid" tells us that [Weak Onset] is really just a version of [Strong Onset] that can be violated minimally. In OT, minimal violation is a general property of all constraints, so it isn't necessary to build it into the definition of this or any other specific constraint.

Language differences will be a particular focus of our attention in chapter 5. Chapters 2 and 4 lay the foundation for studying this important topic.

QUESTION

18 What would it take to prove that some markedness constraint was literally absent from the grammars of some languages, rather than merely low-ranking? When answering this question, feel free to make any necessary assumptions about the other constraints in Con.

EXERCISE

19 Show that even low-ranking faithfulness constraints are universally present in the grammars of all languages. The material in §1.6 offers a hint about how to make this argument.

1.8 The Version of OT Discussed in This Book

In this and subsequent chapters, I am describing a version of OT that can be called "standard" or "classic." Standard or classic OT incorporates almost all of Prince and Smolensky's (1993/2004) main ideas. There is only one systematic difference between this standard theory and what Prince and Smolensky say: how faithfulness is implemented. The standard theory formulates faithfulness constraints like Max and Dep using correspondence theory (McCarthy and Prince 1995, 1999). These constraints have replaced Prince and Smolensky's original faithfulness constraints Parse and Fill, which were formulated somewhat differently. (Correspondence theory, Parse, and Fill will be explained in §4.6.)

As I noted in §1.3, OT itself does not say anything specific about the constraints in Con, particularly the markedness constraints. Markedness constraints embody substantive claims about phonology, syntax, or some other linguistic domain. OT is a formal system in which notions like constraint priority are rigorously defined, but it does not say what the constraints are. Likewise, OT itself does not say anything about the nature of representations, though it provides a framework in which the well-formedness of representations can be evaluated using violable constraints.

Because OT itself does not specify what the constraints are, research in OT is primarily focused on developing and improving hypotheses about the constraints in Con in order to understand and eventually solve specific empirical problems. Exploring the results of ranking permutation, improving or rejecting old constraints, and positing new constraints are familiar activities to anyone working in this theory.

This book, particularly in chapters 4 and 5, offers plenty of guidance about how to do these things with maximal effectiveness.

Another type of OT research explores the effects of various possible changes in OT's basic assumptions. What if OT had derivations? Can a language have more than one constraint ranking? Work that addresses questions like these will be introduced in chapter 6, along with pointers to the literature.

A third type of research deals in formal analysis of OT, including learnability, logic, and computation. Some of this work is discussed in §2.11 and §2.12.

1.9   Suggestions for Further Reading

Among the article-length overviews of OT are Archangeli (1997), Legendre (2001), McCarthy (2003b, 2007c), Prince and Smolensky (1997, 2003), Smolensky, Legendre, and Tesar (2006), and Tesar, Grimshaw, and Prince (1999). Kager (1999) is a textbook that focuses on applications of OT to several phonological phenomena: syllabification, stress, reduplication, and cyclicity. Yip (2002) is a textbook about tone with information about how OT can be applied to tonal phenomena. McCarthy (2002) is a guide to OT's main concepts and the results that follow from them. It also includes an extensive bibliography, with references organized by topics at the end of each chapter.

Anyone who works through *Doing Optimality Theory* is ready for more advanced reading, starting with Prince and Smolensky (1993/2004). The next step after that depends on the individual reader's interests. If they tend toward phonology, then the papers collected in McCarthy (2003a) are probably the best place to start. Two other useful anthologies, Lombardi (2001) and Féry and van de Vijver (2003), are focused on segmental and syllabic phonology, respectively. Readers of a syntactic bent could not do better than to consult two anthologies of papers on OT syntax, Legendre, Grimshaw, and Vikner (2001) and Sells et al. (2001). In addition, there are now several anthologies on OT semantics and pragmatics (Blutner et al. 2005, Blutner and Zeevat 2004, de Hoop and de Swart 1999), and one on historical linguistics (Holt 2003). The roots of OT in cognitive science, as well as applications to phonology, syntax, and other areas, are the topic of another anthology, Smolensky and Legendre (2006).

Some of the most important work on OT is available for free on the Rutgers Optimality Archive (http://roa.rutgers.edu). ROA, which was created by Alan Prince in 1993, is an electronic repository of "work in, on, or about OT." It's a fabulous resource for the student as well as the veteran scholar. To find ROA papers on specific topics, you can use ROA's built-in function for searching abstracts, but it's better to use Google, which searches the body of papers as well. Use the Google directive *site:roa.rutgers.edu* in the search string – e.g., *metathesis site:roa.rutgers.edu* will locate all of the ROA postings that mention metathesis anywhere in the text.

Notes

1 Nowadays, the preferred name for this Yokuts dialect is Yowlumne. I retain the earlier name since it is much more familiar to most linguists.

2 According to Newman (1944: 29) and most subsequent analysts, final vowel deletion is limited to CV suffixes like /-kʔa/ and /-mi/. I believe it is more accurate to say that overt alternations are limited to these suffixes, since longer or shorter suffixes do not present opportunities for alternations.

3 Kathryn Flack informs me that "DON'T EPenthesize" is in use as a mnemonic for DEP.

4 A somewhat forced mnemonic for MAX: "MAke expressed."

2

How to Construct an Analysis

Doing linguistic analysis in OT is different from doing linguistic analysis in other theories. The differences include everything from choosing a problem to work on to writing up the results. The goal of this chapter and the next is to explain how to do these things well in OT. This chapter is structured around four main topics: choosing appropriate data to work on, getting from the data to an OT analysis, constraint ranking, and finding and fixing problems with the analysis. It also contains sections about two closely related topics: constraint-ranking algorithms and the logic of OT.

Developing an analysis and writing it up are somewhat different tasks. This chapter is about the process of developing an analysis. Chapter 3 is about how to write up the results.

2.1 Where to Begin

2.1.1 Choosing a problem to work on

The first step is to find some data to analyze. This might seem too obvious to mention, but it's actually a very important point, since the *kind* of data chosen really matters. How we frame the problem affects the likelihood that we will be successful in solving it.

Some kinds of data are much more likely to lead to successful, insightful analyses than others. It depends on the theory. Dissertations on phonology in the 1960s and 1970s often followed the *SPE* model of trying to construct a comprehensive analysis of all the alternations in a single language. Shorter works, including term papers or problem sets, were smaller versions of the same thing: an analysis of all the alternations in Latin third declension nouns, for instance. That approach made sense in the *SPE* theory of phonology, where the goal of the analysis was to construct and order a set of language-particular rules. Success depended on generating all of the correct forms using maximally simple rules.

OT is different. An OT grammar is a ranking of universal constraints, but relatively few of those constraints are presently known to us with certainty. In all but the simplest cases, then, analysis and theorizing are linked: the analyst must sometimes modify old constraints or posit new ones, in addition to ranking a set of given constraints. Any OT analysis is a partial theory of CON as well as a description of some facts. The ultimate goal of the analysis is to support claims about the universal properties of CON. Success depends on how well the evidence does that.

Contemporary syntax also has to deal with the problem of simultaneously analyzing and theorizing. The solution adopted by most syntacticians is to focus the analysis and the accompanying theorizing on a specific construction in one or more languages – e.g., dative subjects in Icelandic, or multiple *wh*-questions. The same solution makes sense for anyone doing OT. As we will see in chapter 5, theorizing about CON is most successful when it's informed by the study of a phenomenon or some related phenomena in multiple languages. To get a handle on, say, the universal markedness constraints that govern syllable-initial consonant clusters, it's necessary to look at observed restrictions on these clusters in various languages. In principle, any proposal to modify CON needs this sort of support.

In practice, such thoroughness is often impossible. When doing a problem set or writing a paper, you may not have enough time to survey a phenomenon in multiple languages. Sometimes, you have to make do with something less: analyze – and if necessary theorize about – a specific phenomenon in an individual language. As you acquire more knowledge of previously proposed constraints and of similar phenomena in other languages, the processes of analysis and theorizing become somewhat easier. But even then it's no less true that studying phenomena is the best way to proceed.

It should now be clear why the *SPE*-era model of research is inappropriate in OT phonology. A language is a somewhat arbitrary collection of phenomena, some of which coexist only by virtue of the accidents of history. Even the phonology of the Latin third declension is an arbitrary collection; it is, after all, just the set of alternations that happen to be conditioned by the suffixes of that declension.[1] For a phonologist to try to analyze all of the alternations in the Latin third declension is a bit like a syntactician trying to analyze all of the six-word sentences in a language. The task isn't meaningful.

A personal note. When I first began working in OT, I didn't know any better. I stumbled into a research project that involved a large chunk of the phonology of a single language. I was lucky that the various phenomena had cross-linguistic relevance, and it certainly helped that I had a first-rate collaborator, so in the end it turned out OK. But what was supposed to be a modest article-length project ended up expanding into a book (McCarthy and Prince 1993b). One shouldn't rely on luck in such matters.

Which phenomena make good research topics? The answer obviously depends on the size of the project, but let's focus on the standard unit of academic currency, the 10–20 page term paper. The phenomenon should be reasonably self-contained. A pretty good test of this is whether the scope of the project can be described in a single sentence that uses only the terminology of the field in which the paper is being written. "Analyze all of the data in the phonology section of Hale and Buck's Latin grammar" is a terrible topic. "Analyze the alternations in Latin third declension nouns" isn't a good topic for a phonology paper because the scope is being defined in morphological terms. "Voicing alternations in Russian" or "Onset clusters in English" are topics whose scope is appropriately defined in phonological terms. This test won't work perfectly for topics at the interface of two grammatical components, such as phonology and morphology or morphology and syntax, but even then the scope should be definable using terminology that is usual in such interface studies.

With an ideal OT research topic, the phenomenon will hint at the possibilities of constraint interaction, even prior to any analysis. In phonology, the existence of regular alternations tells us immediately that markedness constraints are crucially dominating faithfulness constraints, since regular alternations are only possible when some underlying form is mapped unfaithfully to its output. For example, the [p]~[b] alternation in Latin [urps]~[urbis] 'city~gen.' (from /urb/) means that some markedness constraint requiring voicing agreement dominates faithfulness to voicing.

In both phonology and syntax, any sort of *nonuniformity* is a solid indicator of constraint interaction. Nonuniformity is systematically inconsistent behavior. A clue to inconsistent behavior is the appearance of phrases like "except when" or "only when" in descriptions.

"Yawelmani deletes final vowels except when they are preceded by a consonant cluster." "Icelandic verbs with dative subjects have nominative objects only when the object is in the third person." These examples of inconsistent behavior are systematic, and thus are good cases of nonuniformity, because they involve regular patterns rather than arbitrary lexical exceptions. In OT, nonuniformity is always a consequence of constraint interaction, as we saw with the Yawelmani example in §1.6. In fact, phonological alternations are just a special case of nonuniformity: Latin consonants are faithful to their voicing except before a voiceless consonant.

Phenomena that do not involve alternations or nonuniformity may be harder to study and are therefore less suitable as topics for time-limited projects like term papers. "Onset clusters in English" is an example of a topic that fails this test. There are very few overt alternations involving restrictions on English onset clusters.[2] There is some nonuniformity, but it isn't very easy to recognize without also studying onset restrictions in other languages. (An example of nonuniformity is the absence of [tl] and [dl] onsets, when all other stop + liquid onsets are allowed.) This is the sort of problem that is best studied with a cross-language survey like Baertsch (2002). It's probably too big a task for the typical term-paper research project.

2.1.2   Formulating a descriptive generalization

People will often say that a theory or analysis accounts for some data. But this is really an oversimplification. Theories and analyses account for *generalizations*. Generalizations are based on data, but generalizations and data aren't the same thing. Someone might say that their analysis accounts for why *bnag* isn't a word of English or why coreference is impossible in *John saw him*, but what they really mean is that their analysis accounts for some generalization about phonotactics or coreference. The specific word *bnag* or sentence *John saw him* are no more necessary to the argument than *pnutch* and *Mary saw her*.

A *descriptive generalization* is the essential intermediate step between data and analysis. Good descriptive generalizations are accurate characterizations of the systematic patterns that can be observed in the data. They may not require any formalization or theoretical constructs beyond the usual linguistic terminology. Precision is much more important than fancy apparatus. The ultimate test of a descriptive generalization is this: any competent linguist who sees the generalization but has never seen the data ought to be able to invent data that are completely consistent with the generalization. These imaginary dialogues give a sense of what I have in mind:

> "Yawelmani deletes final vowels except when they are preceded by a consonant cluster." "OK, so you mean that underlying /tasidu/ becomes [tasid], but underlying /patakta/ remains [patakta], not *[patakt]. I get it."

> "Icelandic verbs with dative subjects have nominative objects only when the object is in the third person." "So you're telling me that something like *To-you liked he* is OK, but *To-you liked we* is not. Very interesting."

Proceeding straight from the data to the analysis, without taking time to formulate an accurate descriptive generalization, is never a good idea. The descriptive generalization mediates between the data and the analysis; it's what the analysis is an analysis of. The temptation to get it over with by going straight from data to constraint ranking should be resisted fiercely, like any of Satan's blandishments. A good descriptive generalization will make the whole task of analysis much easier. It will allow both the author and the readers to see whether the analysis achieves its goals. And it will help show the way to improvement when the analysis falls short of its goals. This is especially true for problem sets and term papers, since the course instructor needs to see where the student has gone astray. Is the generalization right but the analysis wrong? Is this a good analysis of a bad generalization? Without having the student's descriptive generalization to compare with the student's analysis, the instructor can only conjecture.

Since descriptive generalizations are stated in ordinary language rather than some formalism, there can be many ways of saying the same thing. Stating the generalization in the right way can make the task of analysis much easier. A descriptive generalization that has been constructed with the theory in mind can be a big help. A good descriptive generalization will foreshadow the analysis. An excellent descriptive generalization will make the analysis seem almost inevitable.

When formulating a descriptive generalization intended to lead to an OT analysis, there are two important things to remember. First, OT analyses are constructed out of markedness and faithfulness constraints. Ideally, descriptive generalizations will contain statements about target output configurations and unfaithful mappings related to those configurations. Compare the following generalizations that describe the same situation in different ways:

(i) Words cannot end in vowels. This requirement is enforced by deletion.
(ii) Delete word-final vowels.

The generalization in (ii) is appropriate for an analysis in rule-based phonology, but it isn't helpful when an OT analysis is the goal. It's unhelpful because the relationship between the descriptive generalization and the ultimate analysis is highly indirect: the generalization describes a process, but the ultimate analysis is the ranking *V# >> MAX. The generalization in (i) is much better suited to an OT analysis. The descriptive statement "words cannot end in vowels" points straight toward the markedness constraint *V#, and the phrase "enforced by deletion" hints at *V#'s relationship to MAX.

The problem with using the language of processes or rules, as in (ii), is that OT has no analogous notion. A rule describes an input configuration – the rule's structural description, such as a word-final vowel – and an operation to perform on it – the rule's structural change. OT analyses are constructed out of constraints that ban certain output configurations and constraints that require identity in input–output mappings. Formulating descriptive generalizations in the right way helps to avoid faulty analyses with types of constraints that are impossible in OT (like "delete word-final vowels," which isn't a constraint at all).

The terms *repair* or *repair strategy* are sometimes used in the OT literature to refer to phenomena like epenthesis, as in the statement "Epenthesis repairs violations of *C^{unsyll}." I do not recommend using the word "repair" when formulating descriptive generalizations or otherwise talking about OT. It comes from a different theory of phonology, the Theory of Constraints and Repair Strategies (Paradis 1988a, 1988b). Repair is well-defined in that other theory, but it isn't well-defined in OT. Use *mapping* or *unfaithful mapping* instead.

Another thing to remember when formulating descriptive generalizations is that OT is based on constraint ranking. As I mentioned in §2.1.1, the phrases "except when" and "only when" are often the way that descriptions hint at constraint ranking. In Yawelmani, the descriptive generalization in (i) above has to be qualified because of examples like /xat-k$^?$a/ → [xat.k$^?$a], *[xat.k$^?$]. The best way to do this is to state the descriptive generalization using a simple formula that includes the phrase "except when" and a counterfactual condition describing the unwanted output configuration:

Words cannot end in vowels, and this requirement is enforced by deletion, except when an unsyllabified consonant would result.

This generalization calls to mind the markedness constraint $*C^{unsyll}$, and the phrase "except when" suggests how it should be ranked. Words cannot end in vowels, except for the effect of $*C^{unsyll}$. So $*C^{unsyll}$ must dominate $*V\#$. In the ultimate analysis, the ranking is $*C^{unsyll}$ >> $*V\#$ >> Max.

The "except when" + counterfactual formula works well for this and many other generalizations about blocking effects. The essence of a blocking effect is that some expected behavior isn't observed under certain conditions. In an OT analysis, the expected behavior is defined by a markedness-over-faithfulness ranking like $*V\#$ >> Max. Satisfaction of the markedness constraint is blocked whenever it conflicts with another constraint that is ranked even higher, as in $*C^{unsyll}$ >> $*V\#$.

Blocking effects aren't limited to phonology. The Icelandic phenomenon mentioned above is an example of a syntactic blocking effect. That's clear when we state the descriptive generalization in the recommended way:

When the subject is dative, the object is nominative, except when a first or second person nominative object would result.

This generalization suggests the constraint ranking that we actually find in an OT analysis by Hrafnbjargarson (2004): a constraint against first and second person nominative objects dominates and thereby overrides the constraint requiring nominative objects with dative subjects. (For the higher-ranking constraint's rationale, see the discussion of Aissen (2003) in §4.7.3.)

Descriptive generalizations may need to deal with systems of priorities that are deeper than a single "except when" clause. For example, a dialect of Bedouin Arabic is subject to the following descriptive generalization (after Al-Mozainy 1981):

Low vowels are prohibited in nonfinal open syllables. This requirement is enforced by raising the vowel to high (/katab/ → [kitab] 'he wrote'),

except when the result would contain a sequence of a low consonant and a high vowel (/ʕabad/ → [ʕabad], *[ʕibad] 'he worshipped')

except when the result would contain a sequence of a low vowel followed by a high vowel in the next syllable (/ħalim/ → [ħilim], *[ħalim] 'he dreamt').

The structure of this generalization is *(low vowels prohibited (except when … (except when …)))*, as the indentation indicates. This generalization leads to a ranking with the markedness constraint against *[ħalim]'s *aCi* sequence ranked at the top, followed by the constraint against *[ʕibad]'s *ʕi* sequence, and then a constraint against low vowels in nonfinal open syllables. Faithfulness to vowel height is at the bottom.

The moral is that care and attention paid to constructing a good descriptive generalization that is attuned to OT's basic theoretical premises will be lavishly repaid when it comes time to construct the actual analysis. A wrongly formulated generalization, even if it's a correct description of the facts, can place the analysis almost hopelessly out of reach.

2.1.3 Getting from the generalization to an analysis

Even with a good descriptive generalization as an intermediate step, the distance between the data and the analysis can seem daunting. Perhaps the hardest thing is deciding which constraints are going to be important in the analysis. At this early stage, the decisions are tentative and subject to later revision as the details of the analysis emerge, but one must start somewhere. Where?

When the data involve phonological alternations, start with the faithfulness constraints. They are the best place to start because faithfulness constraints are more limited in variety and better understood than markedness constraints. (This isn't to say that the theory of faithfulness constraints is fully settled, since it's not. But it's on a firmer footing than the theory of markedness constraints.) At this early stage in the process of analysis, it's enough to focus on just the three basic types of faithfulness constraints in (1). These constraints are ubiquitous in the phonological OT literature, and versions of them appear in many OT syntax papers as well.

(1) Basic faithfulness constraints (McCarthy and Prince 1995, 1999)
    a. MAX prohibits deletion.
    b. DEP prohibits epenthesis.
    c. IDENT(F) is a family of constraints, one for each distinctive feature F, that prohibit changing feature values.

When doing an analysis, you can use your descriptive generalization to deduce which basic faithfulness constraints are being violated. If voicing alternates, then IDENT([voice]) is violated. If there is deletion or epenthesis, then MAX or DEP is violated.[3] This will also tell you something about the ranking. Any faithfulness constraint that is violated must be dominated by at least one markedness constraint. (This will be explained in §5.2.) Faithfulness constraints that are obeyed are also important, but it's easier to wait until the analysis is farther along before trying to identify the faithfulness constraints that are consistently obeyed and also important to the analysis. (This will be discussed in §2.5.)

As we saw in the previous section, descriptive generalizations are also useful for identifying the active markedness constraints. When the generalization describes prohibited output configurations like an unsyllabified consonant or a word-final vowel, then markedness constraints forbidding these configurations are obviously implicated.

At this point in the analytic process, frustration or even panic can sometimes develop. From the descriptive generalization, it's fairly clear what the markedness constraint must *do*, but it isn't so clear what the markedness constraint is *called*. What is this constraint's name? Has anyone proposed it before? How exactly is it defined? Is it universal, as OT constraints are supposed to be?

These are all reasonable questions. Sometimes they can be answered simply by consulting the list of common phonological markedness constraints in §4.8. If not, don't worry about it. When the analysis is just getting started, it's OK to construct ad hoc markedness constraints without worrying about whether they have been proposed previously, what they are "officially" called, and whether they are active in other languages. Those questions can wait. The only important thing at this point is that the ad hoc markedness constraint needs to really *be* a markedness constraint.

Markedness constraints can only do one thing: prohibit certain output configurations. They must not mention any property that isn't represented in output candidates. Markedness constraint definitions must never mention the input. They must not use words like "contrast" or "phoneme" that pertain to entire phonological systems rather than individual words. They cannot use verbs like "delete," "replace," "move," etc. Failure to heed this advice is a fatal error, even when a temporary, ad hoc markedness constraint is involved. It's fatal because such a constraint strays so far outside the boundaries of the theory. OT itself does not say much about constraints, but it says that there are only two types of them: constraints that evaluate individual output forms, and constraints that require individual output forms to be identical to their inputs. Perhaps eventually we'll decide that markedness and faithfulness constraints aren't enough, but an ad hoc constraint introduced early in the process of analysis isn't the appropriate place to pioneer a new version of OT.

Another bit of advice is to strive for precision in constraint definitions. Precision doesn't require elaborate formalization, or indeed any formalization. Precision does mean, however, that any knowledgeable but unsympathetic reader can apply the constraint to any candidate and know exactly whether and by how much it's violated. A good strategy to ensure this is to begin every constraint definition with the phrase "Assign one violation mark for every . . ."

The danger with an insufficiently precise constraint definition is that the interpretation and hence the effect of the constraint can vary slightly as the analysis progresses. I and probably everyone else who works in OT have occasionally imagined a constraint with a wonderfully flexible definition that undergoes unnoticed changes as each new piece of data is examined. The result is an analysis that is internally inconsistent and very hard to fix.

Chapter 4 has lots more about defining and justifying constraints.

2.1.4 Summary

Are all of these preliminaries really necessary? In my experience, they really do make a difference. When I've skipped steps and rushed the process, I've usually found that I have to go back and fill in the gaps, particularly when the system involves more than about three constraints interacting. When I read papers, I find that the absence of clear descriptive generalizations makes the work impenetrable, and it's often accompanied by mistakes in the formal OT analysis. The preliminary steps take time, but they save effort and improve accuracy and clarity in the long run.

EXERCISES

1   "A pretty good test of this is whether the scope of the project can be described in a single sentence that uses only the terminology of the field in which the paper is being written." Give brief descriptions of two possible research topics that fail this test and two that pass it.

2   Give an example of nonuniformity in phonology or syntax.

3   Read the abstracts of five works posted on ROA. Which describe good OT research projects and which do not, according to the criteria in this section? Explain your answer.

4   Explain why the following descriptive generalizations aren't suitable for an OT analysis and then fix them.

a.   "Word-finally, the vowels /i/ and /u/ are lowered to [æ] and [a], respectively." (Lardil)
b.   "A long vowel in a closed syllable becomes short: /CVːC/ → [CVC]." (Yawelmani)
c.   "Move *wh* to [Spec, CP]." (English)

5   Skim three papers on ROA until you locate a descriptive generalization. Is it clear and OT-friendly? Explain your answer.

6   The following statements are all bad examples of ad hoc markedness constraints that someone might formulate early in the process of doing an analysis. For each of them, explain what is wrong with it. Formulate better constraints to replace them. (In each case, you'll need at least two constraints and a ranking between them. Don't be reluctant to make up constraints, as long as you define them properly.)

a.   A nasal consonant assimilates in place of articulation to a following consonant.
b.   Subjects raise to [Spec, IP].
c.   Word-final consonants become voiceless, except for /b/, because [p] isn't a sound of the language.

7   What does the following descriptive generalization suggest about relevant constraints and their ranking in an OT analysis?

"Syllables cannot end in consonants. This requirement is enforced by epenthesizing [ə], except that there is no epenthesis word-finally."

8   Formulate an OT-friendly descriptive generalization for the following data from Maori (Hale 1973, Hohepa 1967). Then explain what this descriptive generalization suggests about the constraints and their ranking in an OT analysis.

Underlying root	*No suffix* 'active'	*Root+/ia/* 'passive'	*Root+/aŋa/* 'gerundive'	
/weroh/	[wero]	[werohia]	[werohaŋa]	'stab'
/hopuk/	[hopu]	[hopukia]	[hopukaŋa]	'catch'
/arum/	[aru]	[arumia]	[arumaŋa]	'follow'
/maur/	[mau]	[mauria]	[mauraŋa]	'carry'
/afit/	[afi]	[afitia]	[afitaŋa]	'embrace'

9 Formulate an OT-friendly descriptive generalization for the following data from Palauan (based on a problem set in Schane and Bendixen 1978). Then explain what this descriptive generalization suggests about the constraints and their ranking in an OT analysis.

Underlying root	No suffix	Root+/k/ 'my'	Root+/mam/ 'our'	
/ʔabu/	[ʔáb]	[ʔəbúk]	[ʔəbəmám]	'ashes'
/mada/	[mád]	[mədák]	[mədəmám]	'eyes'
/keri/	[kér]	[kərík]	[kərəmám]	'question'
/ʔuri/	[ʔúr]	[ʔərík]	[ʔərəmám]	'laughter'
/ʔara/	[ʔár]	[ʔərák]	[ʔərəmám]	'price'
/buʔi/	[búʔ]	[bəʔík]	[bəʔəmám]	'spouse'
/duʔa/	[dúʔ]	[dəʔák]	[dəʔəmám]	'skill'
/badu/	[bád]	[bədúk]	[bədəmám]	'rock'

2.2 How to Rank Constraints

Ranking establishes priority relationships among constraints: higher-ranking constraints take precedence over lower-ranking ones. These precedence relationships are important in situations of *constraint conflict*, where two constraints make competing demands on the output of the grammar. All inferences about constraint ranking are ultimately based on conflicts between pairs of constraints.

There are three indispensable elements to any valid ranking argument:

(i) *A conflict* For two constraints to be directly rankable, they must conflict; that is, they must disagree in their assessment of a pair of competing output candidates derived from the same input. For instance, Yawelmani /ʔilk-hin/ has competing candidate output forms [ʔi.lik.hin] and *[ʔil.k.hin]. The markedness constraint *C^{unsyll} and the faithfulness constraint DEP disagree in their assessment of these forms, since *C^{unsyll} favors [ʔi.lik.hin] and DEP favors *[ʔil.k.hin]. As it happens, the conflict in this case is between satisfying one constraint and violating the other, but that isn't a necessary element of a ranking argument. Constraints that are violated by both candidates can also conflict, as long as there is disagreement about which candidate each constraint favors.

(ii) *A winner* One member of this pair of competing candidates must be the actual output form for the given input – the winner, in short. The constraint that favors the winner, *C^{unsyll}, must dominate the constraint that favors the loser, DEP. No conclusions about ranking can be drawn from comparing losers. The reason: we know that the winner is better than all of the losers, but we have no evidence about whether any loser is better than any other loser.

(iii) *No disjunction* The ranking argument is secure only if there is no third constraint that could also be responsible for the winner beating the loser. In the Yawelmani example, such a constraint would have to meet two conditions to be problematic: like *C^unsyll, it would have to favor [ʔi.lik.hin] over *[ʔil.k.hin]; and it would also have to be able to dominate *C^unsyll. (I will give an example and explain this concept more fully later in this section.)

Because ranking arguments are so important, it's unwise to claim rankings without first doing the arguments needed to back them up. It might sometimes be tempting to skip this step – why not assert some ranking based on an intuition about how things work and then use the ranking to analyze further data? Do not give in to this temptation. It can lead to several different errors:

- asserting CONST1 >> CONST2 when in fact the ranking is CONST2 >> CONST1;
- asserting CONST1 >> CONST2 when the evidence only supports CONST1 >> CONST2 *or* CONST3 >> CONST2;
- asserting CONST1 >> CONST2 when there is no evidence for ranking these constraints either way.

Problems like these are very common and can be found in the work of some of the best linguists and in the pages of the best journals. For instance, an article that was published in 2004 in one of the best-edited and most widely admired linguistics journals contains a mistake of the last type. The language in question allows onsetless syllables, and this leads the author to infer correctly that the faithfulness constraints MAX and DEP dominate ONSET. But the author says that the ranking in this language is MAX >> DEP >> ONSET. This is a mistake.

In a language with onsetless syllables, hypothetical /apa/ becomes surface [a.pa] and not *[pa], with deletion. This pair of candidates presents a conflict between MAX, which favors [a.pa], and ONSET, which favors *[pa]. Since [a.pa] is the actual output – the winner – we have the elements of a proper argument that MAX dominates ONSET. Similarly, the pair [a.pa] and *[ʔa.pa] presents a conflict between DEP and ONSET; since [a.pa] wins, DEP must also dominate ONSET. But these forms don't supply an argument for ranking MAX above DEP. It's true that Max and Dep disagree in their assessments of *[pa] and *[ʔa.pa], but neither of these forms is the winner. From the evidence, we do not know how these constraints are ranked, and it's wrong to assert the Max >> Dep ranking for which there is no foundation.

What is the source of this error? Probably the author is making the incorrect assumption that the constraints must be totally ordered or else the analysis will be incomplete. Since a total ordering seems to be required, the author supplies one even though there is insufficient evidence to support it. This assumption is unjustified. It's perfectly OK if the process of analysis leads to a partial ordering: Const1 and Const3 both dominate Const2, but the ranking between Const1 and Const3 is unknown. It's also perfectly OK if the process of analysis leads to a disjunction: Const1 or Const3 dominates Const2, but which of them dominates Const2 is unknown.

Occasionally, someone will object: "Max >> Dep >> Onset isn't exactly wrong. Since it just overspecifies the known rankings, it's completely consistent with the data." Regardless of whether it's "wrong," it's unwise to assert rankings for which there is no support. Suppose we later find evidence for Dep >> Max. If we forget that the Max >> Dep ranking was asserted with no evidence, it will seem like there is a contradiction in the rankings when there is not. (I speak from painful experience when I say that it's easy to forget which rankings were previously assumed without proof.) The worst thing about this objection, though, is that it rather trivializes the task of analysis in OT. It implies that cranking out the facts is the sole goal of the enterprise.

To really grasp what is going on in an analysis, we need to know and understand the *crucial* constraint rankings – those that make a difference in the outcome. Without that understanding, we cannot competently challenge the analysis with additional candidates or inputs. Nor can we hope to advance broader theoretical goals, such as evaluating some claimed advantage of OT or testing a proposal about one or more of the constraints in Con. Sound ranking arguments are therefore essential for any real progress in OT.

Ranking arguments are illustrated with *tableaux*. Back when Prince and Smolensky first introduced OT, only one type of tableau was in common use. The *violation tableau*, exemplified in (2), has one row for each candidate being compared and one column for each constraint involved in the comparison. (We saw these earlier in chapter 1.) The constraints are listed in the top row in ranking order, from highest-ranking to lowest-ranking. The candidates are listed in the first column, with the winning candidate usually listed first. The winner is indicated with an arrow → or a pointing hand ☞. Information about constraint violations is given by the asterisks. For example, the asterisk in row (b) beneath the constraint *C^{unsyll} means that *[ʔil.k.hin] incurs one violation mark from this constraint. The double asterisk in row (c) means that *[ʔi.li.ki.hin] has two DEP violations.

(2)   Violation tableau

	*C^{unsyll}	DEP
a. → ʔi.lik.hin		*
b. ʔil.k.hin	*	
c. ʔi.li.ki.hin		**

Tableau (2) contains all of the indispensable information – candidates, violations, and rankings – but tableaux are often supplied with annotations that make them easier to read. Tableau (3) is the same as (2), but with the helpful annotations added. The exclamation point ("!") only appears in loser rows. It signals the highest-ranking constraint that disfavors that loser relative to the winner – that is, the constraint that is active by virtue of knocking that loser out of the competition for optimality. There is an exclamation point in row (b) where *C^{unsyll} disfavors *[ʔil.k.hin] relative to the winner [ʔi.lik.hin], and there is another one in row (c) because DEP favors the winner over *[ʔi.li.ki.hin]. Another convention followed in (3) is the appearance of the input above the candidates. This is helpful for assessing faithfulness violations, and it's a good reminder that tableaux can only compare candidates from the same input.

(3)   Violation tableau with annotations

/ʔilk-hin/	*C^{unsyll}	DEP
a. → ʔi.lik.hin		*
b. ʔil.k.hin	*!	
c. ʔi.li.ki.hin		**!

Tableau (3) has a shaded cell to the right of the cell with the exclamation point in row (b). Shading is another of these helpful annotations in tableaux, and here it indicates that *[ʔil.k.hin]'s performance on DEP is irrelevant to the outcome, precisely because this candidate earned an exclamation point from *C^{unsyll}. In other words, cells that are shaded are those that can have no effect on the outcome because the competition has been decided by higher-ranking constraints. Cells in both loser rows and winner rows can be shaded, and shaded cells can contain violation marks or not. Tableau (4) exemplifies this – neither candidate's performance on DEP matters, since higher-ranking *C^{unsyll} is completely decisive over just this pair of candidates. A warning: mistakes in the use of shading are surprisingly common, even in published work, so don't worry too much if you sometimes can't make sense of the shading in papers that you read.

(4) Shading example

/ʔilk-hin/	*C^{unsyll}	DEP
a. → ʔi.lik.hin		*
b. ʔil.k.hin	*!	

Violation tableaux are very common in the literature, and they usually include all of the helpful annotations. Minor variations on this format are also occasionally encountered: replacing the asterisks with the number of violations or the actual offending element (k in row (b) of (4)); and transposing the tableau, with constraints in rows and candidates in columns, to allow room for more constraints but fewer candidates.

Prince (2002a) introduced a different tableau format, the *comparative tableau*. While the original tableaux focus on constraint violations, comparative tableaux focus on favoring relations. For each losing candidate in the tableau, we ask of each constraint whether it favors the winner over this loser (W), or favors this loser over the winner (L), or favors neither (blank). The W and L symbols are entered into the corresponding cells of the tableau, as shown in (5).

(5) Comparative tableau

/ʔilk-hin/	*C^{unsyll}	DEP
a. → ʔi.lik.hin		
b. ʔil.k.hin	W	L
c. ʔi.li.ki.hin		W

The W and L symbols are limited to loser rows because they represent how a loser compares with the winner on each constraint. To illustrate, let's work through tableau (5) systematically. In row (b), *C^{unsyll} favors the winner [ʔi.lik.hin] over the loser *[ʔil.k.hin]. Therefore, W is entered into the cell at the intersection of the *[ʔil.k.hin] row and the *C^{unsyll} column. The next cell to the right has an L because DEP favors *[ʔil.k.hin] over the winner. Since *C^{unsyll} dominates DEP, the winner-favoring W takes precedence over the loser-favoring L. In row (c), *C^{unsyll} favors neither the winner nor the loser *[ʔi.li.ki.hin], so the cell in the *C^{unsyll} column is left blank. DEP favors the winner because this loser has more epenthesis, so the bottom-right cell gets a W.

Because every loser row in (5) has a W and that W is to the left of (= dominates) every L, this tableau shows that the winner [ʔi.lik.hin] beats the losers *[ʔil.k.hin] and *[ʔi.li.ki.hin] with these constraints as they are ranked. Every time a constraint favors some loser, there is a higher-ranking constraint that favors the winner over that loser.

With examples of even moderate complexity, it can be difficult to fill in the Ws and Ls of a comparative tableau without first constructing a violation tableau. The solution is to use the *combination tableau,* which includes information about violations as well as the W and L annotations of the comparative tableau. To make a combination tableau, first construct a violation tableau like (2), and then add the W and L annotations to the loser rows. The result is shown in (6):

(6) Combination tableau

/ʔilk-hin/	*C^{unsyll}	DEP
a. → ʔi.lik.hin		*
b. ʔil.k.hin	*W	L
c. ʔi.li.ki.hin		**W

The combination tableau is the ideal instrument for constructing and presenting ranking arguments, and we will be using it for that purpose throughout this book. It practically guarantees that the first two requirements of a valid ranking argument are met: constraint conflict and a winner. For example, tableau (7) presents an argument for ranking *C*unsyll above DEP in Yawelmani. The cells with W and L in row (b) tell us that these constraints conflict over the choice of the winner. For the winner to win, the constraint with the W must be ranked higher than the constraint with the L. That is exactly what we seek in a ranking argument.

(7)   A ranking argument in a combination tableau

/ʔilk-hin/	*C^unsyll	DEP
a. → ʔi.lik.hin		*
b. ʔil.k.hin	*W	L

The combination tableau is also useful in determining whether the third condition on valid ranking arguments is met. The third condition says that we can legitimately conclude that CONST1 must dominate CONST2 only if there is no third constraint CONST3 that could be doing the same work as CONST1. Suppose just for the purposes of this discussion that there is a markedness constraint against [lk] consonant clusters. This otherwise highly dubious constraint, which I'll call *lk, favors [ʔi.lik.hin] over *[ʔil.k.hin]. It therefore has the same favoring relation as *C^unsyll on this pair of candidates. It has the potential to undermine the argument that *C^unsyll dominates DEP. In (8), I show the result of adding *lk to tableau (7). (The broken line between columns will be explained shortly.) Because both *C^unsyll and *lk have W in (8), we cannot know for certain which of them dominates DEP. In other words, we know that some W must dominate the L, but we don't know which W is doing the work. If all we had were tableau (8), then we would be stuck with a disjunctive statement about ranking: *C^unsyll or *lk dominates DEP. (This disjunction can be resolved – see exercise 11)

(8)   Tableau (7) with hypothetical *lk added

/ʔilk-hin/	*C^unsyll	*lk	DEP
a. → ʔi.lik.hin			*
b. ʔil.k.hin	*W	*W	L

We now have two main tableau formats. Brasoveanu and Prince (2005: 3–5) have a good way of explaining which tableau format to use depending on the situation. They distinguish between the *ranking problem* and the *selection problem*. The comparative or combination format is best for the ranking problem, whereas the violation format is best for the selection problem.

In the ranking problem, the winner is already known and we are trying to figure out which ranking will produce that winner. The ranking problem arises whenever we are trying to analyze some data: the winners are known because they are the data of the language, and we are trying to figure out a ranking that will account for the data. We've already seen why the comparative or combination format is best for making ranking arguments.

In the selection problem, the ranking is already known but the winner is not. This situation arises when we are trying to determine what our analysis predicts about additional data that weren't available when the analysis was first constructed. It also arises in the study of language typology, where we want to check a ranking to determine which candidate wins (see chapter 5). When the winner isn't known in advance of tableau construction, the comparative format can't be used first, since it presumes that we already know which candidate wins.

Tableaux aren't perfect. Their most important limitation is that they cannot represent all ranking situations. Tableau format presents the constraints as if they were in a total ordering: a constraint is ranked lower than the constraints to its left and higher than the constraints to its right. In real analyses, however, a total ordering of the constraints cannot usually be established. There are several reasons why this happens.

One possible reason why a total ordering cannot be established is that we haven't yet found an example or thought of a loser that would show the constraints in conflict. Some of the analytic techniques described in this chapter will help to resolve such uncertainties.

Another possible reason is that the constraints never conflict over the choice of winner anywhere in the language. That's the problem with the unsupported claim about ranking in the journal aricle that I mentioned: MAX and DEP dominate ONSET, but their ranking with respect to one another is unknown and perhaps unknowable, based on data from that language. Rankings like this are often represented graphically using something called a *Hasse diagram*. ("Hasse" is pronounced ['hɑsə].) The Hasse diagram in (9) shows that MAX and DEP both dominate ONSET, but it shows them as unranked with respect to one another because there is no strictly downward path between them. In tableaux, situations like this are usually indicated by drawing a broken line between columns with unranked constraints. See tableau (10) for an example.

(9) Hasse diagram: {MAX, DEP} >> ONSET

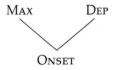

(10) Tableau: {MAX, DEP} >> ONSET

/apa/	MAX	DEP	ONSET
a. → a.pa			*
b. pa	*W		L
c. ʔa.pa		*W	L

Sometimes, however, the known information about ranking cannot be accurately represented in a tableau, even with the aid of the broken-line convention. Tableau (11) shows a situation where the broken-line convention is insufficient. In this hypothetical example, we know that ONSET dominates MAX-V and that NO-CODA dominates DEP-V. (MAX-V and DEP-V are vowel-specific versions of MAX and DEP – see §2.10.3.) But the tableau seems to be telling us that *both* ONSET and NO-CODA dominate *both* MAX-V and DEP-V, and that is more than we can legitimately infer from this example. The Hasse diagram (12) accurately represents the known rankings. The tableau formats in (13) can be used in a situation like this.

(11) Bad tableau: ONSET >> MAX-V; NO-CODA >> DEP-V

/apak/	ONSET	NO-CODA	MAX-V	DEP-V
a. → pa.kə			*	*
b. pak		*W	*	L
c. a.pa.kə	*W		L	*

(12)   Hasse diagram: Onset >> Max-V; No-Coda >> Dep-V

Onset	No-Coda
│	│
Max-V	Dep-V

(13)   Tableau formats for Onset >> Max-V; No-Coda >> Dep-V

/apak/	Onset	Max-V	No-Coda	Dep-V
a. → pa.kə		*		*
b. pak		*	*W	L
c. a.pa.kə	*W	L		*

or

/apak/	Onset	Max-V	No-Coda	Dep-V
a. → pa.kə		*		*
b. pak		*	*W	L
c. a.pa.kə	*W	L		*

Even Hasse diagrams are inadequate when the known rankings involve a disjunction (Prince 2006a: 53–55). For instance, there is no way of representing the disjunctive ranking information in (8) using a Hasse diagram, since these diagrams have no means of expressing *or*. The OTSoft constraint ranking program adds labels to the lines in a Hasse diagram as a way of indicating disjunctions (Hayes, Tesar, and Zuraw 2003). See (14) for how OTSoft would represents the ranking information in (8), and §2.11 for more about OTSoft.

(14)   OTSoft labeled diagram for (*C^unsyll >> Dep) ∨ (*lk >> Dep)

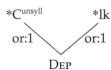

EXERCISES

10   If a winning candidate violates none of the constraints under discussion, is it potentially useful for ranking purposes? What if it violates all of the constraints under discussion? Explain your answers. (Hint: The two situations aren't symmetric.)

11   Tableau (8) leads to a disjunctive statement about ranking: at least one of *C^{unsyll} and *lk dominates DEP. This disjunction can be resolved by showing that one of *C^{unsyll} and *lk couldn't possibly dominate DEP because it's dominated *by* DEP. Do this by constructing a ranking argument based on the winner~loser pair [ʔil.kal]~*[ʔi.li.kal] 'might sing'.

12   Below, you are given the underlying and surface forms of some words of Tibetan (from a problem set in Halle and Clements 1983).[4] You are also given a somewhat random assortment of losing candidates for comparison with the actual surface forms (the winning candidates). Use this material to construct arguments for the following constraint rankings:

*COMPLEX-ONSET >> MAX
DEP >> MAX
DEP >> NO-CODA
MAX >> NO-CODA

NO-CODA is violated by syllable-final consonants, such as the [g] of [ʤig]. *COMPLEX-ONSET is violated by initial clusters, such as the [bʃ] of *[bʃi].

Underlying	Surface	Losers	
/bʃi/	[ʃi]	*[bʃi]	'four'
		*[ib.ʃi]	
		*[bi.ʃi]	
/rgu/	[gu]	*[rgu]	'nine'
		*[ir.gu]	
		*[ri.gu]	
/gʤig/	[ʤig]	*[gʤig]	'one'
		*[gʤi.gi]	
		*[gi.ʤi.gi]	

13   Now assume one more constraint, DEP$_{init-\sigma}$, that is violated by any epenthetic segment in the first syllable of a word. Does the existence of this additional constraint affect the ranking arguments that you have already constructed?

14 Do all of the following tasks for each of the following violation tableaux. Consider each tableau separately, and assume that it includes all of the constraints that could possibly be relevant to evaluating these candidates.

a. Translate the violation tableau into comparative format.
b. Determine what constraint rankings, if any, are supported by the tableau.
c. Draw Hasse diagrams for the rankings, if possible. If not, explain why.

Tableau 1

	CONST1	CONST2
a. → Cand1	**	****
b. Cand2	***	*****

Tableau 2

	CONST1	CONST2
a. → Cand1	*	***
b. Cand2	**	***

Tableau 3

	CONST1	CONST2	CONST3
a. → Cand1	*	**	*
b. Cand2	*	***	
b. Cand3	**	**	

Tableau 4

	CONST1	CONST2	CONST3
a. → Cand1	*	**	*
b. Cand2	*	***	

15 Translate each of the following comparative tableaux into a violation tableau. Since there are infinitely many violation tableaux that are consistent

with any specific comparative tableau, the exercise needs to be made more specific to ensure a unique outcome. Therefore, you should assume that the winner violates each constraint exactly once, and you should add the minimum number of marks to loser rows so as to produce the desired result. (Bonus questions: Why are there infinitely many violation tableaux that are consistent with any specific comparative tableau? And why do the further specifications of the task ensure a unique outcome?)

Tableau 1

	CONST1	CONST2	CONST3
a. → Cand1			
b. Cand2	W		L
b. Cand3		W	L

Tableau 2

	CONST1	CONST2	CONST3	CONST4
a. → Cand1				
b. Cand2	W	L	L	
b. Cand3		W		L

2.3 Working through an Analysis in Phonology

To pull the various techniques together and get some practical experience, we'll systematically work through an example of moderate complexity. The example involves two interacting phenomena in Yawelmani, vowel shortening in closed syllables and deletion of final vowels. Because my goal here is to show how to construct an analysis, I'll be explaining the process of doing an analysis in detail. A warning: This is advice about how to *do* an analysis, but not advice about how to *write up* an analysis. Doing an analysis and writing it up are different tasks. In chapter 3 I'll explain the best way to write up this analysis in a paper.

The vowel shortening data appear in (15). The forms in (a) show that an underlying long vowel changes into a surface short vowel in a closed syllable – that is, in contexts ___CCV and ___C#. (The ___C# context isn't included in these examples but will be seen shortly.) The forms in (b) are there to justify the underlying long vowels in the roots; they show the same roots with a vowel-initial suffix, which allows the underlying vowel length to emerge.

(15) Yawelmani closed syllable shortening (Kenstowicz and Kisseberth 1979: 83)

	Underlying	*Surface*	
a.	/laːn-hin/	[lan.hin]	'hear (nonfuture)'
	/ṣaːp-hin/	[ṣap.hin]	'burn (nonfuture)'
b.	/laːn-al/	[laː.nal]	'hear (dubitative)'
	/ṣaːp-al/	[ṣaː.pal]	'burn (dubitative)'

Final vowel deletion is exemplified in (16). The forms in (a) show the effect of final vowel deletion in words ending in /. . . V-CV/. The forms in (b) show final vowel deletion being blocked in words ending in /. . . VC-CV/. The (b) forms also prove that the suffixes have a /-CV/ shape in underlying representation. Another thing to notice about (a) is vowel shortening: when final vowel deletion creates a final closed syllable, the long vowel is shortened as expected.

(16) Yawelmani final vowel deletion (Kenstowicz and Kisseberth 1979: 98)

	Underlying	*Surface*	
a.	/taxaː-kʼa/	[ta.xakʼ]	'bring!'
	/taxaː-mi/	[ta.xam]	'having brought'
b.	/xat-kʼa/	[xat.kʼa]	'eat!'
	/xat-mi/	[xat.mi]	'having eaten'

The first step in the analysis is to formulate OT-friendly descriptive generalizations, following the guidelines in §2.1.2. In (17), (a) and (b) are descriptive statements analogous to OT markedness constraints. So is the first clause of (d). In (c), there is a statement about the unfaithful mapping that occurs to satisfy (a) and (b).

(17) Descriptive generalizations for Yawelmani
    a. No syllable is larger than CVC or CVː. (I.e., *CVCC, *CVːC, etc.)
    b. Unsyllabified consonants are prohibited.
    c. (a) and (b) are enforced by vowel shortening.

d. Words cannot end in vowels, and this requirement is enforced by deletion, except when the result would be inconsistent with (a) or (b).

Good descriptive generalizations hint at which constraints are involved in the analysis. Clause (a) of the generalization tells us that all Yawelmani words obey some markedness constraint(s) that are violated by CVCC and CVːC syllables. We could interrupt the analysis at this point to research the topic of syllable-structure constraints, but a better move is to put the matter aside and simply formulate an ad hoc constraint that is violated by any syllable that is too big. Call it *COMPLEX-SYLLABLE (*COMP-SYLL). The other markedness constraints alluded to in (17) have already been introduced, *C^{unsyll} and *V#. As for faithfulness, we know that deletion is a violation of MAX, but the faithfulness constraint associated with vowel shortening is less certain. We can call it IDENT(long) for now, although ultimately we might want to adopt something like MAX(mora) instead. It's OK to leave this detail unresolved, because our goal right now is to get a handle on the Yawelmani system rather than explore the typology and theory of vowel shortening processes.

Now that we have a hypothesis about the constraints that are involved, we can move on to the ranking. It's easiest to begin the ranking process with a faithfulness violation. Any faithfulness violation must be compelled by a higher-ranking markedness constraint, so if we start with a faithfulness violation, we immediately know that we need to locate a conflicting markedness constraint to make the other half of the ranking argument. It's also a good idea, whenever possible, to start with an example that violates just one faithfulness constraint, putting off the complicated cases until more of the analysis is secure. The shortening examples like /laːn-hin/ → [lan.hin] in (15) are perfect: they violate a faithfulness constraint, IDENT(long), and this is the only faithfulness constraint that they violate. So the first question the analysis will answer is this: Which markedness constraint or constraints dominate IDENT(long)?

The answer is already there in clause (c) of the descriptive generalization: *COMPLEX-SYLLABLE and *C^{unsyll}. We'll start with *COMPLEX-SYLLABLE. Since ranking arguments are based on comparing candidates, we need a winner and a loser. We have already chosen the winner, [lan.hin]. It's derived from /laːn-hin/ by violating IDENT(long), and it satisfies *COMPLEX-SYLLABLE. To make the ranking argument, we need a loser that does better than the winner on IDENT(long) and worse than the winner on *COMPLEX-SYLLABLE. Since the winner has only one violation of IDENT(long), the loser must not have any violations of this constraint. And since the winner has no violations of *COMPLEX-SYLLABLE, the loser must have at least one violation of this constraint.

A loser that meets both of these criteria is *[laːn.hin]. It has no violations of IDENT(long), and it has one violation of *COMPLEX-SYLLABLE because it contains a CVːC syllable. (I will say lots more about how to construct useful losers in §2.5.) We now have a winner~loser pair for the ranking argument illustrated in tableau (18).

(18) Ranking argument: *COMPLEX-SYLLABLE >> IDENT(long)

/laːn-hin/	*COMP-SYLL	IDENT(long)
a. → lan.hin		*
b. laːn.hin	*W	L

The argument that *C^{unsyll} also dominates IDENT(long) requires a different loser, *[laː.n.hin], with a syllabically unparsed [n]. This candidate is structurally distinct from *[laːn.hin], so it violates *C^{unsyll} but not *COMPLEX-SYLLABLE. Since *[laː.n.hin] obeys IDENT(long), it can serve as the basis for another ranking argument. This argument is represented by tableau (19).

(19) Ranking argument: *C^{unsyll} >> IDENT(long)

/laːn-hin/	*COMP-SYLL	*C^{unsyll}	IDENT(long)
a. → lan.hin			*
b. laː.n.hin		*W	L

Why does (19) include *COMPLEX-SYLLABLE, which is certainly not the focus of attention in this tableau? We know from the explanation of ranking in §2.2 that three factors are essential for valid ranking arguments: constraint conflict, a winner~loser comparison, and no other constraint that could do the same job. This third factor is the reason for including *COMPLEX-SYLLABLE in (19): we need to make sure that it doesn't undermine the ranking argument. In fact, it doesn't, since it favors neither the winner nor the loser. Furthermore, we also need to go back and make sure that $*C^{unsyll}$ doesn't undermine the ranking argument in (18). Tableau (20) does that: it shows that $*C^{unsyll}$ favors neither the winner nor the loser in this competition.

(20) No effect of $*C^{unsyll}$ on *COMPLEX-SYLLABLE >> IDENT(long) argument

/laːn-hin/	*COMP-SYLL	$*C^{unsyll}$	IDENT(long)
a. → lan.hin			*
b. laːn.hin	*W		L

In general, whenever a constraint is introduced into an analysis, its potential effects on *all* existing claims about ranking need to be considered. That means that new ranking arguments may need to include constraints that had been discussed earlier (like (19)), and old ranking arguments need to be rechecked with the new constraint (like (20)). I have been very fastidious in (19) and (20), since I have insisted on including constraints that favor neither the winner nor the loser. Constraints that favor neither a winner nor a loser cannot possibly affect a ranking argument (see §2.7 for the explanation), so it isn't strictly necessary to include them in these tableaux. Nonetheless, their presence in tableaux (19) and (20), and in the summary tableaux at the end of the analysis ((31)–(34)), serves as a good reminder of an important point: the ranking argument is solid precisely because no other constraint does the job. Seeing *COMPLEX-SYLLABLE's blank column in (19) emphasizes this important point: our confidence in the argument for ranking $*C^{unsyll}$ over IDENT(long) rests on knowing that *COMPLEX-SYLLABLE cannot do the job of favoring the winner over *[laː.n.hin].

We now turn to the vowel deletion phenomenon exemplified in (16). These examples have both final vowel deletion and vowel shortening: /taxaː-kʔa/ → [ta.xakʔ]. Since we already have the hypothesis that the ranking in (20) accounts for vowel shortening, we should first check whether that hypothesis also accounts for these new cases of shortening. To do that, we'll compare the winner with losers that differ from it only by virtue of having a long vowel: *[ta.xaːkʔ] and *[ta.xaː.kʔ].

(21) Shortening analysis verified

/taxaː-kʔa/	*Comp-Syll	*Cᵘⁿˢʸˡˡ	Ident(long)
a. → ta.xakʔ			*
b. ta.xaːkʔ	*W		L
c. ta.xaː.kʔ		*W	L

Tableau (21) might look like an illegitimate move because the candidates have lost their final vowels but the tableau doesn't explain why. In fact, this tableau is perfectly legitimate. We are doing the right thing by building up the analysis gradually, one piece at a time. Tableaux like (21) are an inevitable consequence of taking that approach. What makes (21) legitimate is that *all* of the candidates have lost the final vowel. In other words, (21) presupposes that an analysis of final vowel deletion will be forthcoming and therefore sets deletion aside to focus on shortening. This move is legitimate because the constraints that we haven't discussed yet – *V# and Max – favor neither the winner nor the losers.

Next, we'll analyze final vowel deletion. From clause (d) of the descriptive generalization (17) and from previous discussion, we know that deletion is a consequence of satisfying the markedness constraint *V#. Since *V# favors [ta.xakʔ] over faithful *[ta.xaː.kʔa], it must dominate Max. Can [ta.xakʔ] and *[ta.xaː.kʔa] be compared on just *V# and Max, or do we have to include other constraints in the tableau? To answer this question, we review the constraints that we already have – *Complex-Syllable, *Cᵘⁿˢʸˡˡ, and Ident(long) – and ask whether any of them favors the winner or the loser in this pair of candidates. Since Ident(long) favors the loser, it has to be included in the tableau. Like Max, Ident(long) is ranked below *V#, as (22) shows.

(22) Ranking argument: *V# >> Max, Ident(long)

/taxaː-kʔa/	*V#	Max	Ident(long)
a. → ta.xakʔ		*	*
b. ta.xaː.kʔa	*W	L	L

Tableau (22) shows that a ranking argument can contain two loser-favoring constraints and still be valid. Because of how EVAL works, *every* loser-favoring constraint must be dominated by *some* winner-favoring constraint. (In a comparative tableau, every L must have some W to its left.) Since the mapping /taxaː-k$^?$a/ → [ta.xak$^?$] is doubly unfaithful, two faithfulness constraints favor the faithful loser *[ta.xaː.k$^?$a]. The constraint *V# must dominate both of them to ensure that [ta.xak$^?$] is optimal.[5] (Candidate comparisons with more than one *winner*-favoring constraint are more problematic – see §2.5 and §2.12 on disjunctions.)

Since we have just introduced two additional constraints, we need to make sure that they do not affect either of our previous ranking arguments, (19) and (20). They do not, since neither *V# nor MAX favors a winner or a loser in those arguments.

There is one thing left in our descriptive generalization, the blocking of final vowel deletion after consonant clusters: [xat.k$^?$a]. From the "except when" clause of the generalization, we know that the markedness constraints *COMPLEX-SYLLABLE and *C^{unsyll} define the conditions where final vowel deletion is blocked. *V# must be dominated by both of these constraints, as shown in (23) and (24).

(23)   Ranking argument: *COMPLEX-SYLLABLE >> *V# (>> MAX)

/xat-k$^?$a/	*COMP-SYLL	*V#	MAX
a. → xat.k$^?$a		*	
b. xatk$^?$	*W	L	*W

(24)   Ranking argument: *C^{unsyll} >> *V# (>> MAX)

/xat-k$^?$a/	*C^{unsyll}	*V#	MAX
a. → xat.k$^?$a		*	
b. xat.k$^?$	*W	L	*W

Tableaux (23) and (24) also include MAX. The reason for including MAX is that it also favors the winner. (None of the other constraints considered so far favors the winner or losers in these tableaux) Winner-favoring constraints have the potential to undermine ranking arguments by offering an alternative explanation for why the winner wins. But since we already know that MAX is ranked below *V#, it does not threaten these ranking arguments at all. By including MAX in the tableau, we verify that it's ranked too low to undermine the argument.

Since we have now completed an initial pass through the entire descriptive generalization, it's appropriate to summarize the proven rankings in (25) and assess the overall analysis. This diagram shows two constraints on syllable well-formedness, *COMPLEX-SYLLABLE and *C^{unsyll}, dominating the markedness constraint *V# and, through it, the faithfulness constraint IDENT(long). The result is a triggering effect (shortening) and a blocking effect (final vowel deletion). In addition, *V# dominates MAX, so there is final vowel deletion whenever the top-ranked constraints allow it.

(25)   Summary ranking for Yawelmani (preliminary)

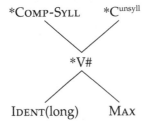

It might seem as if we could quit now after a bit of self-congratulation, but actually we still have more work to do. The next step is to check all of the pairs of constraints that aren't ranked with respect to one another. Do these constraints ever conflict? If so, the analysis is incomplete until they have been ranked. Checking all of the pairs of unranked constraints is an excellent way of discovering interactions that we might have overlooked.

One unranked pair is *COMPLEX-SYLLABLE and *C^{unsyll}. As far as we know, neither of these constraints is ever violated by surface forms of Yawelmani. They are *unviolated constraints*. Unviolated constraints can never be ranked with respect to one another because ranking requires conflict, and for there to be conflict the winner must violate one of the constraints. No winner in Yawelmani ever violates either of these constraints, so they never conflict and neither dominates the other. In fact, since they are never violated, *no* constraint dominates them. Unviolated constraints are *undominated*.

The other unranked pair is IDENT(long) and MAX. All of the ranking arguments that we have considered so far involve a markedness constraint and a faithfulness constraint (triggering) or two markedness constraints (blocking). Since IDENT(long) and MAX are both faithfulness constraints, they present a different kind of conflict: what is the best way of being unfaithful? When there is choice between shortening and deletion, which is preferred? Again, we need an input where both constraints are potentially relevant, and again that input is /taxaː-kˀa/. The actual output form [ta.xakˀ] violates both IDENT(long) and MAX, once each. For the ranking argument, then, we need a loser that violates one of these constraints more than [ta.xakˀ] does and one of them less. Since the input has only one long vowel, it's impossible to incur any more violations of IDENT(long), so the loser we seek must have *fewer* violations of IDENT(long) (i.e., none) and *more* violations of MAX (i.e., at least two).

One possibility that comes to mind is *[ta.xaː]. It fulfills both requirements, since it has no violations of IDENT(long) and two violations of MAX. It would seem to be perfectly suited for the ranking argument in tableau (26). But this argument is invalid. Although the argument involves constraints that conflict over the choice of the winner, the constraints aren't active on this pair of candidates. The reason is that a higher-ranking constraint, *V#, has the same favoring relation as MAX. In (27) I have included shading to emphasize this point about constraint inactivity.

(26) *Invalid* ranking argument: MAX >> IDENT(long)

/taxaː-kˀa/	MAX	IDENT(long)
a. → ta.xakˀ	*	*
b. ta.xaː	**W	L

(27) Why (26) is invalid

/taxaː-kˀa/	*V#	MAX	IDENT(long)
a. → ta.xakˀ		*	*
b. ta.xaː	*W	**W	L

To fully grasp why the ranking argument in (26) is invalid, it helps to think about the following question: Would the result change if IDENT(long) and MAX were in the opposite order? The answer is no, because the result is determined by *V#, which has already been shown to dominate both IDENT(long) and MAX. This is why ranking arguments have to be considered in the context of the full system and why we must always include other winner-favoring constraints in ranking tableaux.

Since *[ta.xaː] isn't the foundation of a valid ranking argument, we need to look at a candidate with even more deletion, *[tax]. This candidate violates MAX more than the winner [ta.xakʔ] does, and it satisfies IDENT(long) – maybe. When I introduced IDENT(long) earlier in this section, I was (deliberately) vague about how it's defined. I ignored my own advice about the need to be precise when defining constraints. We have now run into one of the consequences of vagueness: we don't know whether deleting a long vowel violates IDENT(long) as well as MAX.[6] If deleting a long vowel violates both of these constraints, then there is no ranking argument. Tableau (28) shows the unrankable configuration: both candidates violate IDENT(long) equally, so there is no conflict between MAX and IDENT(long).

(28)   No ranking argument under one definition of IDENT(long)

/taxaː-kʔa/	MAX	IDENT(long)
a. → ta.xakʔ	*	*
b. tax	***W	*

On the other hand, if IDENT(long) is defined so that it prohibits only literal vowel shortening, then we can make the valid ranking argument in (29):

(29)   Ranking argument: MAX >> IDENT(long) under another definition

/taxaː-kʔa/	MAX	IDENT(long)
a. → ta.xakʔ	*	*
b. tax	***W	L

Let us assume that (29) is correct. (On the general problem of deciding among competing constraint definitions, see chapter 5.) We can then revise the Hasse diagram to reflect the new ranking arguments.

(30) Summary ranking for Yawelmani (final for this section)

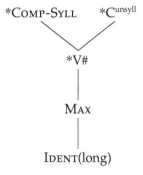

This is also the point when we should check that all of the original data have been correctly analyzed. The best way to do this is with summary tableaux that challenge the full constraint hierarchy with all of the relevant inputs and candidates. Since the original data were organized into four groups in (15) and (16), we should have one summary tableau for each group. That means constructing tableaux for the inputs /laːn-hin/, /laːn-al/, /taxaː-kʼa/, and /xat-kʼa/. Besides the winners, of course, the tableaux should contain all of the losers that appeared in ranking arguments. There are some other losers here as well.

(31) Summary tableau: /laːn-hin/ → [lan.hin]

/laːn-hin/	*Comp-Syll	*C^{unsyll}	*V#	Max	Ident(long)
a. → lan.hin					*
b. laːn.hin	*W				L
c. laː.n.hin		*W			L

(32) Summary tableau: /laːn-al/ → [laː.nal]

/laːn-al/	*Comp-Syll	*C^{unsyll}	*V#	Max	Ident(long)
a. → laː.nal					
b. la.nal					*W

(33) Summary tableau: /taxaː-k^{ʔ}a/ → [ta.xak^ʔ]

/taxaː-k^{ʔ}a/	*Comp-Syll	*C^{unsyll}	*V#	Max	Ident(long)
a. → ta.xak^ʔ				*	*
b. ta.xaː.k^{ʔ}a			*W	L	L
c. ta.xaːk^ʔ	*W			*	L
d. ta.xaː.k^ʔ		*W		*	L
e. ta.xaː			*W	**W	L
f. tax				***W	L

(34) Summary tableau: /xat-k^{ʔ}a/ → [xat.k^{ʔ}a]

/xat-k^{ʔ}a/	*Comp-Syll	*C^{unsyll}	*V#	Max	Ident(long)
a. → xat.k^{ʔ}a			*		
b. xatk^ʔ	*W		L	*W	
c. xat.k^ʔ		*W	L	*W	

Since every loser-favoring constraint has to be dominated by some winner-favoring constraint, we check that every L has some W to its left (across a solid line). There is nothing wrong with having W dominated by an L, as in row (c) of (34), provided that the L is dominated by another W. The simplest ranking arguments are rows with a single W and one or more Ls, since that lone W must dominate all of the Ls for the correct form to win. Rows that contain only Ws, such as (b) in (32), are uninformative about ranking (see exercise 18). In §2.12, we'll see in detail how to analyze the ranking information in a tableau row.

EXERCISES

16 The constraint domination relation is transitive: if Const1 dominates Const2 and Const2 dominates Const3, then Const1 must also dominate Const3. Sometimes, rankings that are inferred from transitivity of domination can also be supported by direct ranking arguments. List all of the pairwise constraint rankings that can be inferred from transitivity in (30). For each ranking in the list, give a direct ranking argument if one exists.

17   Using the loser *[xa.tik^{ʔ}], with epenthetic [i], give a ranking argument for
DEP and some other constraint in (30). Could you have made this argument
using the loser *[xat.k^{ʔ}i] instead?

18   Is there any ranking of these constraints that would allow candidate (b)
in (32) to be the winner? What about candidate (e) in (33)? Explain your answers.

2.4   The Limits of Ranking Arguments

Ranking settles constraint conflicts about which candidate is optimal.
When there are no such conflicts, direct ranking arguments are impossible. Knowing when *not* to attempt a ranking argument will avoid frustration and potential errors.

We have already seen one situation where ranking is impossible:
Unviolated constraints cannot be ranked with respect to one another.
In Yawelmani, no surface form ever violates *COMPLEX-SYLLABLE or
*C^{unsyll}, so these constraints never conflict over the output of the gram-
mar. They always agree about the choice of the winner, since every
winner obeys both of them. Without conflict, there can be no ranking.
This is a very common situation, since most grammars contain a
number of unviolated constraints. For example, most phonotactic
regularities are a consequence of unviolated markedness constraints,
and contrasts that are never neutralized are attributable to unviolated
faithfulness constraints. Identifying the unviolated constraints is a
useful method of narrowing down the set of potentially problematic
candidates, as we will see in §2.5.

Direct ranking arguments are also impossible when two constraints
are in a *stringency relation* (de Lacy 2002, Prince 1997b, 1997c).
Stringency is a kind of subset relation on constraint violations. It's a
bit like the notion of lesser included offenses in criminal law. Any theft
is a crime of larceny. If the theft is accompanied by a threat of force,
it's also a crime of robbery. Larceny is therefore a lesser included offense
of robbery – every robbery is also a larceny, but some larcenies (e.g.,
pick-pocketing) aren't robberies. Somewhat confusingly, in OT parlance
the law against larceny would be described as more stringent than the
law against robbery. It's more stringent because it prohibits more
activities. (The more stringent punishment for the crime of robbery has
nothing to do with stringency in the OT sense.)

Formally, constraint CONST1 is more stringent than constraint
CONST2 if every violation of CONST2 is also a violation of CONST1, but

there are some violations of Const1 that aren't violations of Const2. In other words, Const1 is more stringent or severe in its assessments than Const2 is, since the Const1 violations are a proper superset of the Const2 violations. Other terms used to describe stringency relations are *superset-subset relation, general-specific relation, elsewhere* or *Elsewhere Condition relation,* and *Paninian relation.* (The Sanskrit grammarian Paːɳini was the first person to write about general and specific relations among linguistic principles (Joshi and Kiparsky 1970).) These various terms are practically interchangeable, and all can be found in the literature.

An example of two syntactic markedness constraints in a stringency relation is given in (35), and two phonological faithfulness constraints in a stringency relation are defined in (36). In (35), T-Gov is the more stringent of these two constraints. Every trace that isn't governed is also not lexically governed, but there can be traces that are governed but not lexically governed, so the violations of T-Gov are a proper superset of the violations of T-Lex-Gov. As for (36), the onset consonants that are unfaithful to voicing are a proper subset of all consonants that are unfaithful to voicing. Ident([voice]) is therefore the more general – and hence the more stringent – of these two constraints.[7]

(35) Markedness constraints in a stringency relation (after Grimshaw 1997: 374)
    a. T-Gov
       Assign one violation mark for every trace that is not governed.
    b. T-Lex-Gov
       Assign one violation mark for every trace that is not lexically governed.

(36) Faithfulness constraints in a stringency relation (after Lombardi 1995/2001)
    a. Ident([voice])
       Assign one violation mark for every output segment that differs from its input correspondent in the feature [voice].
    b. Ident$_{Onset}$([voice])
       Assign one violation mark for every output segment in syllable onset position that differs from its input correspondent in the feature [voice].

Constraints in a stringency relation never conflict with one another. For two constraints to conflict, they must disagree in their assessments, with each constraint favoring a different candidate. Since every violation of the specific constraint is also a violation of the general constraint, conflict isn't possible. The stringency relation is illustrated in (37) using the violations assigned by IDENT([voice]) and IDENT$_{Onset}$([voice]) when underlying /bad/ devoices one or both of its consonants. The subset relation is clear: every violation of IDENT$_{Onset}$([voice]) is also a violation of IDENT([voice]), but not vice versa. Because there is no conflict, no ranking argument can possibly be constructed using any pair of the candidates in (37).

(37) Stringency illustrated

/bad/	IDENT([voice])	IDENT$_{Onset}$([voice])
a. bat	*	
b. pad	*	*
c. pat	**	*

Although constraints in a stringency relationship aren't directly rankable, statements about how they are ranked are surprisingly common in the literature. These statements always put the more specific constraint on top, as in IDENT$_{Onset}$([voice]) >> IDENT([voice]). It's important to realize that no direct argument could ever support this ranking, so any author who gives a ranking like this is either mistaken or is perhaps thinking about a ranking that can be inferred from transitivity of domination.

As we saw in exercise 16, the constraint domination relation is transitive: if direct ranking arguments have established CONST1 >> CONST2 and CONST2 >> CONST3, then CONST1 >> CONST3 follows automatically. Two constraints in a stringency relation can only ever be ranked by transitivity through one or more constraints that are outside the stringency relation. For example, IDENT$_{Onset}$([voice]) and IDENT([voice]) may be rankable by transitivity in German and other languages with coda devoicing (Lombardi 1999). The word /bad/ 'bath' undergoes final devoicing, producing [bat]. Assume that coda devoicing is attributed to a general markedness constraint against all voiced stops and fricatives, *VOICE. Since onsets do not devoice but codas do, *VOICE must be ranked below the less stringent constraint IDENT$_{Onset}$([voice]) and above the more stringent one, as illustrated in (38) and (39).

(38) Ranking argument: *Voice >> Ident([voice])

/bad/	*Voice	Ident([voice])
a. → bat	*	*
b. bad	**W	L

(39) Ranking argument: Ident_{Onset}([voice]) >> *Voice (>> Ident([voice]))

/bad/	Ident_{Onset}([voice])	*Voice	Ident([voice])
a. → bat		*	*
b. pat	*W	L	**W

Given these two ranking arguments, the ranking Ident_{Onset}([voice]) >> Ident([voice]) can be inferred from transitivity even though it cannot be proven by direct arguments. Since a direct argument for this ranking is impossible, however, it's misleading to simply assert Ident_{Onset}([voice]) >> Ident([voice]) as one of the premises of an analysis. It isn't literally wrong, but it fosters confusion about ranking and the basis for it.

There is another situation that frequently leads to unfounded assertions about ranking. Suppose our analysis is progressing nicely, with several constraints already ranked by solid arguments. Then we discover a losing candidate that ties with the winner on all of the constraints that have been considered so far. What do we do? We bring in an additional constraint that favors the winner over the problematic loser and thereby breaks the tie.

How is the tie-breaking constraint ranked? The natural intuition is that the tie-breaking constraint should be ranked low, perhaps below all of the constraints that the intended winner violates. This intuition probably comes from the way that ties are broken in sports or elections. The main event takes place, and if the main event fails to produce a unique winner, the special tie-breaking mechanism is invoked. In sports or elections, the tie-breaker is performed only if the normal decision-making processes have failed to produce a unique winner. This natural intuition is completely wrong for the OT analysis, however.

Constraints that only break ties are unrankable with respect to the constraints responsible for the tie. Tableau (40) represents a tie schematically. (Assume that the four constraints have been ranked on the basis of other evidence.) Even though this is intended to be a combined comparative and violation tableau, there are no W or L annotations precisely because both candidates tie on all constraints.

(40) Tied candidates

	Const1	Const2	Const3	Const4
→ cand1		**		*
cand2		**		*

Since *cand1* is the intended winner, we introduce an additional constraint, Const5, that favors *cand1* over *cand2*. As the tableaux in (41) show, Const5 can be ranked anywhere and *cand1* still wins. That means there is no argument here for ranking Const5 at the bottom or anywhere else in the hierarchy.

(41) Free ranking of tie-breaker

	Const5	Const1	Const2	Const3	Const4
→ cand1			**		*
cand2	*W		**		*

or

	Const1	Const5	Const2	Const3	Const4
→ cand1			**		*
cand2		*W	**		*

or

	Const1	Const2	Const5	Const3	Const4
→ cand1		**			*
cand2		**	*W		*

or

	Const1	Const2	Const3	Const5	Const4
→ cand1		**			*
cand2		**		*W	*

or

	Const1	Const2	Const3	Const4	Const5
→ cand1		**		*	
cand2		**		*	*W

The intuitive idea that tie-breaking constraints should be low-ranked is wrong because it's based on a false analogy. In elections or sports, the chronology is fixed: the main event occurs, the results are examined, and the tie-breaking event takes place only if necessary. In the OT analysis, however, the original ranking in (40) has no privileged status as the chronologically prior "main event." Rather, (40) is just the array of constraints that we happened to arrive at first when constructing the analysis. The chronology is just part of the analyst's experience of doing the analysis, so it has no theoretical status.

While we're on the topic of ties, this is a good opportunity to point out a somewhat common misconception about constraint ranking. The misconception is illustrated in the violation tableau (42), which is loosely based on the analysis of Yawelmani. Even though *C^{unsyll} and *V# crucially conflict in the choice of the winner, they are shown as unranked with respect to one another. Candidates (a) and (b) perform equally well on these tied constraints, so the choice goes to the next constraint down in the hierarchy, Max.

(42)   A misconception about constraint ranking

/xat-k$^?$a/	*Comp-Syll	*C^{unsyll}	*V#	Max
a. → xat.k$^?$a			*	
b. xat.k$^?$		*		*!
c. xatk$^?$	*!			*

The misconception is that the broken line between *C^unsyll and *V#
in (42) allows their violation marks to be pooled together, as if they
were a single constraint. This isn't how EVAL works. *C^unsyll and
*V# are separate constraints, so their violation marks can never be
combined. They are in conflict in (42), and conflicting constraints
must be ranked.

We have seen that there are three circumstances where direct ranking arguments are impossible: undominated constraints, constraints
in a stringency relationship, and constraints that only break ties. This
doesn't exhaust the possibilities. There are pairs of constraints that
never conflict because they deal with completely unrelated properties
of language, so there is no way that satisfaction of one could force
violation of the other. I have in mind something like IDENT([voice])
and a constraint requiring phonological phrases to contain two
phonological words, although with sufficient ingenuity it might be
possible to bring even these two constraints into conflict. Finally,
sometimes constraints may remain unranked out of ignorance: we
can imagine how the constraints would conflict, but we can find
no pertinent data in the language under analysis. More about this
in §2.5.

EXERCISES

19 None of the following violation tableaux presents a valid argument that
CONST1 dominates CONST2. For each tableau, explain why there is no valid
ranking argument.

Tableau 1

	CONST1	CONST2
a. → cand1		*
b. cand2	*	*

Tableau 2

	CONST1	CONST2
a. → cand1		
b. cand2	*	

Tableau 3

	CONST3	CONST1	CONST2
a. → cand1			*
b.　cand2	*	*	

20　To each of these tableaux, add a losing candidate that would support a valid argument that CONST1 dominates CONST2. If this isn't possible, explain why.

2.5　Candidates in Ranking Arguments

Figuring out which losing candidates need to be considered is probably the hardest thing about doing analysis in OT. There are two aspects of this problem, one arising in the early stages of analysis and the other arising later on. In the early stages, losing candidates are needed for the ranking arguments that emerge from our descriptive generalizations. In the later stages, the analysis needs to be challenged with losing candidates that might reveal its inadequacies. Typically, these other losers are disfavored by constraints that were not suggested by the original descriptive generalization. They might even be disfavored by constraints that haven't yet been proposed by anyone.

In this section, I describe techniques for dealing with both of these problems, beginning with the first of them. In the early stages of doing an analysis, the descriptive generalization gives an approximate sense of which constraints are involved and how they are ranked, and the task is to devise formal ranking arguments to confirm these suspicions. The data of the language are the winners, so appropriate losers are needed.

This problem arose at several points in the analysis of Yawelmani in §2.3. For instance, the descriptive generalization in (17) leads us to suspect that the ranking *C^{unsyll} >> IDENT(long) is part of the grammar of this language. To argue for this ranking, we need a winner that violates IDENT(long), and to keep things simple, it would be best if it violates no other faithfulness constraints. A form that meets these requirements is [lan.hin], from underlying /laːnhin/.

This ranking argument also requires a loser. For the ranking argument to work, the loser must do worse than [lan.hin] on *C^{unsyll} and better on IDENT(long). We can use these two requirements in a kind of procedure for finding the loser we need (see (43)). Start with the winner [lan.hin]. Now eliminate its violation of the lower-ranking constraint, IDENT(long), yielding *[laːn.hin]. Next, add a violation of the higher-ranking constraint, *C^unsyll. There are many ways to do this – *[laː.n.hin], *[laːn.hi.n], *[l.aːn.hin], *[laːn.hin.ʔ] (with epenthetic unsyllabified glottal stop) – but, as we'll see shortly, there's also a good strategy for picking the right one, *[laː.n.hin].

(43) Constructing a loser to argue for *C^unsyll >> IDENT(long)
      Winner   [lan.hin]
      Remove IDENT(long) violation   [laːn.hin]
      Add *C^unsyll violation   [laː.n.hin]

The procedure just described can be generalized to a technique for finding losers to support ranking arguments. Given a suspected constraint ranking CONST1 >> CONST2 and a winner [w], we want to find a loser *[l] to prove the ranking. Starting from [w], eliminate one or more CONST2 violations and add one or more CONST1 violations *without adding violations of any other constraints, except for those that are already known to be ranked below CONST1*. The result is *[l].

The highlighted clause in the preceding paragraph is how we know that *[laː.n.hin] and not *[laːn.hi.n], *[l.aːn.hin], or *[laːn.hin.ʔ] is the right loser to make the ranking argument. Recall the third condition on valid ranking arguments in §2.2: to prove CONST1 >> CONST2 using winner [w] and loser *[l], there can be no constraint CONST3 that (a) also favors [w] over *[l] and (b) isn't independently known to be dominated by CONST1. In other words, there can be no third constraint that could do CONST1's job of favoring the correct candidate as winner. Right now, we are looking for a technique that can be used when the analysis is just getting started, so we need a criterion that isn't quite as exact as this formal condition. "Without adding violations of any other constraints, except those that are already known to be ranked below CONST1" is such a criterion. The unwanted losers *[laːn.hi.n], *[l.aːn.hin], and *[laːn.hin.ʔ] violate various combinations of *COMPLEX-SYLLABLE, ONSET, and DEP, and none of these constraints is already known to be ranked below *C^unsyll. The loser we need, *[laː.n.hin], adds no violations other than *C^unsyll.

For practice, we can apply this technique to the other Yawelmani ranking arguments in §2.3:

(44) (= 18) *COMPLEX-SYLLABLE >> IDENT(long)

/laːn-hin/	*COMP-SYLL	IDENT(long)
a. → lan.hin		*
b. laːn.hin	*W	L

The winner is [lan.hin]. This ranking argument and the next one involve a markedness constraint dominating a faithfulness constraint. Eliminating a CONST2 violation is therefore a matter of restoring whatever property of the underlying representation the winner has lost – in this case, vowel length. Since the loser has to add a violation of *COMPLEX-SYLLABLE but no other constraints that could dominate *COMPLEX-SYLLABLE, it must be *[laːn.hin].

(45) (= 22) *V# >> MAX, IDENT(long)

/taxaː-kʔa/	*V#	MAX	IDENT(long)
a. → ta.xakʔ		*	*
b. ta.xaː.kʔa	*W	L	L

The winner is [ta.xakʔ] from /taxaː-kʔa/. The loser must eliminate the winner's MAX and IDENT(long) violations, gain a *V# violation, and avoid acquiring violations of other constraints that could dominate *V#. The loser that does all this is *[ta.xaː.kʔa].

(46) (= 23) *COMPLEX-SYLLABLE >> *V# (>> MAX)

/xat-kʔa/	*COMP-SYLL	*V#	MAX
a. → xat.kʔa		*	
b. xatkʔ	*W	L	*W

The winner is [xat.kʔa] from /xat-kʔa/. Starting from the winner [xat.kʔa], we need to eliminate the *V# violation and add a violation of *COMPLEX-SYLLABLE. The loser that fulfills this requirement is [xatkʔ]. It adds a MAX violation as well, and this could make it unsuitable for

the ranking argument, but we have already established that *V#
dominates Max, so there is no problem.

(47)   (= 29) Max >> Ident(long)

/taxaː-kʔa/	Max	Ident(long)
a. → ta.xakʔ	*	*
b. tax	***W	L

The winner is [ta.xakʔ]. Removing the Ident(long) violation and
adding another Max violation would yield *[ta.xaː]. This is unsuitable,
however, because it also adds a violation of *V#, and *V# is already
known to dominate Max. Adding a second Max violation does the job;
*[tax] is the basis for a valid ranking argument.

I want to emphasize that this is a useful analytic technique, but it
isn't quite a formal algorithm. There is as yet no purely mechanical
procedure for eliminating a Const2 violation and adding a Const1
violation. How exactly this is to be done in each case depends on the
constraints involved, the representational assumptions in which those
constraints are embedded, and so on. Furthermore, the technique does
not specify how to avoid adding violations of other constraints that
might dominate Const1. Still, the Yawelmani example suggests a
general strategy: the locations of the withdrawn Const2 violation and
the added Const1 violation are probably fairly close together.

Another caveat is that the "other constraints," whose violations
must not change, may not be completely known when a ranking argument is first constructed. Early in the process of analysis, we might
be unable to say whether Const1 or Const3 dominates Const2. Later
on, other evidence might show that Const2 dominates Const3, in
which case the argument for ranking Const1 over Const2 should
be revisited. On the other hand, a constraint introduced later in the
process of analysis can cast a shadow on a ranking argument that
had previously been OK. That is why it's so important to do summary
tableaux like (31)–(34). Summary tableaux provide a final check on
the soundness of the analysis.

At the beginning of this section, I also identified a second issue that
arises in candidate selection: challenging and improving the analysis
by finding losing candidates that threaten to tie or beat the intended
winner. Overlooking one of these candidates "invites theoretical disaster,

public embarrassment, and unintended enrichment of other people's careers" (McCarthy and Prince 1993b: 13).

Perhaps the most common and straightforward situation goes like this. An argument has been developed that some markedness constraint dominates some faithfulness constraint, like *C^{unsyll} >> IDENT(long). In the argument for this ranking, the winner [lan.hin] was compared with the loser *[laː.n.hin]. But what about a loser that avoids a violation of both of the constraints involved in the ranking argument, such as *[laː.ni.hin], with epenthetic [i]? Unless something is said, *[laː.ni.hin] threatens the intended winner because it obeys IDENT(long), which the winner violates, and it also obeys *C^{unsyll}, which the loser violates.

It is all too easy to overlook candidates like *[laː.ni.hin]. Karttunen (2006) describes a problem of this type: three excellent phonologists worked out and published an analysis of Finnish stress but overlooked a candidate that beat the intended winner. As Karttunen says, "The specter of an unexpected competitor suddenly emerging to eliminate the desired winner is the bane of OT analyses."

Karttunen's solution is to take the problem out of the hands of the analyst by implementing a candidate-generation algorithm (like GEN, but more limited) and using the grammar to check all of the resulting candidates against the intended winner. In the Finnish stress case, even with the algorithm limited to producing candidates that differ only in foot and syllable structure, the number of candidates is extremely large (nearly 22 million for one input), so the task is truly out of the hands of the analyst and must be done on a computer.

The weakness of this analytic technique is that it's only as good as the algorithm that generates the candidates. With an extremely well-studied and narrowly circumscribed phenomenon like Finnish stress, it's a reasonably straightforward task to devise an appropriate algorithm. But the techniques recommended in this book are intended for situations where the analysis isn't known in advance and the phenomenon itself may be imperfectly understood. In those situations, devising a suitable candidate-generation algorithm would be a significant research project that couldn't even be started until the analysis was very far along.

Even if using a candidate-generation algorithm is sometimes impractical, there is a useful idea here: as much as possible, we should attempt to explore the range of candidates *systematically*, in search of those that cause problems. This task isn't as difficult as it might seem. Once we have established that a constraint is undominated, we can ignore all candidates that violate it, since they will never threaten the winner. For example, as the analysis of Yawelmani continues, there is no reason to keep worrying about candidates that violate *COMPLEX-SYLLABLE or *C^{unsyll}, since we are reasonably certain that these constraints are undominated and therefore unviolated by any winner. Similarly, if we observe that some language never has deletion, it's usually enough to incorporate that observation into one or two ranking arguments involving MAX. After that, we can stop worrying about candidates with deletion, since they will never threaten to embarrass us.

The losing candidates that should concern us are those that violate only dominated constraints. For example, Yawelmani has epenthesis in some circumstances (/ʔilk-hin/ → [ʔi.lik.hin] in example (2) in chapter 1). This tells us that DEP is crucially dominated in this language. With that in mind, we should go back to the tableaux in §2.3 and ask whether any of the winners would be threatened by a candidate that violates DEP. (Exercise 17 asked you to do that.) For example, *[laː.ni.hin] threatens [lan.hin], since it obeys IDENT(long) without violating any of the undominated constraints. The solution to this problem is to rank DEP above IDENT(long) (see (48)). Likewise, epenthesizing a final consonant offers an alternative way of satisfying *V#, so *[ta.xaː.kʲaʔ] threatens [ta.xakʲ]. This shows that DEP also dominates MAX (see (49)).

(48)   Ranking argument: DEP >> IDENT(long)

/laːn-hin/	DEP	IDENT(long)
a. → lan.hin		*
b. laː.ni.hin	*W	L

(49)   Ranking argument: DEP >> MAX (>> IDENT(long))

/taxaː-kʲa/	DEP	MAX	IDENT(long)
a. → ta.xakʲ		*	*
b. ta.xaː.kʲaʔ	*W	L	L

So, to explore the range of candidates systematically in search of losers that threaten the winners, proceed like this. Each time the process of analysis discloses some constraint that is crucially dominated, look back at the winners in all of the tableaux that have been created up to that point. Manipulate each winner by adding one or more violations of the newly disclosed constraint. Does this suggest a loser that ties with or beats the winner on the other constraints? If so, then some ranking work needs to be done. Don't neglect the possibility of adding the violation in different places, such as [ʔi.lik.hin] versus *[ʔil.ki.hin]. And don't overlook the possibility of purely structural differences, such as *[laːn.hin] versus *[laː.n.hin].

Prince and Smolensky (1993/2004: 139) describe another technique for finding potentially problematic losers, the *Method of Mark Eliminability* (MME). Start with a summary tableau in violation or combination format. Look at every violation mark incurred by the winner. Think of all of the ways of avoiding that violation mark, and make sure that all of those alternatives do worse than the winner on some higher-ranking constraint. This method works because the winner's violation marks are the only thing that can get it into trouble. The only constraints that can possibly favor a loser are those that the winner violates, so those are the only constraints that could cause problems.

In tableau (50), for example, the winner has two marks, a violation of MAX and a violation of IDENT(long). According to the MME, we need to ask about ways of avoiding the winner's MAX violation. Candidate (b) does that, but it violates higher-ranking *V#, so it isn't a problem. Another candidate that obeys MAX is *[ta.xaː.kʼaʔ]. As we saw in (49), it requires another constraint that isn't in this tableau, DEP. We do the same for the winner's IDENT(long) violation. This leads us to candidates (c)–(f), which the analysis already handles nicely, as well as a more distant possibility like *[ta.xaː.ʔikʼ]. DEP causes it to lose as well.

(50)   Tableau (33) to illustrate the MME

/taxaː-kʼa/	*COMP-SYLL	*C^unsyll	*V#	MAX	IDENT(long)
a. → ta.xakʼ				*	*
b. ta.xaː.kʼa			*		
c. ta.xaːkʼ	*			*	
d. ta.xaː.kʼ		*		*	
e. ta.xaː			*	**	
f. tax				***	

This section concludes with three final rules of thumb for checking candidates:

- *Check for other ways of becoming less marked.* Whenever a markedness constraint dominates a faithfulness constraint, there is probably some other way of being unfaithful that would also do better on that markedness constraint. When doing an analysis, it's important that we think of these alternatives and deal with them by ranking. Since there are only so many ways of being unfaithful – Dep violation, Max violation, Ident violation, and perhaps a few more – it's usually possible to do a quick mental or paper-and-pencil scan for potentially problematic candidates. For instance, if the winner violates Dep, we need to ask ourselves questions like "Would violating Max or Ident produce the same markedness improvement?" If so, then probably Max and/or Ident need to be ranked above Dep.
- *Be careful with rankings where Max is crucially dominated.* The reason to worry is that it's possible to do better on almost any markedness constraint by violating Max. In fact, it's theoretically possible to vacuously satisfy all markedness constraints by deleting the entire input. Therefore, if Max is dominated, it's very important to check the analysis for losers that might improve satisfaction of markedness constraints ranked above Max by deleting some or all of the input segments. (For an explanation of vacuous satisfaction, see the boxed text at the end of this section.)
- *Always make sure that the analysis can handle the fully faithful candidate.* It's present in every candidate set; in fact, there may be more than one fully faithful candidate in the set because of possible structural differences like syllabification. The fully faithful candidate obeys every single faithfulness constraint, so it's crucial that it be ruled out for markedness reasons, if it isn't optimal.

Explanation: Vacuous satisfaction of a constraint

A constraint against structure s with property p is vacuously satisfied by any candidate that contains no instances of structure s. It's non-vacuously satisfied by any candidate that contains some instances of structure s, none of which have property p. For instance, a candidate with no syllables vacuously satisfies Onset. Eval treats nonvacuous satisfaction and vacuous satisfaction exactly the same, so this difference has no theoretical status, but it's occasionally mentioned in the literature.

EXERCISES

21 Using the following data from Diola Fogny ([dʲolɑ fonʲi]) (Sapir 1965), construct arguments for these three constraint rankings:

Agree(Place) >> Ident(Place)
Dep >> Ident(Place)
Max >> Ident(Place)

Although you wouldn't normally do this when writing up an analysis, for the purpose of this exercise explain how you obtained the losing candidates used in your ranking arguments.

The markedness constraint Agree(Place) is violated once by each consonant cluster that isn't homorganic, such as *[mt]. The faithfulness constraint Ident(Place) is violated once by any consonant that has a different place of articulation in underlying and surface representation, such as the /m/ of /nadʒum-to/, which maps to surface [n].

Underlying	Surface	
/ni-maŋ-maŋ/	[ni.mam.maŋ]	'I want'
/ni-ŋan-ŋan/	[ni.ŋaŋ.ŋan]	'I cried'
/nadʒum-to/	[na.dʒun.to]	'he stopped'
/ni-gam-gam/	[ni.gaŋ.gam]	'I judge'
/na-tiŋ-tiŋ/	[na.tin.tiŋ]	'he cut through'
/ku-boɲ-boɲ/	[ku.bom.boɲ]	'they sent'

22 Construct a summary tableau for Diola Fogny and use the MME and other methods described in this section to look for potentially problematic losers. Explain your work as you go along, and if you find any problematic losers, try to account for them.

2.6 Harmonic Bounding

In the previous section, we looked at some techniques for making sure that the analysis can deal with the full range of losing candidates that might challenge it. There are also losers that are certain *not* to cause any problems for the analysis. These are the losers that cannot win no matter how the constraints are ranked. They are said to be *harmonically bounded* (Samek-Lodovici 1992, Samek-Lodovici and Prince 1999).[8]

In a violation tableau, if *cand1* has a proper subset of *cand2*'s violation marks, then *cand2* cannot beat *cand1* under any ranking of the constraints in that tableau. We then say that *cand2* is harmonically bounded by *cand1* under that constraint set.[9] In the violation tableau (51), I've added the harmonically bounded candidate *[ta.xa] to the bottom of tableau (33). This added candidate (row (g)) is harmonically bounded by the winning candidate, (a). Candidate (a) has one violation of MAX and one of IDENT(long); candidate (g) has these violations, plus another MAX violation and a *V# violation. Dotted lines are used in this tableau to emphasize that harmonic bounding isn't dependent on ranking. Only the constraints, the input, and the candidates matter in determining harmonic bounding relations.

(51) Tableau (33) in violation format with *[ta.xa] added

/taxaː-k$^?$a/	*COMP-SYLL	*C^{unsyll}	*V#	MAX	IDENT(long)
a. → ta.xak$^?$				*	*
b. ta.xaː.k$^?$a			*		
c. ta.xaːk$^?$	*			*	
d. ta.xaː.k$^?$		*		*	
e. ta.xaː			*	**	
f. tax				***	
g. ta.xa			*	**	*

As it happens, there is another candidate in (51) that harmonically bounds (g). This candidate, (e), has a violation of *V# and two violations of MAX; candidate (g) has these, plus a violation of IDENT(long). This shows that a loser can harmonically bound another loser. Saying that (a) or (e) harmonically bounds (g) doesn't mean that (a) or (e) always wins regardless of the ranking. That's not true. Instead, it means that there is no ranking where (g) wins, because (a) and (e) will always do better than (g), even if they themselves are not the winners.

When a loser is harmonically bounded by the winner, then no constraint favors that loser over the winner. This is apparent when we add the Ws and Ls to (51), creating (52). It's obvious from this tableau why no ranking of the constraints can induce (g) to win. Therefore, (g) can't give us any information about how to rank these constraints.

(52) Tableau (51) in combination format

/taxaː-kʼa/	*Comp-Syll	*C^unsyll	*V#	Max	Ident(long)
a. → ta.xakʼ				*	*
b. ta.xaː.kʼa			*W	L	L
c. ta.xaːkʼ	*W			*	L
d. ta.xaː.kʼ		*W		*	L
e. ta.xaː			*W	**W	L
f. tax				***W	L
g. ta.xa			*W	**W	*

Just to be perfectly clear, harmonic bounding is always determined relative to some set of constraints and some set of candidates from a common input. The harmonic bounding of *[ta.xa] in (52) means that the input /taxaː-kʼa/ can never map to the output *[ta.xa] under any ranking of the constraints *Complex-Syllable, *C^unsyll, etc. It certainly doesn't mean that *[ta.xa] can't be the winner for *any* input – for instance, the mapping /taxa/ → [ta.xa] isn't harmonically bounded. Nor does it mean that /taxaː-kʼa/ → [ta.xa] is impossible under any imaginable set of constraints.

Harmonic bounding is important for three reasons. First, harmonically bounded candidates need to be recognized as a potential distraction from the task of ranking constraints. When presenting an analysis, for example, there is usually no reason to include harmonically bounded candidates, since they are not informative about ranking. There will be more said about this in §2.12. Second, discovering that the intended winner is harmonically bounded by some loser is a serious problem. At a minimum, solving this problem requires introducing a constraint that breaks the bounding relation by favoring the winner over the loser that threatens to bound it. Chapter 4 deals with that topic. Third, harmonic bounding is important in studying language typology. Since a harmonically bounded candidate cannot win under any ranking, it is predicted to be impossible in any language, if all relevant constraints have been considered. We will see much more about typology in chapter 5.

23 How many harmonically bounded candidates are there for a given input? Explain your answer.

EXERCISE

24 Invent harmonically bounded candidates for tableaux (31) and (34), just as I did with tableau (33). What about tableau (32)?

2.7 Constraints in Ranking Arguments

Imagine the following situation. The analysis is looking pretty good and even seems almost finished. Then we find out about another constraint that might be relevant to the phenomenon being analyzed. Does this constraint need to be incorporated into the analysis, or can it be disregarded?

Prince (2002a: 276) has a succinct answer, couched in the terminology of comparative tableaux:

> The answer is that we may omit from discussion all and only those constraints assessing *blank*: these are the ones that do not enter into the comparative evaluation. If – with an excessive concern for conciseness, or through mere oversight, or because we prefer the expositional strategy of withholding key information – we ignore a constraint that assesses L, we have lost track of a constraint that *must be dominated* and our argument is dangerously incomplete. If we ignore a constraint that assesses W, we have (as long as some other constraint assesses L) produced a ranking argument that is too strong and may be literally false.

In other words, if we add this constraint to the tableaux in our analysis, what does it do? Does it favor the winner or a loser? Does it favor neither, so there are no Ws or Ls in its column (= "assessing *blank*")? Only in the last case can it be safely ignored.

When the added constraint favors a loser, then it threatens to undermine the analysis by causing the wrong candidate to win. In that case, the constraint has to be discussed, and it has to be ranked below some winner-favoring constraint. To illustrate, I'll add a constraint to the analysis of Yawelmani in §2.3. The hypothetical constraint $\text{Max}_{\text{stem-final}}$ prohibits deletion of a stem-final segment, such as the vowel of the suffix /-kʔa/.[10] If we add this constraint to the Yawelmani summary tableau (33), we get (53). Since the ranking of

MAX$_{stem-final}$ isn't yet known, I have placed it to the right of the ranked portion of the tableau, as in (13).

(53)   Added MAX$_{stem-final}$

/taxaː-k$^?$a/	*Comp-Syll	*C^{unsyll}	*V#	Max	Ident(long)	MAX$_{stem-final}$
a. → ta.xak$^?$				*	*	*
b. ta.xaː.k$^?$a			*W	L	L	L
c. ta.xaːk$^?$	*W			*	L	*
d. ta.xaː.k$^?$		*W		*	L	*
e. ta.xaː			*W	**W	L	*
f. tax				***W	L	*

It is clear from (53) that MAX$_{stem-final}$ favors the loser (b). Now that we are aware of the existence of this constraint, we are obliged to deal with it in the analysis precisely because it favors a loser. The way to deal with it is simple: rank it below the highest-ranking (and here, only) constraint that favors the winner over (b), *V#. That ranking argument is given in (54). As usual, we include all of the known winner- or loser-favoring constraints in the tableau.

(54)   Ranking argument: *V# >> MAX$_{stem-final}$

/taxaː-k$^?$a/	*V#	MAX$_{stem-final}$	Max	Ident(long)
a. → ta.xak$^?$		*	*	*
b. ta.xaː.k$^?$a	*W	L	L	L

When the newly introduced constraint favors a winner, it can undermine a preexisting ranking argument by offering an alternative explanation for why the winner is optimal. Yawelmani again supplies an example. Stress normally falls on the penultimate syllable (Newman 1944: 28), so the metrical stress foot is two syllables long.[11] (For more about feet and stress, see §4.5.2.) Some languages have only disyllabic feet, with monosyllabic feet ruled out by the constraint Foot-Binarity(syllable) (Ft-Bin(syll)). If we add this constraint to the analysis, we have two alternative rankings represented by the two tableaux in (55), because Foot-Binarity(syllable) favors the disyllabic winner [xat.kʔa] over the monosyllabic losers.

(55) Ranking disjunction
   *Comp-Syll, *C^{unsyll} >> *V#

/xat-kʔa/	*Comp-Syll	*C^{unsyll}	*V#	Max	Ft-Bin(syll)
a. → ('xat.kʔa)$_{foot}$			*		
b.　　('xatkʔ)$_{foot}$	*W		L	*W	*W
c.　　('xat.kʔ)$_{foot}$		*W	L	*W	*W

or

Ft-Bin(syll) >> *V#

/xat-kʔa/	Ft-Bin(syll)	*V#	Max	*Comp-Syll	*C^{unsyll}
a. → ('xat.kʔa)$_{foot}$		*			
b.　　('xatkʔ)$_{foot}$	*W	L	*W	*W	
c.　　('xat.kʔ)$_{foot}$	*W	L	*W		*W

The problem with (55) is that now there are two possible explanations for why (b) and (c) lose. There is the explanation that we accepted earlier: *Complex-Syllable and *C^{unsyll} dominate *V#. And there is a new explanation: Foot-Binarity(syllable) dominates *V#. Previously, we could say for sure that both *Complex-Syllable and *C^{unsyll} dominate *V#, but now we are left with a disjunction: both *Complex-Syllable and *C^{unsyll} dominate *V#, or Foot-Binarity(syllable) dominates *V#.

Ranking disjunctions are sometimes irresolvable, but before giving up, there are some promising lines of inquiry to pursue. Sometimes the disjunction can be cleared up by finding a different loser or even a different input that separates the effects of the winner-favoring constraints in the disjunction. The definitions of the constraints often help to suggest what that loser or input should look like.

For example, *Complex-Syllable and *C^{unsyll} are constraints on the organization of segments into syllables, while Foot-Binarity(syllable) is a constraint on the organization of syllables into feet. Since they deal with such different matters, it should be possible to come up with competing candidates where the constraint on one side of the disjunction is inactive, so we can see the pure effect of the constraint on the other side of the disjunction. To see the effect of *COMPLEX-SYLLABLE and *C^{unsyll} without interference from FOOT-BINARITY(syllable), we need a competition where both the winner and loser contain at least two syllables. An example is given in (56). Since FOOT-BINARITY(syllable) assesses *blank* in this tableau, we can safely conclude that *COMPLEX-SYLLABLE and *C^{unsyll} really do dominate *V#.

(56)   Tableau for [haj.wis.k$^?$a] 'don't laugh!' (Newman 1944: 118)

/hajwis-k$^?$a/	*COMP-SYLL	*C^{unsyll}	*V#	MAX	FT-BIN(syll)
a. → haj.('wis.k$^?$a)$_{foot}$			*		
b. ('haj.wisk$^?$)$_{foot}$	*W		L	*W	
c. ('haj.wis.k$^?$)$_{foot}$		*W	L	*W	

Another way to pull apart this ranking disjunction is to show that FOOT-BINARITY(syllable) must be ranked too low to dominate *V#. In fact, it has to be ranked below MAX, and since we already know that MAX is ranked below *V#, it follows that FOOT-BINARITY(syllable) cannot possibly dominate *V#. The argument for ranking FOOT-BINARITY(syllable) below MAX is based on the observation that Yawelmani has some monosyllabic content words, such as [ti?] 'house (subjective)' (Newman 1944: 240). The word [ti?] violates FOOT-BINARITY(syllable) and obeys MAX. To make the ranking argument, we require a losing candidate that obeys FOOT-BINARITY(syllable) and violates MAX. The idea, which goes back to the beginning of OT (Prince and Smolensky 1993/2004: 57), is that FOOT-BINARITY(syllable) can be vacuously satisfied by deleting all of the segmental material in the input. With no segments to parse, there are no syllables, no feet, and no phonological word – hence, vacuous satisfaction of FOOT-BINARITY(syllable). The ranking argument is given in (57).

(57)   Ranking argument: MAX >> FOOT-BINARITY(syllable)

/ti?/	MAX	FT-BIN(syll)
a. → ('ti?)$_{foot}$		*
b. Ø	***W	L

In summary, constraints that favor losers need to be dealt with in the analysis because they threaten the winner, and constraints that favor winners need to be dealt with because they threaten the previously established rankings. The threat from loser-favoring constraints needs to be eliminated by ranking them below winner-favoring constraints, and any disjunctions that come from winner-favoring constraints need to be resolved whenever possible. Constraints that favor neither winners nor losers can be ignored at no peril to the analysis. In many cases, these constraints might simply be irrelevant to the phenomenon under discussion, and including them in the analysis would be a distraction.

EXERCISES

25   In exercise 21, you were not asked to consider the potential effect of $\text{MAX}_{\text{stem-final}}$ on the analysis of Diola Fogny. Now you are. Can it be omitted from discussion, according to Prince's criteria? Explain your answer. (You should assume that all of the assimilating nasal consonants in the data are stem-final, so this constraint is at least potentially relevant.)

26   Assume that there is a markedness constraint *ŋ that is violated by velar nasals. Can this constraint be omitted from discussion of Diola Fogny, according to Prince's criteria? Explain your answer.

2.8   Inputs in Ranking Arguments

Which inputs need to be dealt with in an analysis? The answer might seem obvious: the analysis needs to deal with the inputs for all of the data that are being analyzed. It is of course correct that the analysis needs to deal with all of those inputs, but that isn't enough. In phonology especially, the data sets that are the focus of an analysis are paradigms with alternations, such as (15) and (16). The inputs for data sets like these are sometimes insufficient for constructing a solid OT analysis. There are two reasons for this.

First, because the data set was probably constructed with a focus on forms that alternate, it may be biased toward inputs that map to unfaithful output forms. In an OT analysis, however, inputs that map to *faithful* output forms are also relevant to the analysis, since they tell us which markedness constraints are crucially dominated. For example, Yawelmani /ʔilk-al/ → [ʔil.kal] shows that the language has codas, so No-Coda must be dominated by Max and Dep, to rule out unfaithful codeless candidates like *[ʔi.ka] and *[ʔi.li.ka.li]. Similarly, the faithful mapping /laːn-al/ → [laː.nal] shows that long vowels are permitted in open syllables, so the markedness constraint against long vowels must be ranked below IDENT(long). Faithful input–output mappings like these are relevant to the analysis because of the assumption that all constraints are universally present in the grammars of all languages (§1.3). It's important to discover which markedness constraints a language violates, since those constraints must be ranked below faithfulness. The only way to discover these constraints is to look at faithful input–output mappings. Like Sherlock Holmes's "curious incident of the dog in the night-time,"[12] the inputs where nothing happens can be crucial.

Second, the inputs that are involved in alternations almost never include all of the logical possibilities that the grammar must treat unfaithfully. One of OT's basic hypotheses is that constraint ranking is the *only* systematic difference between languages (§1.7). If this is true, then languages cannot differ systematically in their lexicons. This has important implications for what inputs need to be considered, what the grammar must do with them, and what ranking arguments we therefore need to construct.

The idea that languages cannot differ systematically in their lexicons is called *richness of the base* (Prince and Smolensky 1993/2004: 205, 225). This phrase is a little obscure, so I will first explain its origin. The word "base" refers to the input to the grammar, since in early syntactic theory the base was the phrase structure component that produced inputs to the transformational component.[13] The word "richness" is used here in the sense of "profusion." In OT, the base (= lexicon, as input to the grammar) contains a profusion of diverse forms because it isn't subject to any language-particular restrictions.

If richness of the base is assumed, then OT cannot rely on certain analytic techniques that are common in other theories. In phonology, for example, non-OT analyses frequently employ devices like lexical redundancy rules, morpheme-structure constraints, or lexical underspecification – e.g., /bn/ is prohibited morpheme-initially in English, or voicing is lexically unspecified in labials in Arabic (which has [b] but not [p]). Similar ideas are common in contemporary syntactic theory as well – e.g., the claim that languages differ systematically in whether their *wh*-words carry a feature that requires movement to [Spec, CP]. Because of richness of the base, these methods of analysis aren't available in OT. Instead, all aspects of well-formedness are under the control of EVAL and the constraint hierarchy, and all systematic differences between languages can and must be obtained only from differences in constraint ranking.

There are two main arguments in support of richness of the base. One is parsimony: since ranking can differ from language to language, the strongest hypothesis is that ranking is the *only* possible difference between languages. The other argument goes back to the study of phonological conspiracies in the 1970s (see §1.1). Researchers at that time noticed that restrictions on the lexicon often had the same effect as the phonological rules. For example, Yawelmani has a morpheme structure constraint that prohibits initial consonant clusters, and it also has a phonological rule of epenthesis that eliminates unsylabifiable clusters (see (58)). This kind of conspiracy was referred to as the *Duplication Problem*, since the restrictions on the lexicon duplicate the effects of the rules (Clayton 1976, Kenstowicz and Kisseberth 1977). Some researchers proposed to solve the Duplication Problem by eliminating restrictions on the lexicon and using just rules or output constraints to account for all generalizations. Richness of the base is OT's instantiation of this idea. See McCarthy (2002: 68–91) for further explanation of the Duplication Problem.

As a practical matter, richness of the base means that the grammar has to deal with a much wider range of inputs than the analyst might normally consider. Even though English has no words that alternate in a way that would require the underlying form /bnæg/, the grammar of English still has to handle the input /bnæg/. "Handle," in this context, means "account for the unpronounceability of the faithful candidate *[bnæg]." The grammar must be designed so that it selects something other than unpronounceable *[bnæg] as the most harmonic member of /bnæg/'s candidate set. In this way, it's the grammar alone, rather than the grammar aided by restrictions on the lexicon, that accounts for the set of possible words or grammatical sentences of English or any other language.

In general, the grammar of every language has to map every possible input to some well-formed output. (We'll see an interesting twist on this idea in §6.5.) To check whether the grammar really does this, the analyst needs to ask questions that are sometimes not very obvious from the data being studied. In phonology, it's necessary to ask about inputs containing various configurations that are unpronounceable in the language, such as initial clusters in Yawelmani. Nothing in the Yawelmani data would suggest that inputs with initial clusters are important, since there is no reason to set up underlying representations with initial clusters. In syntax, similar questions have to be asked about inputs where case is assigned inappropriately or required verbal arguments are missing or there are unwanted instances of dummy elements like English unstressed *do*. (See Smolensky, Legendre, and Tesar (2006: 529) for an example of richness of the base in syntax.) In general, it isn't enough that the analysis works when the inputs are well-behaved; the analysis has to work over all possible inputs.

In actual practice, the analyst's job isn't nearly so daunting. The important thing is to make sure that the analysis does not rely on convenient regularities in the inputs. Because these regularities are so often unstated, even in theories that allow language-particular restrictions on inputs, it takes some effort to realize that they're there. But no analysis in OT is complete until the inputs have been checked for regularities. If input regularities are found, the analysis needs to be fixed so that it can handle, in the sense used above, inputs that do not conform to these regularities.

Let's look at the Yawelmani example once again. The active markedness constraints – *COMPLEX-SYLLABLE, $*C^{unsyll}$, and *V# – limit the shapes of syllables and words. We therefore need to make sure that the inputs do not exhibit any convenient regularities of syllable or word shape that might be helping the analysis along. Since the analysis has only been checked with underlying representations that were obtained from the data sets (15) and (16), we shouldn't be surprised to find that there are significant regularities in the inputs. These regularities disclose holes in the analysis that need to be filled.

So far, the Yawelmani analysis has focused on roots with the shapes CVC, CVːC, and CVCVː. The gaps are fairly obvious. For example, what about roots like CVCC or VC? Often, such questions can be answered simply by looking at more data. For instance, further data like (58) show that Yawelmani has underlying CVCC roots and that these roots undergo vowel epenthesis before consonant-initial suffixes. This tells us something about the ranking of DEP.

(58)   Yawelmani epenthesis (Kenstowicz and Kisseberth 1979: 85)

		Underlying	*Surface*	
	a.	/ʔilk-hin/	[ʔi.lik.hin]	'sing (nonfuture)'
		/lihm-hin/	[li.him.hin]	'run (nonfuture)'
	b.	/ʔilk-al/	[ʔil.kal]	'sing (dubitative)'
		/lihm-al/	[lih.mal]	'run (dubitative)'

The question about VC roots is harder to answer. Yawelmani has no vowel-initial syllables or words, so an input VC root must not be mapped to a faithful output form – i.e., hypothetical /ap-hin/ cannot become *[aphin], since *[aphin] isn't pronounceable in this language (Newman 1944: 27). But the only way for *[aphin] to lose is for some other candidate to win, and there is no evidence from alternations to tell us what that other candidate is.[14] We might conjecture that it's [ʔaphin], but this really is nothing but a conjecture. On how to deal with questions like this, see §2.10.4.

Richness of the base is particularly important when analyzing systems of contrast and neutralization. Take Yoruba, for example. Vowels contrast in nasalization except after a nasal consonant, where all vowels neutralize to nasal (Pulleyblank 1988: 258). Thus, [a], [ã], [ba], [bã], and [mã] are allowed, but not *[ma]. Traditional analyses would rule out *[ma] by ruling out /ma/ from the input, using something like a morpheme structure constraint or lexical underspecification. Richness of the base requires that the grammar do all of the work of explaining the ill-formedness of *[ma]. In particular, the grammar of Yoruba must treat /ma/ unfaithfully, mapping it to something well-formed like [mã].

A grammar that does exactly that is given in (60) and (61). This grammar is based on the three constraints in (59). The markedness constraint $*V_{[+nasal]}$ is a general, context-free constraint against nasal vowels. The other markedness constraint, $*NV_{[-nasal]}$, prohibits oral vowels in a specific context, when they are preceded by a nasal consonant. In other words, $*V_{[+nasal]}$ is a general force in opposition to nasal vowels, whereas $*NV_{[-nasal]}$ exerts a pressure in their favor in the right environment. The third constraint in (59) requires faithfulness to input nasality.

(59) Nasality constraints (McCarthy and Prince 1995)
    a. $*V_{[+nasal]}$
        Assign one violation mark for every nasalized vowel.
    b. $*NV_{[-nasal]}$
        Assign one violation mark for every sequence of a nasal consonant followed by a nonnasalized vowel.
    c. Ident([nasal])
        Assign one violation mark for every segment that changes its value for the feature [nasal] between input and output.

Since the grammar maps /ma/ to [mã], the pro-nasal constraint $*NV_{[-nasal]}$ must dominate the anti-nasal constraint $*V_{[+nasal]}$ as well as the faithfulness constraint. This ranking result is shown in (60).

(60)   Yoruba: $*NV_{[-nasal]}$ >> IDENT([nasal]), $*V_{[+nasal]}$

/ma/	$*NV_{[-nasal]}$	IDENT([nasal])	$*V_{[+nasal]}$
a. → mã		*	*
b. ma	*W	L	L

Tableau (60) presents an incomplete picture, however, because it doesn't yet explain why there is a nasality contrast in [a] vs. [ã] and [ba] vs. [bã]. That requires the further ranking in (61): faithfulness to nasality in the input overrides the anti-nasal force of $*V_{[+nasal]}$.

(61)   Yoruba: ($*NV_{[-nasal]}$ >>) IDENT([nasal]) >> $*V_{[+nasal]}$

/bã/	$*NV_{[-nasal]}$	IDENT([nasal])	$*V_{[+nasal]}$
a. → bã			*
b. ba		*W	L

This analysis treats the distribution of nasalized vowels in Yoruba as a fact about surface forms: there is no nasalization contrast after nasal consonants because the markedness constraint $*NV_{[-nasal]}$ dominates the faithfulness constraint IDENT([nasal]), but there is a nasalization contrast elsewhere because IDENT([nasal]) dominates $*V_{[+nasal]}$. In a traditional analysis, neutralization of a contrast is dealt with by a restriction on the inputs to the grammar: vowels preceded by nasal consonants must be nasal or must be underspecified for nasality. In OT, contrast or the lack of it is determined by the grammar, so contrast and distribution are facts about surface structure alone.

This sort of reasoning and analysis isn't limited to phonology; similar things need to be said to account for the distribution of unstressed *do* in English (§2.9). In general, if some linguistic item has a restricted distribution, then faithfulness to that item is ranked below some markedness constraint or constraints that control the distribution. In Yoruba, $*NV_{[-nasal]}$ controls the distribution of nasality in vowels but $*V_{[+nasal]}$ does not. That is why Yoruba neutralizes the contrast in one environment (after a nasal consonant) and preserves it elsewhere.

The same method of analysis is applicable when there is no contrast at all. Madurese has [a], [ba], and [mã], but not *[ã], *[bã], or *[ma]

(Stevens 1968).[15] In Madurese, then, there is perfect complementary distribution, so there is no environment where nasality is contrastive in vowels. This means that IDENT([nasal]) is ranked below both of the markedness constraints, as shown in (62) and (63).

(62) Madurese: $*NV_{[-nasal]} >> *V_{[+nasal]}$, IDENT([nasal])

/ma/	$*NV_{[-nasal]}$	$*V_{[+nasal]}$	IDENT([nasal])
a. → mã		*	*
b. ma	*W	L	L

(63) Madurese: $(*NV_{[-nasal]} >>)$ IDENT([nasal]) $>> *V_{[+nasal]}$

/bã/	$*NV_{[-nasal]}$	$*V_{[+nasal]}$	IDENT([nasal])
a. → ba			*
b. bã		*W	L

Richness of the base is the source of more confusion and misunderstanding than any other aspect of OT. One misunderstanding is the belief that richness of the base requires all languages to have identical lexicons. Actually, richness of the base says that there are no *systematic* differences in lexicons. In other words, linguistic patterns or generalizations cannot be attributed to lexical differences. Richness of the base does not exclude the possibility of unsystematic differences in lexicons, of which there are many. Languages unsystematically differ in the meanings that they associate with specific segmental sequences; the meaning *felis catus* is associated with the segment sequence [kæt] in English but not other languages. Lexicons are full of accidental properties like this, and richness of the base says nothing about them.

Another misunderstanding is the idea that richness of the base requires absurd underlying representations. Suppose the grammar of English maps /ŋkæt/ to [kæt], because the markedness constraint violated by *[ŋkæt]'s initial cluster dominates MAX. This doesn't mean that the underlying representation for the actual word [kæt] is /ŋkæt/. The underlying representation for [kæt] is /kæt/, of course. When children acquire English, they have no reason to set up any other underlying representation for [kæt].[16]

This misunderstanding is the result of failing to distinguish between inputs and underlying representations. The set of inputs is a construct of the theory: it's simply the result of freely combining all of the representational primitives, such as features, in all possible ways. But underlying representations are a construct of learners: they are inferences about the shared properties of a group of related words. The actual underlying representations that some learner has acquired are a finite subset of the infinite set of phonological inputs. In general, richness of the base says nothing about how to analyze specific surface forms; it's about the general structure of the language rather than individual words or sentences.

Another source of confusion is the incorrect assumption that the inputs of the rich base must be transformed into actual words of the language. On this view, English phonology couldn't map /bnæg/ to, say, [blæg] because there is no such word in the language. This assumption is wrong because it misconceives the goal of phonological analysis. We aren't concerned with the phonology of the *actual* words of the language so much as the *possible* words. Clearly, [blæg] is a phonologically possible word of English,[17] and our analysis should say as much. In this respect, the goal of phonology is much like the goal of syntax. The goal of a syntactic analysis of English is to construct a grammar of all possible sentences and not, say, just the sentences that have been uttered since the beginning of modern English around 1550.

A final source of confusion about richness of the base is the incorrect assumption that it somehow overrides the theory of representations. An anonymous reviewer for the same widely-admired journal mentioned in §2.2 faulted an author for not considering inputs with underspecification, since this was supposedly required by richness of the base. This complaint would only make sense if the author had assumed the possibility of underspecified representations, which he did not. You are free to assume *universal* restrictions on inputs, such as full specification, without running afoul of richness of the base.

Richness of the base presents a special problem of indeterminacy in some analyses. See §2.10.4 for an explanation of this problem and some suggestions about how to deal with it.

27 The data in (58) tell us something about the ranking of DEP in Yawelmani. What do they tell us? In exercise 17, you saw other evidence for how DEP is ranked in this language. Considering both sources of evidence and everything

you know about Yawelmani's constraint hierarchy from §2.3, is there a problem? What is it? How could you solve it?

28 Hawai'ian has no consonant clusters whatsoever. From this fact alone, what (if anything) can we conclude about constraint ranking in Hawai'ian?

29 In Nancowry (Radhakrishnan 1981), nasal and oral vowels contrast in all environments, so all of the following are well-formed: [a], [ã], [ba], [bã], [ma] and [mã]. Analyze Nancowry using the constraints in (59). Be sure to present ranking arguments like (60)–(63).

30 In Spanish, the voiced stops [b, d, g] are in complementary distribution with their fricative counterparts [β, ð, ɣ]. Using the following data (from a problem set in Halle and Clements 1983), formulate a descriptive generalization and construct an OT analysis that is consistent with richness of the base.

[aɣrio]	'sour'	[komuniðað]	'community'
[gustar]	'to please'	[deðo]	'finger/toe'
[xweɣo]	'game'	[droɣas]	'drugs'
[alβondiɣas]	'meatballs'	[seða]	'silk'
[gastos]	'expenses'	[ganaðo]	'cattle'
[gonsales]	a surname	[usteð]	'you (sg. polite)'
[jaɣa]	'sore, boil'	[bastante]	'plenty'
[uβa]	'grape'	[brinkar]	'to jump'
[futbol]	'soccer'	[suβo]	'I climb'
[alɣo]	'something'	[uβo]	'there was'
[sombra]	'shade'	[kluβ]	'club'
[saβino]	'cypress'	[karβon]	'coal'
[kaβe]	'it fits'	[berðe]	'green'

2.9 Working through an Analysis in Syntax

The methods of analysis described here are equally applicable to syntax. Since I am not a syntactician, I will be using a published analysis as an example, Grimshaw's (1997) account of *do* support in English. What I say here shouldn't be taken as an accurate summary of Grimshaw's work; rather, it's a pedagogically oriented partial restatement that focuses on illustrating the various analytic techniques that I've been presenting here.

The data that will be analyzed are given in (64). (See Grimshaw's article for additional relevant data, such as *Who ate apples?*.)

(64)　*Do*-support data
  a.　Robin ate apples.
  　　*Robin did eat apples. (Unstressed *did*.)
  b.　What did Robin eat?
  　　*Robin ate what? (As interrogative, not echo question.)
  　　*What Robin ate?
  　　*What Robin did eat?
  c.　What will Robin eat?
  　　*Robin will eat what?
  　　*What will Robin do eat?
  　　*What does Robin will eat?

Within each group of sentences, *do* is either required (b) or forbidden (a, c). This is the central insight that any analysis should somehow express.

As an initial hypothesis, we can assume that each of the groups of sentences in (64) constitutes a mini candidate set. Thus, *Robin ate apples* competes with **Robin did eat apples*, but neither competes with the sentences in (b) or (c) or any other sentences. Later in this section, we will see how the principles of OT allow us to determine the extent of a candidate set and thereby to make inferences about the input and GEN in syntax.

The first step is to reduce the data to OT-friendly descriptive generalizations. Descriptive generalizations, it should be emphasized, aren't agnostic about matters like representational assumptions. The Yawelmani descriptive generalizations in (17) were couched in terms of syllables, and the idea that there are syllables, though widely accepted, is a hypothesis about phonological representation, not an obvious truth. The same goes for the representational assumptions that underlie (65).

(65)　Descriptive generalizations for English *do*-support
  a.　The *wh*-phrase is in [Spec, CP]. This requirement is enforced by *wh*-movement: [$_{CP}$ *What$_i$ will$_j$* [$_{IP}$ *Robin* e$_j$ [$_{VP}$ *eat* t$_i$]]].
  b.　CP must have a head. This requirement is enforced by:
  　　(i)　moving the auxiliary: [$_{CP}$ *What$_i$ will$_j$* [$_{IP}$ *Robin* e$_j$ [$_{VP}$ *eat* t$_i$]]]. or else
  　　(ii)　inserting and moving *do*: [$_{CP}$ *What$_i$ did$_j$* [$_{IP}$ *Robin* e$_j$ [$_{VP}$ *eat* t$_i$]]].
  c.　Unstressed *do* is forbidden, except when required by clause (ii) of (b).

The next step is to account for one aspect of this phenomenon, *wh*-movement. The descriptive generalization in (a) suggests the need for a markedness constraint that is violated by any *wh*-word that isn't in [Spec, CP]. This constraint is OPERATOR-IN-SPECIFIER (OP-SPEC), and it's violated once by every syntactic operator that isn't in specifier position. Since *wh*-phrases are syntactic operators (i.e., they take their scope from their position in the syntax), they are subject to this constraint. Movement violates a constraint against traces, which is called STAY. Since there is *wh*-movement, OPERATOR-IN-SPECIFIER must dominate STAY.

To make this ranking argument formally, we look first for a grammatical sentence that shows the conflict in the simplest possible way, by obeying OPERATOR-IN-SPECIFIER and violating STAY once. There are none in the data set (64), because *wh*-movement is always accompanied by subject-auxiliary inversion. Thus, there are always two STAY violations, one for the trace of *wh* and one for the trace of the auxiliary. A sentence with two STAY violations is just as serviceable for a ranking argument, however. We can therefore use [$_{CP}$ *What$_i$ will$_j$* [$_{IP}$ *Robin* e$_j$ [$_{VP}$ *eat* t$_i$]]] as the winner. The loser it competes with should violate OPERATOR-IN-SPECIFIER and incur fewer than two violations of STAY. Withdrawing both violations of STAY leads us to *[$_{IP}$ *Robin will* [$_{VP}$ *eat what*]], with a *wh*-phrase that isn't in specifier position. The result is tableau (66).

(66) Ranking argument: OPERATOR-IN-SPECIFIER >> STAY

	OP-SPEC	STAY
a. → [$_{CP}$ *What$_i$ will$_j$* [$_{IP}$ *Robin* e$_j$ [$_{VP}$ *eat* t$_i$]]]		**
b. [$_{IP}$ *Robin will* [$_{VP}$ *eat what*]]	*W	L

Constituents require heads, according to one of the earliest ideas about constituent structure (Harris 1946). In an OT context, it's natural to regard this requirement as a violable constraint, OBLIGATORY-HEADS (OB-HD). Under the hypothesis that inversion is movement of the auxiliary to head position, OBLIGATORY-HEADS must dominate STAY. For the ranking argument, we first look for a grammatical sentence that obeys OBLIGATORY-HEADS and violates STAY just once. For the reason given in the last paragraph, we end up using a sentence that incurs two STAY violations, the same as in the previous ranking argument. For the loser, we want an ungrammatical sentence that violates OBLIGATORY-HEADS and has fewer than two violations of STAY. Furthermore, for the ranking argument to be valid, the loser must not violate OPERATOR-IN-SPECIFIER, since we have already shown that OPERATOR-IN-SPECIFIER dominates STAY. This narrows the possibilities down to *[CP What_i __ [IP Robin will [VP eat t_i]]], which is the losing candidate in the ranking argument (67). (Point of clarification: OBLIGATORY-HEADS is satisfied by traces, so in candidate (a), the trace of *will* is the head of IP.)

(67)   Ranking argument: OBLIGATORY-HEADS >> STAY

	OB-HD	OP-SPEC	STAY
a. → [CP What_i will_j [IP Robin e_j [VP eat t_i]]]			**
b. [CP What_i _ [IP Robin will [VP eat t_i]]]	*W		*L

According to clause (c) of the descriptive generalization (65), *do* appears only when it's needed. In OT, if some linguistic item *i* appears only when it's needed, then CON must include a constraint that *i* violates. Given this, the situations where *i* is needed can be defined by higher-ranking constraints that demand its presence. The constraint that *do* violates is called FULL-INTERPRETATION (FULL-INT), which Legendre (2001: 5) defines as "Lexical items must contribute to the interpretation of a structure." Since *do* is a lexical item that contributes nothing to the interpretation – it's a semantically empty, dummy element – it violates this constraint.

FULL-INTERPRETATION is violated in English when the alternative is a violation of OBLIGATORY-HEADS, as shown in tableau (68). The difference between the winner and loser in this tableau is clear: the winner contains *do* and the loser does not. Furthermore, because *do* moves, the winner violates STAY more than the loser does. The loser pays a price for this: its CP and IP are headless.

(68)   Ranking argument: OBLIGATORY-HEADS >> FULL-
       INTERPRETATION, STAY

	OB-HD	OP-SPEC	FULL-INT	STAY
a. → [CP What_i did_j [IP Robin e_j [VP eat t_i]]]			*	**
b. [CP What_i _ [IP Robin _ [VP eat t_i]]]	**W		L	*L

Most of the examples in (64) have been discussed, but not the contrast in (a): *Robin ate apples* versus **Robin did eat apples*. Grimshaw adopts the VP-internal subject hypothesis (Kitagawa 1986, Koopman and Sportiche 1991, Zagona 1982 and others), so in terms of her representational assumptions there is a contrast in the positions occupied by the subject in [$_{VP}$ *Robin ate apples*] and ***[$_{IP}$ *Robin$_i$ did* [$_{VP}$ t$_i$ *eat apples*]], with the subject raised to [Spec, IP]. Of the four constraints we have discussed, two of them (STAY and FULL-INTERPRETATION) favor [$_{VP}$ *Robin ate apples*] in this competition, and the other two (OBLIGATORY-HEADS and OPERATOR-IN-SPECIFIER) equally favor both candidates. In a situation like this, ***[$_{IP}$ *Robin$_i$ did* [$_{VP}$ t$_i$ *eat apples*]] cannot win no matter how these constraints are ranked – it is harmonically bounded by the winner under this constraint set. The absence of Ls in tableau (69) emphasizes this point.

(69) Harmonic bounding of ***[$_{IP}$ *Robin$_i$ did* [$_{VP}$ t$_i$ *eat apples*]]

	OB-HD	OP-SPEC	FULL-INT	STAY
a. → [$_{VP}$ *Robin ate* apples]				
b. ***[$_{IP}$ *Robin$_i$ did* [$_{VP}$ t$_i$ *eat apples*]]			*W	*W

The ranking results so far are summarized in the Hasse diagram (70):

(70) Hasse diagram for English *do*

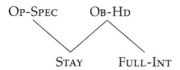

The question we should always ask, when confronted with a diagram like (70), is whether it's possible to discover rankings of any constraint pairs that are as yet unranked. One of the unranked pairs is STAY and FULL-INTERPRETATION. Unfortunately, nothing in data set (64) will help us to rank this pair. The violation of FULL-INTERPRETATION brings with it a violation of STAY in [$_{CP}$ *What$_i$ did$_j$* [$_{IP}$ *Robin* e$_j$ [$_{VP}$ *eat* t$_i$]]], so we cannot use these data to separate the effects of these constraints and thereby make a ranking argument.

Another unranked pair in (70) is OPERATOR-IN-SPECIFIER and OBLIGATORY-HEADS. They do not conflict in data set (64), since all of the grammatical sentences obey both of them. Grimshaw (1997: 396) goes on to show that Operator-in-Specifier is ranked higher, using evidence from subordinate interrogatives: *I know what Robin said* versus **I know what did Robin say*. Subordinate interrogatives have *wh*-movement without inversion, so they separate the effects of these two constraints and thereby make them rankable.

The last unranked pair in (70) is Operator-in-Specifier and Full-Interpretation. Data set (64) provides the evidence needed to rank Operator-in-Specifier over Full-Interpretation. The choice is between *wh*-movement with *do*-support versus no *wh*-movement and hence no need for *do*-support. Tableau (71) shows why *wh*-movement wins.

(71) Ranking argument: Operator-in-Specifier >> Full-Interpretation, Stay

	Op-Spec	Full-Int	Stay
a. → [$_{CP}$ *what*$_i$ *did*$_j$ [$_{IP}$ *Robin*$_k$ e$_j$ [$_{VP}$ t$_k$ *eat* t$_i$]]]		*	***
b. [$_{CP}$ *Robin ate what*]	*W	L	L

The next step is to check the grammar against all of the data and descriptive generalizations. This is particularly important in the present instance because I temporarily delayed mentioning the VP-internal subject hypothesis for expositional reasons. We need to make sure that all of the earlier results remain intact, once that hypothesis is taken into account. As usual, the best way to check the analysis is to construct summary tableaux, one for each of the groups of sentences in (64), and then to examine the tableaux with the descriptive generalizations in mind.

(72) Summary tableau: *Robin ate apples.*

	Op-Spec	Ob-Hd	Stay	Full-Int
a. → [$_{VP}$ *Robin ate apples*]				
b. *[$_{IP}$ *Robin*$_i$ *did* [$_{VP}$ t$_i$ *eat apples*]]			*W	*W

(73) Summary tableau: *What did Robin eat?*

	Op-Spec	Ob-Hd	Stay	Full-Int
a. → $[_{CP}$ *What$_i$ did$_j$* $[_{IP}$ *Robin$_k$* e$_j$ $[_{VP}$ t$_k$ *eat* t$_i$]]]			***	*
b. $[_{VP}$ *Robin ate what*]	*W		L	L
c. $[_{CP}$ *What$_i$ _ $[_{VP}$ *Robin eat* t$_i$]]		*W	*L	L
d. $[_{CP}$ *What$_i$ _ $[_{IP}$ *Robin$_k$ did* $[_{VP}$ t$_k$ *eat* t$_i$]]]		*W	**L	*

(74) Summary tableau: *What will Robin eat?*

	Op-Spec	Ob-Hd	Stay	Full-Int
a. → $[_{CP}$ *What$_i$ will$_j$* $[_{IP}$ *Robin$_k$* e$_j$ $[_{VP}$ t$_k$ *eat* t$_i$]]]			***	
b. $[_{IP}$ *Robin$_k$ will* $[_{VP}$ t$_k$ *eat what*]]	*W		*L	
c. $[_{CP}$ *What$_i$ will$_j$* $[_{IP}$ *Robin$_k$* e$_j$ $[_{XP}$ *do* $[_{VP}$ t$_k$ *eat* t$_i$]]]]			***	*W
d. $[_{CP}$ *What$_i$ does$_j$* $[_{IP}$ *Robin$_k$* e$_j$ $[_{XP}$ *will* $[_{VP}$ t$_k$ *eat* t$_i$]]]]			***	*W

We'll work through these summary tableaux in the usual way. First, check that the intended winners really do win. Is there a W in every loser row, and is every L dominated by some W? Yes to both. Second, check the tableaux against the descriptive generalizations. There is *wh*-movement to [Spec, CP] because Operator-in-Specifier dominates Stay ((73) and (74)). CP always has a head because Obligatory-Heads dominates Full-Interpretation and Stay (73). *Do* only appears when it's needed because Full-Interpretation rules out candidates with unnecessary *do* ((72) and (74)). In other words, Full-Interpretation enforces a kind of economy of *do* – it's prohibited except when it's needed to satisfy Operator-in-Specifier or Obligatory-Heads, the two constraints that dominate Full-Interpretation.

Earlier in this section, I promised some discussion of the nature of the candidate set and the input in OT syntax. From the basic principles of OT, we know that the candidates derived by Gen from a given input compete to be the surface realization of that input. The basic principles also tell us that a candidate loses because some other candidate wins. Part of the reason why *Robin did eat apples* is ungrammatical is that some competing candidate, derived from the same input, is more harmonic. By the same token, two grammatical sentences like *What did Robin eat?* and *What will Robin eat?* need to have different inputs, so they aren't forced to compete with one another.[18] If they did compete, then *What did Robin eat?* would lose because of its violation of FULL-INTERPRETATION. Unless it could be obtained from some other input, the grammar would wrongly predict that it's ungrammatical.

From these premises, it's possible to make inferences about the input, GEN, and the candidate set. Those inferences were implicit in the tableaux, but now we need to make them explicit. Tableaux (72), (73), and (74) each contain a nonexhaustive list of candidates derived from a common input. The members of each candidate set have identical lexical material and verbal argument structure, but they differ in whether there is movement and whether the functional projections CP and IP are present. This process of reasoning leads Grimshaw to conclude that the input consists of the lexical items and their verbal argument structure, while GEN has freedom to do movement and to build extended projections. Although this by no means answers all of our questions about the syntactic input and GEN, it nicely illustrates how one goes about finding the answers by starting from the basic principles of OT.

Any discussion of the input naturally leads to questions about faithfulness: What are the faithfulness constraints in OT syntax? The answer is a bit unclear because constraints like STAY or FULL-INTERPRETATION have the function but not the form of faithfulness constraints. In trace theory, movement isn't a process but a relationship between an element and its trace, and STAY is formulated to detect traces in the output rather than differences between input and output. In this respect, STAY is just like the original phonological faithfulness constraints PARSE and FILL in Prince and Smolensky (1993/2004) (see §4.6.4).

Because OT is a theory of constraint interaction rather than a theory of constraints, it isn't limited to phonology or any other specific empirical domain. In fact, even this tiny fragment of OT syntax reveals a close parallel between syntax and phonology. Because constraints can be active even when they are dominated, FULL-INTERPRETATION rules out unnecessary uses of nonemphatic *do* in *Robin did eat apples* and *What will Robin do eat?* (see (72) and (74)). That is why *do* has an only-when-needed distribution: it's forbidden except when higher-ranking constraints compel its presence. The same thing happens in phonology. In St'at'imcets (formerly Lillooet), the vowel [ə] appears only when it's needed for markedness reasons, in words that would otherwise be vowelless and in clusters that would otherwise violate sonority-sequencing requirements (van Eijk 1997). Gouskova (2003) develops an analysis of St'at'imcets in which the economy of [ə] is explained in virtually the same way as the economy of English *do*: a markedness constraint that [ə] violates is dominated by constraints that demand [ə]'s presence, with faithfulness to [ə] at the bottom.

QUESTION

31 Should the syntactic GEN be allowed to delete and/or insert lexical items (i.e., nouns, verbs, and adjectives)? What consequences, good or bad, would this have?

EXERCISES

32 As the text notes, no literal faithfulness constraints are included in Grimshaw's analysis. For the purpose of this exercise, assume that inputs can contain *do*, that it can be deleted or inserted, and that deletion and insertion of *do* violate syntactic versions of the faithfulness constraints MAX and DEP, respectively. Show how these constraints must be ranked relative to the other constraints in Grimshaw's analysis.

33 The text describes Grimshaw's view of the nature of the input and GEN in OT syntax. Bakovic and Keer (2001) take a different view. Read their article (available as #384 on ROA) and compare the approaches.

2.10 Finding and Fixing Problems in an Analysis

2.10.1 How to check an analysis for problems

Perhaps "all grammars leak" (Sapir 1921: 38), but it's useful to be able to find the leaks and sometimes plug them up. This section explains how to diagnose and repair the problems that sometimes arise in an OT analysis. The focus here is on problems that can be corrected by modest changes in the analysis itself. Problems that might require bigger changes in CON are discussed in chapter 4.

Problems usually emerge when the analysis is being checked. In the sections on Yawelmani phonology and English *do*-support, we saw some strategies for checking an analysis. The following procedure builds on those strategies.

(i) *Summarize the ranking arguments.* Put the tableaux into combination format if you have not already done so. Go through the tableaux and make a list of all the ranking arguments with the corresponding example numbers of the tableaux, similar to (75). Then use this list to construct a ranking diagram. It is helpful to label each descending line with the example number of the supporting ranking argument, as I have done in (76). Make sure you include any constraints that are active but not (yet) ranked; these constraints will appear in the diagram but won't have any connections with other constraints.

(75) Ranking arguments in §2.9
    OPERATOR-IN-SPECIFIER >> STAY (66), (71)
    OBLIGATORY-HEADS >> STAY (67), (68)
    OBLIGATORY-HEADS >> FULL-INTERPRETATION (68)
    OPERATOR-IN-SPECIFIER >> FULL-INTERPRETATION (71)

(76) Hasse diagram for (75)

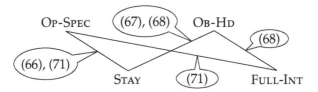

(ii) *Check the ranking results for paradoxes.* Make sure that every ranking argument in the list corresponds to a strictly downward path in the diagram. This path may pass through another constraint, if a ranking is supported by both a direct argument and by transitivity of domination, but a downward path must exist for every ranking argument. Take note of any discrepancies, since these are *ranking paradoxes*, where there is a contradiction between different sources of information about ranking.

After fixing any paradoxes using the guidelines in §2.10.3, go back to step (i) and add the new ranking argument(s) to the summary.

(iii) *Check for unranked constraints.* Checking the diagram for unranked constraints is a good way of finding additional ranking arguments. Two constraints in a Hasse diagram are unranked if there is no strictly downward path between them. For each pair of constraints, try to construct a ranking argument using the techniques we have seen throughout this chapter. If this is successful, go back to (i) and add the new ranking argument(s) to the summary.

(iv) *Construct summary tableaux.* A summary tableau presents a winner and a variety of relevant losers as they are evaluated by all of the constraints in the analysis. The summary tableaux should be representative of the data set, the descriptive generalizations, and the ranking arguments. In general, there should be one summary tableau for each natural grouping of the data and/or each clause of the descriptive generalization and/or each distinct winner appearing in a ranking argument. (Typically, these three criteria converge on the same result.) At a minimum, every loser that appears in a ranking argument should also appear in a summary tableau.

(v) *Add losers to the summary tableaux.* Using the techniques in §2.5, look for additional losing candidates that might challenge the winner in each summary tableau.

(vi) *Check the summary tableaux for consistency.* The comparative format makes the process of checking tableaux very easy: make sure that every loser row contains a W, and make sure that every L is dominated by some W. Discrepancies mean that either some loser ties with the intended winner for optimality (a loser row with no Ws or Ls), or some loser beats the intended winner (a loser row with an undominated L). This usually indicates an inadequacy in the constraint system, which can often be corrected using the methods in chapter 4.

After fixing any such problems, go back to (i) and add the new ranking arguments to the summary.

(vii) *Check the validity of the ranking arguments.* An argument for ranking Const1 over Const2 is invalid if some other constraint Const3 could do the work of Const1. Although the techniques of analysis illustrated in §2.3 and §2.9 will usually avoid such problems, the summary tableaux provide the last opportunity to check. In §2.10.2 we will see how to do this check.

The following subsections fill in many of the details of how to check an analysis and how to fix any problems that emerge.

EXERCISE

34   Below, I have collected (and slightly modified) all of the constraint ranking tableaux from the McCarthy and Prince (1993b) analysis of various phenomena in Axininca Campa, an Arawakan language of Peru (Payne 1981).

Perform all of the checks on this analysis except for (vii), which hasn't been explained yet. Be sure to explain what you are doing as you go along. To avoid giving any hints, the tableaux appear in a somewhat illogical order and shading and "!" are omitted. They are violation tableaux because comparative tableaux had not yet been invented in 1993, and they are 2 × 2 tableaux because that was the normal form of ranking arguments at that time. (See §3.3 for an explanation of the change.)

The tableaux include three constraints that we have not yet encountered. ALIGN-RIGHT(stem, syllable) requires every stem-final segment to be syllable-final (McCarthy and Prince 1993a, Prince and Smolensky 1993/2004: 127); it is violated in *[iŋ.ko.mai] because the final [a] of the root (and stem) [koma] falls in the middle of a syllable (tableau 1), and it is violated in [noñ.ʧʰi.ka.wai.ti] because the final [k] of the root/stem [ʧik] is syllable-medial (tableau 8). DEP$_{init-σ}$ is violated when the word-initial syllable contains an epenthetic segment. CODA-COND is a cover constraint that is violated by any coda consonant except for a nasal coda that precedes a homorganic stop or affricate in onset position. Thus, *[noñ.ʧʰik.wai.ti] in tableau 6 violates CODA-COND because of its [k] but not because of its [ñ].

Tableau 1

/i-N-koma-i/ 'he will paddle'	ALIGN-RIGHT(stem, syllable)	DEP
a. → iŋ.ko.ma.ti		*
b. iŋ.ko.mai	*	

Tableau 2

/i-N-koma-i/	DEP$_{init-σ}$	ONSET
a. → iŋ.ko.ma.ti		*
b. tiŋ.ko.ma.ti	*	

Tableau 3

/i-N-koma-i/	MAX	ONSET
a. → iŋ.ko.ma.ti		*
b. ko.ma.ti	**	

Tableau 4

/i-ɴ-koma-i/	Onset	Dep
a. → iŋ.ko.ma.ti	*	*
b. iŋ.ko.ma.i	**	

Tableau 5

/i-ɴ-koma-i/	Max	Dep
a. → iŋ.ko.ma.ti		*
b. iŋ.ko.ma	*	

Tableau 6

/no-ɴ-ʧʰik-wai-i/ 'I will continue to cut'	Coda-Cond	Dep
a. → noñ.ʧʰi.ka.wai.ti		**
b. noñ.ʧʰik.wai.ti	*	*

Tableau 7

/no-ɴ-ʧʰik-wai-i/	Max	Dep
a. → noñ.ʧʰi.ka.wai.ti		**
b. noñ.ʧʰi.wai.ti	*	*

Tableau 8

/no-ɴ-ʧʰik-wai-i/	Coda-Cond	Align-Right(stem, syllable)
a. → noñ.ʧʰi.ka.wai.ti		*
b. noñ.ʧʰik.wai.ti	*	

2.10.2 Problem 1: An invalid ranking argument

Suppose we think that we have a good argument for ranking CONST1 over CONST2 by comparing the winner [w] with the loser *[l]. We cannot be certain of this argument, however, until we have checked whether there is some third constraint CONST3 that could also explain why [w] beats *[l]. Part of checking an analysis involves looking at all the ranking arguments and making sure that none of them is subverted by considerations like this.

Here's a procedure for doing this check. The list of ranking arguments includes CONST1 >> CONST2. Look through all of the summary tableaux for a loser row where CONST1 assigns W, CONST2 assigns L, and no other constraint assigns W. If such a row exists, then no constraint in the analysis has the potential to subvert the argument for CONST1 >> CONST2. You can safely move on to checking the next ranking argument in the list. (I suggest you take a moment to think about why rows with only one W are so useful.)

Alternatively, the search might turn up only rows where CONST1 assigns W, CONST2 assigns L, and some other constraint CONST3 also assigns W. To determine whether CONST3 really does affect the argument for CONST1 >> CONST2, look at all of the information about how CONST3 is ranked. There are three possible outcomes:

First, you might find that CONST1 dominates CONST3. If so, then there is nothing to worry about: CONST1 definitely does dominate CONST2.

Second, you might find that CONST3 dominates CONST1. If so, then there is no argument for ranking CONST1 above CONST2, since CONST3 is sufficient to account for all of the winner~loser pairs that CONST1 would account for. (This gets a little more complicated when several constraints together dominate CONST1, but the general idea is the same.) This situation was illustrated in (27), which is repeated here as (77). Since *V# dominates MAX, *V# and not MAX is active in favoring the winner over the loser in this tableau. Unless there is some independent, valid argument that MAX dominates IDENT(long), we are obliged to simply drop any claim about the ranking of these two constraints.

(77) No argument for MAX >> IDENT(long) because *V# >> MAX

/taxaː-kʔa/	*V#	MAX	IDENT(long)
a. → ta.xakʔ		*	*
b.　 ta.xaː	*W	**W	L

Third, you might find that the ranking of Const3 with respect to Const1 is unknown. Because the ranking of Const1 and Const3 is unknown, either one of them could be responsible for overruling Const2 by favoring the winner. All that can be said with certainty is that Const1 or Const3 dominates Const2. An example of a ranking argument with this property is given in (78). This poorly chosen loser can at best tell us that one of Operator-in-Specifier or Obligatory-Heads dominates Stay.

(78)   Disjunctive ranking result

	Op-Spec	Ob-Hd	Stay	Full-Int
a. → $[_{CP}$ *What*$_i$ *will*$_j$ $[_{IP}$ *Robin*$_k$ e$_j$ $[_{VP}$ t$_k$ *eat* t$_i$]]]			***L	
b. $[_{CP}$ _ $[_{IP}$ *Robin*$_k$ *will* $[_{VP}$ t$_k$*eat what*]]]	*W	*W	*L	

If tableau (78) were the best that we could do, then it would deserve a place in our analysis. But it would be better to try to separate the effects of Operator-in-Specifier and Obligatory-Heads by finding a loser that only one of them disfavors (see §2.7 on how to do this). As soon as we have a tableau that tells us definitively that one of Operator-in-Specifier and Obligatory-Heads dominates Stay, then tableau (78) is useless and may be discarded. That is because the disjunctive ranking result in this tableau is entailed by either of the pairwise rankings that make it up: if we have a tableau showing unambiguously that Const1 dominates Const3, there is no point in presenting a argument that shows that Const1 or Const2 dominates Const3. For more about entailment and disjunction in constraint ranking argumentation, see §2.12.

2.10.3   Problem 2: A ranking paradox

A ranking paradox is a set of two or more inconsistent rankings. In the simplest case, there is evidence for Const1 >> Const2 and other evidence for Const2 >> Const1. More complicated examples involve transitivity of domination – e.g., there are direct ranking arguments for Const1 >> Const2, Const2 >> Const3, and Const3 >> Const1. In this section, we will see an example of a ranking paradox and a way to resolve it.

In previous discussion of Yawelmani, we saw a ranking argument that places DEP above MAX (49). This argument is repeated in (79). The point of this ranking is to explain why *V# is satisfied by deletion of a final vowel rather than epenthesis of a final consonant. By ranking DEP higher, we rule out the epenthesis option.

(79) Ranking argument: DEP >> MAX (>> IDENT(long))

/taxaː-k$^?$a/	DEP	MAX	IDENT(long)
a. → ta.xak$^?$		*	*
b. ta.xaː.k$^?$aʔ	*W	L	L

Yawelmani also has vowel epenthesis in triconsonantal clusters. (The data were given in (58).) This shows that MAX dominates DEP, as the ranking argument (80) certifies. (The other constraints favor neither the winner nor the loser in this tableau, so we can omit them.)

(80) Ranking argument: MAX >> DEP

/ʔilk-hin/	MAX	DEP
a. → ʔi.lik.hin		*
b. ʔil.hin	*W	L

We have, then, two seemingly impeccable ranking arguments leading to exactly opposite conclusions. Situations like this aren't rare, nor are they grounds for despair. On the contrary: a ranking paradox is an opportunity for fresh discovery. Ranking paradoxes often reveal inadequacies in the constraint system. They often tell us that something is wrong with our assumptions about CON and even point toward the solution. (A confession: I don't always experience the unadulterated joy of discovering a ranking paradox, particularly when my analysis is rather far along.)

A ranking paradox may tell us that we need another constraint, and it can also specify some of the properties of that constraint. Suppose we assume that the correct ranking is DEP >> MAX. Then the MAX >> DEP ranking argument in (80) must be eliminated. To eliminate that argument, we require a novel constraint that does the same work as MAX does in (80): it has to dominate DEP and it has to favor [ʔi.lik.hin] over *[ʔil.hin]. But the novel constraint also has to differ from MAX: it cannot favor *[ta.xaː.kʲaʔ] over [ta.xakʲ]. If it did favor *[ta.xaː.kʲaʔ], the novel constraint would pick the wrong winner in (79), and we would be back where we started.

This process of reasoning has led us to two inferences about the new constraint's favoring relations:

(i) It favors [ʔi.lik.hin] over *[ʔil.hin].
(ii) It does not favor *[ta.xaː.kʲaʔ] over [ta.xakʲ]. (Thus, it either favors [ta.xakʲ] or treats them equally. The analysis will work either way.)

Since we are dealing here with choices among unfaithful mappings, the novel constraint is probably a faithfulness constraint rather than a markedness constraint. It must disfavor consonant deletion (*[ʔil.hin]) but not disfavor vowel deletion ([ta.xakʲ]). From there, it's a small step to the conclusion that the novel constraint prohibits consonant deletion specifically. It's called MAX-C. Ranking MAX-C above DEP allows DEP to dominate the general MAX constraint with no danger of a ranking paradox:

(81) MAX-C at work

/ʔilk-hin/	MAX-C	DEP	MAX
a. → ʔi.lik.hin		*	
b. ʔil.hin	*W	L	*W

(82) MAX-C irrelevant

/taxaː-kʲa/	MAX-C	DEP	MAX
a. → ta.xakʲ			*
b. ta.xaː.kʲaʔ		*W	L

There are other possible approaches to this paradox. Instead of positing MAX-C and MAX, two constraints in a stringency relationship (§2.4), CON could contain MAX-C and MAX-V, two constraints in a disjoint relationship. One might also attempt an analysis based on the assumption that DEP rather than MAX has V- and C-specific versions. The general problem of deciding among options like these is a topic for chapter 5.

As this example shows, ranking paradoxes are one of the ways that we make progress in OT. They show that a constraint system is insufficient, and they often offer excellent clues about how to fix the problem. Encountering a ranking paradox is never a reason to give up on an analysis.

EXERCISES

35 Redo the analysis based on the assumption that DEP rather than MAX has a C-specific version.

36 Ito and Mester (1996) describe a ranking paradox that arises in their analysis of a phenomenon in Danish called *stød*. Stød is glottalization ([+constricted glottis]), indicated by ?. It appears on the first segment that follows the syllable nucleus. It's required in stressed syllables, except that a word-final consonant cannot carry stød. Word-final glides and vowels with stød are allowed, however. The constraints in Ito and Mester's analysis require stød on stressed syllables (HAVE-STØD), forbid stød on word-final segments (*?#), forbid stød on true consonants (i.e., other than glides) (*C?), and prohibit adding or removing stød (IDENT([constricted glottis]), or IDENT([cg]) for short).

Starting from the unranked violation tableaux below, show that there really is a paradox. Then work toward resolving the paradox: identify the favoring relations required of a new constraint, propose a constraint with those favoring relations (it may be rather ad hoc), and show that your constraint really does resolve the paradox.

Tableau 1

/skin/ 'light'	HAVE-STØD	*?#	*C?	IDENT([cg])
a. → skin	*			
b. skin?		*	*	*

Tableau 2

/lamp/ 'lamp'	HAVE-STØD	*?#	*C?	IDENT([cg])
a. → lam?p			*	*
b. lamp	*			

Tableau 3

/skow/ 'forest'	Have-Stød	*ʔ#	*Cʔ	Ident([cg])
a. → skowʔ		*		*
b. skow	*			

Tableau 4

/skowl/ 'shovel'	Have-Stød	*ʔ#	*Cʔ	Ident([cg])
a. → skowʔl				*
b. skowl	*			

2.10.4   Problem 3: Dealing with richness of the base

Unlike the other two problems discussed in this section, the rich-base problem does not emerge from constraint ranking. Since the solution often involves ranking, however, it makes sense to look at this problem now. Under richness of the base (§2.8), every language has (infinitely) many inputs that cannot map faithfully to some well-formed expression of that language. Since every input must map to some output, the grammar has to map these inputs to unfaithful candidates that are well-formed: phonotactically possible words or grammatical sentences. The rich-base problem is this: sometimes there is no evidence to tell us exactly *which* unfaithful candidate is optimal for a given input drawn from the rich base.

For example, Yawelmani /ʔilk-hin/ is an input that must map unfaithfully because the rankings prohibit triconsonantal clusters. Alternations provide evidence of what this input maps to, [ʔi.lik.hin]. As we saw in §2.8, Yawelmani also prohibits vowel-initial syllables, so Onset must dominate some relevant faithfulness constraint. But there is no evidence from alternations that will tell us which faithfulness constraint Onset dominates. That is, there is no evidence from paradigms to tell us whether a hypothetical input drawn from the rich base, such as /apak/, will map most harmonically to [ʔapak] or [pak].

Sometimes, all uncertainty can be eliminated by looking at independently motivated rankings. From (82) we know that Dep dominates

MAX in Yawelmani. Given this ranking, the more harmonic candidate from /apak/ will be [pak] rather than *[ʔapak]. This is shown by (83), which is a violation tableau because this is an instance of the selection problem rather than the ranking problem (§2.2). The independently motivated ranking is determining the winner.

(83)   Choosing the winner for hypothetical /apak/

/apak/	ONSET	DEP	MAX
a. → pak			*
b. ʔapak		*!	
b. apak	*!		

Since the analysis of different phenomena in the same language must lead to a single, internally consistent ranking, results about ranking obtained in one context are applicable in another. That general property of OT legitimates the move in (83). Rankings aren't specific to particular constructions or contexts; they are global properties of the grammar. A language can have truly different constraint hierarchies only insofar as it has distinct grammatical modules, such as the phonological and syntactic modules.

In the OT literature, you may also see attempts to use external evidence to solve rich-base problems. External evidence is any kind of data that isn't usually available to language learners, such as how words borrowed from other languages are adapted. Vowel-initial words borrowed into Yawelmani's near relative Gashowu have epenthetic glottal stop (84). (Presumably there are similar data in Yawelmani, though Newman happens not to cite any relevant examples.)

(84)   Gashowu vowel-initial loans (Newman 1944: 168)

Source	Gashowu	
apple	[ʔaːpal]	'apple'
apricots	[ʔaːpalkatʃ]	'apricot'
higos (Spanish)	[ʔijguʃ]	'fig'
uvas (Spanish)	[ʔuwbaʃ]	'grape'

This evidence would seem to support the idea that hypothetical /apak/ maps most harmonically to [ʔapak], contradicting the conclusion derived from independently motivated rankings. But there is plenty of evidence from other languages showing that adaptation of loan words does not mirror unfaithful mappings in the regular phonology (see Smith 2006 and references cited there). For instance, Japanese deals with unpronounceable consonant clusters in loans by epenthesizing vowels: *Christmas* → [kurisumasu]. But in the native phonology, clusters are resolved by deletion: /tob-sase/ → [tobase] 'fly (causative)'. The use of epenthesis rather than deletion, as in Yawelmani and Japanese, is apparently a near-universal of loan phonology (Paradis and LaCharité 1997). Loanword adaptation needs to be used cautiously in addressing the rich-base problem.

The rich-base problem is really a problem of indeterminacy: the evidence doesn't include all of the input–output mappings that the grammar must account for. Sometimes other evidence will resolve the question. Sometimes, though, the indeterminacy lingers despite our best efforts.

2.11 Constraint Ranking by Algorithm and Computer

As we saw in §2.10.1, comparative tableaux make it very easy to check that the constraints are correctly ranked: every L must be dominated by some W. When it comes right down to it, constraint ranking really is that simple: every constraint that favors some loser must be dominated by some constraint favoring the winner over that loser. If ranking is so simple, then it might not be too much of a stretch to hope for a simple procedure that analysts (or babies) could use to discover a language's ranking. That procedure is *constraint demotion* (Tesar and Smolensky 1998, 2000).

The main idea in constraint demotion is that a loser-favoring constraint moves down in the hierarchy from some initial ranking until all of its Ls are dominated by Ws, but no further. I will explain one version of constraint demotion, the Recursive Constraint Demotion algorithm (RCD), using Yawelmani as an illustration.

We begin by assembling all of the information that can contribute to ranking into a single table called the *support*, since it supports the inferences about ranking. Following Prince (2002a), the support is a multi-input, unranked comparative tableau. The Yawelmani support table appears in (85). The constraints are as yet unranked – in fact, I have deliberately scrambled them away from the target ranking. (The inputs have been omitted to save space. They're no doubt familiar from previous discussion of this example.)

(85) Support for RCD

Winners	Losers	*V#	*COMP-SYLL	*C^{unsyll}	ID(long)	DEP	MAX-C	MAX
lan.hin	laːn.hin		W		L			
	laː.n.hin			W	L			
	laː.ni.hin				L	W		
	laː.hin				L		W	W
ta.xakʔ	ta.xaː.kʔa	W			L			L
	ta.xaːkʔ		W		L			
	ta.xaː.kʔ			W	L			
	ta.xaː.kʔaʔ				L	W		L
	tax				L		W	W
xat.kʔa	xatkʔ	L	W					
	xat.kʔ	L		W				
	xat	L					W	W
	xa.tikʔ	L				W		W
	xat.kʔaʔ	L				W		
ʔi.lik.hin	ʔilk.hin		W		L			
	ʔil.k.hin			W	L			
	ʔil.hin				L		W	W

The first step in RCD is to identify all of the constraints that favor no losers. These are the constraints that have no Ls in their columns. Constraints that favor no losers are undominated. They belong at the top of the constraint hierarchy. Three such constraints are visible in (85): *COMPLEX-SYLLABLE, *C^{unsyll}, and MAX-C. All other constraints are demoted below them, yielding the constraint hierarchy in (86).

(86) Constraint hierarchy after first pass through RCD
{*COMP-SYLL, *Cᵘⁿˢʸˡˡ, MAX-C} >> {*V#, IDENT(long), DEP, MAX}

The next step is to hide the *COMPLEX-SYLLABLE, *Cᵘⁿˢʸˡˡ, and MAX-C columns in the support, since there is nothing more to learn from them. We also must hide any losers that are disfavored by any of these three constraints. Those losers have been fully accounted for, so their performance on lower-ranking constraints is irrelevant to the ranking. For example, *COMPLEX-SYLLABLE favors the winner over *[laːn.hin], so *[laːn.hin]'s row has to be hidden. The result is shown in (87), with the "hidden" rows and columns shaded. In (88), I've taken the further step of removing them entirely.

(87) Support after first pass through RCD (shading)

Winners	Losers	*V#	*COMP-SYLL	*Cᵘⁿˢʸˡˡ	ID(long)	DEP	MAX-C	MAX
lan.hin	laːn.hin		W		L			
	laː.n.hin			W	L			
	laː.ni.hin				L	W		
	laː.hin				L		W	W
ta.xakʔ	ta.xaː.kʔa	W			L			L
	ta.xaːkʔ		W		L			
	ta.xaː.kʔ			W	L			
	ta.xaː.kʔaʔ				L	W		L
	tax				L		W	W
xat.kʔa	xatkʔ	L	W					
	xat.kʔ	L		W				
	xat	L					W	W
	xa.tikʔ	L				W		W
	xat.kʔaʔ	L				W		
ʔi.lik.hin	ʔilk.hin		W		L			
	ʔil.k.hin			W	L			
	ʔil.hin				L		W	W

(88) Support after first pass through RCD (removal)

Winners	Losers	*V#	Id(long)	Dep	Max
lan.hin	la:.ni.hin		L	W	
ta.xak$^?$	ta.xa:.k$^?$a	W	L		L
	ta.xa:.k$^?$a?		L	W	L
xat.k$^?$a	xa.tik$^?$	L		W	W
	xat.k$^?$a?	L		W	

Now comes the recursive step that gives RCD its name. (A recursive procedure is one that takes its own output as further input. Opening a set of nested matryoshka dolls is an example of a recursive procedure.) Looking only at the considerably diminished support table (88), search again for any constraints that favor no losers. Here, Dep meets this criterion. Dep is therefore placed in the constraint hierarchy below the top-ranked constraints. All of the remaining constraints are demoted below Dep, as shown in (89). Then the Dep column as well as any rows where Dep assesses a W are shaded (90) or removed (91).

(89) Constraint hierarchy after second pass through RCD
{*Comp-Syll, *C^{unsyll}, Max-C} >> Dep >> {*V#, Ident(long), Max}

(90) Support after second pass through RCD (shading)

Winners	Losers	*V#	Id(long)	Dep	Max
lan.hin	la:.ni.hin		L	W	
ta.xak$^?$	ta.xa:.k$^?$a	W	L		L
	ta.xa:.k$^?$a?		L	W	L
xat.k$^?$a	xa.tik$^?$	L		W	W
	xat.k$^?$a?	L		W	

(91) Support after second pass through RCD (removal)

Winners	Losers	*V#	Id(long)	Max
ta.xak$^{\textipa{P}}$	ta.xaː.k$^{\textipa{P}}$a	W	L	L

We again proceed recursively, using (91) as the basis for constraint demotion. *V# is the only remaining constraint that favors no losers, and when we rank it, we have cleared out all of the losers in the support. At that point, any remaining constraints are placed at the bottom of the hierarchy, yielding (92). Because it was created by using the RCD algorithm, this hierarchy is guaranteed to select the correct winners for all of the winner~loser pairs in the original support (85). (Of course, this is no guarantee that this ranking will work if crucial data or competitive losers have been overlooked.)

(92) Constraint hierarchy after final pass through RCD
{*Comp-Syll, *C^{unsyll}, Max-C} >> Dep >> *V# >> {Ident(long), Max}

RCD is primarily intended as a learning theory, but from the perspective of someone doing analysis in OT it also has some useful properties, as well as some limitations. If the candidates and constraints are already known, then RCD is extremely quick and easy to use. It's a simple matter using a word processor to go from a large support table like (85) to (88) and then to (91).

The speed and simplicity of RCD are particularly attractive because of RCD's ability to do *inconsistency detection*. Suppose we have been applying RCD and we reach a point where each of the remaining constraints favors at least one loser. Since there are still some winner~loser pairs that have not yet been accounted for, we have a problem: RCD is stuck. This means it has failed to find a ranking. Since RCD always finds a ranking if there is one to find, this failure means that the constraints we started with are unable to handle all of the winner~loser pairs in the support.

Here is an example where RCD detects inconsistency. For exercise 35, you were asked to solve the Yawelmani ranking paradox by creating a consonant-specific version of Dep rather than Max. RCD permits a quick check on whether this proposal will actually work in the context of the rest of the system. We begin with the support

(93), which is like (85) except that Max-C has been replaced by Dep-C.

(93) Support for RCD (Dep-C instead of Max-C)

Winners	Losers	*V#	*Comp-Syll	*Cunsyll	Id(long)	Dep	Dep-C	Max
lan.hin	laːn.hin		W		L			
	laː.n.hin			W	L			
	laː.ni.hin				L	W		
	laː.hin				L			W
ta.xakʔ	ta.xaː.kʔa	W			L			L
	ta.xaːkʔ		W		L			
	ta.xaː.kʔ			W	L			
	ta.xaː.kʔaʔ				L	W	W	L
	tax				L			W
xat.kʔa	xatkʔ	L	W					
	xat.kʔ	L		W				
	xat	L						W
	xa.tikʔ	L				W		W
	xat.kʔaʔ	L				W	W	
ʔi.lik.hin	ʔilk.hin		W			L		
	ʔil.k.hin			W		L		
	ʔil.hin					L		W

On the first pass through RCD, the three constraints that favor no losers – *Complex-Syllable, *Cunsyll, and Dep-C – are placed at the top of the hierarchy and the others are demoted below them. We then remove those constraints from the support, as well as any rows where they favor the winner. The result is (94).

(94) Support after first pass through RCD

Winners	Losers	*V#	Id(long)	Dep	Max
lan.hin	laː.ni.hin		L	W	
	laː.hin		L		W
ta.xakˀ	ta.xaː.kˀa	W	L		L
	tax		L		W
xat.kˀa	xat	L			W
	xa.tikˀ	L		W	W
ʔi.lik.hin	ʔil.hin			L	W

At this point, RCD stalls. It can go no further because every column contains at least one L, so no constraints can be ranked. Since some winner~loser pairs remain unaccounted for, RCD has detected inconsistency. There is no ranking of these constraints that can account for the remaining winner~loser pairs. The constraints need to be revised in some way or other. Close examination of the residual support table (94) can even suggest how the constraint set needs to be revised. See chapter 4 for discussion.

Although RCD is great for inconsistency detection, it also has some significant limitations as a tool for doing OT analysis. It requires but by itself does not provide informative losing candidates. RCD is therefore useful only when the losers are already known because they have been constructed by systematic analysis or by free combination of some representational primitives. (Both methods were discussed in §2.5.)

Another limitation of RCD is that it produces a constraint hiearchy that gets the right results but is relatively uninformative about constraint interactions. RCD puts the constraints into a *stratified partial ordering*. If I have a group of people and order them by their year of birth, I get a stratified partial ordering (see (95)). People born in the same year are equal in this ordering – they are in the same ranking stratum, and they are younger than the people above them and older than the people below them. Constraint hierarchies obtained from RCD, such as (92), are also stratified partial orderings: the constraints in each stratum are equally ranked, and they are dominated by the constraints to their left and dominate the constraints to their right.

(95) A stratified partial ordering by year of birth

Albert Einstein, Leon Trotsky, Wallace Stevens (1879)

|

John Maynard Keynes, Benito Mussolini, Franz Kafka (1883)

|

Irving Berlin, T. E. Lawrence, Harpo Marx (1888)

|

Ho Chi Minh, Jelly Roll Morton, Agatha Christie (1890)

RCD's stratified partial orderings are different from the rankings proven with ranking arguments. OT constraint hierarchies derived by ranking argumentation can be partial orderings that aren't stratified. (Diagram (70) is an example.) In fact, sometimes the ranking arguments will give ranking information that involves disjunctions, and disjunctions aren't even a partial ordering. (See diagram (14) and the tableaux in (55).) In short, RCD has no way of identifying the *crucial* rankings that make up an analysis. RCD can tell us that an analysis works for a given set of winner~loser pairs, but it does not help much with understanding how it works, how it should be tested and challenged, and how it could be improved.

RCD can be straightforwardly implemented in a computer program, and the freely downloadable OTSoft package includes RCD among its many features (Hayes et al. 2003). (Another very useful package that includes OT software is Praat (Boersma and Weenink 2007).) OTSoft's input consists of a support table like (85), though in violation format rather than comparative format. OTSoft can read these tables from specially formatted text files, but it's easiest to input them as Microsoft Excel spreadsheets. Table (96) reproduces the spreadsheet page corresponding to the support (85) exactly as I entered it into Excel.[19]

(96) Support as spreadsheet for input to OTSoft

	A	B	C	D	E	F	G	H	I	J
1				*V#	*Complex-Syllable	*C/uns	Ident (long)	Dep	Max-C	Max
2				*V#	*Comp-Syll	*C/uns	Id (long)	Dep	Max-C	Max
3	laːnhin	lan.hin	1				1			
4		laːn.hin			1					
5		laː.n.hin				1				
6		laː.ni.hin					1			
7		laːhin							1	1
8	taxaːka	ta.xak	1				1			1
9		ta.xaː.ka		1						
10		ta.xaːk			1					1
11		ta.xaː.k				1				1
12		ta.xaː.ka?						1		
13		tax							1	3
14	xatka	xat.ka	1	1						
15		xatk			1					1
16		xat.k				1				1
17		xat							1	2
18		xa.tik						1		1
19		xat.ka?						1		
20	?ilkhin	?i.lik.hin	1				1			
21		?ilk.hin			1					
22		?il.k.hin				1				
23		?il.hin							1	1

OTSoft expects to find information in specific places in the spreadsheet. Row 1 of (96) contains the full names of the constraints, in any order, beginning in column D. Row 2 contains abbreviated names of the constraints for use in tableaux. The data begin in row 3. Column A is reserved for inputs and column B for output candidates. When the input cell is left blank, it's assumed that the candidate has the same input as the preceding candidate, and thus that they compete with one another. Column C has a "1" next to the winners. The numbers beneath the constraint names simply indicate the number of violations incurred by each candidate on each constraint. Cells with no violation marks can contain 0 or they can be left blank, as in (96).

OTSoft will rank the constraints using RCD, producing a stratified partial ordering. Upon request, it will also determine whether constraints are unnecessary, find pairwise ranking arguments, and diagram the rankings. Prince (2006b) has found certain problems with these latter aspects of OTSoft 2.1, and users should carefully check what OTSoft reports about unnecessary constraints and pairwise ranking arguments. OTSoft's ability to compute factorial typologies is perhaps its greatest asset, though, as we will see in chapter 5.

EXERCISES

37   Do RCD by hand for the analysis of English *do*-support in §2.9.

38   Do RCD by hand for the analysis of Axininca Campa in exercise 34.

39   Do RCD by hand for the inconsistent analysis of Danish in exercise 36. Show how RCD detects this inconsistency.

40   Install OTSoft on your computer (Windows only, unfortunately) and use it to redo one or more of exercises 37, 38, and 39. It's easiest to create the input tableau for OTSoft in an Excel spreadsheet. OTSoft is a free download from www.linguistics.ucla.edu/people/hayes/otsoft/. If you don't have Microsoft Excel, you can use the spreadsheet program Calc in the OpenOffice package to save and edit files in Excel format. OpenOffice is a free download from www.openoffice.org. Alternatively, you can follow the directions included with OTSoft to enter the input tableau as a text file.

2.12   The Logic of Constraint Ranking and Its Uses

One problem that arises during analysis is this: Which winner~loser pairs supply the most information about constraint ranking? When constructing summary tableaux, it would be preferable to select for inclusion the winner~loser pairs that are most informative about the ranking we are trying to prove. When developing an analysis, it can be useful to know whether further study of some class of winners or losers is likely to yield further insight into the constraint hierarchy.

This question and others like it can be answered by looking at the basic logic of OT, which Alan Prince has explored in a series of papers (Brasoveanu and Prince 2005, Prince 2002a, 2002b, 2006a, 2006b). In this section, we will look at how the logic of OT can help with analysis, and in chapter 5 we will see how it applies to language typology. It is important to realize that the methods of inference described here and in chapter 5 are not just useful techniques; their validity has been established in formal proofs.

The logic of OT is based on the properties of ERCs (Prince 2002b: 1–2). This acronym stands for *elementary ranking condition*. An ERC contains all of the information about constraint ranking that is provided by a single winner~loser comparison. An ERC is therefore the same as a single row of a support table like (85) – it contains W, L, or an empty cell for every constraint. In the discussion below, sometimes ERCs will appear in tableau format, and sometimes they will appear in a more compact form as ordered n-tuples of W and L, with e for empty cells. For instance, the first row of (85) can be represented compactly as (e, W, e, L, e, e, e). Bear in mind that ERCs are not ranked; they could not be, since they will be used to determine what the ranking is. The order of the constraints in an ERC is arbitrary but constant across all of the ERCs that we intend to compare or combine.

At the beginning of this section, I posed the question of which winner~loser pairs are most informative about ranking. The question can be restated as follows: When does one ERC *entail* another ERC? A schematic example of entailment is shown in (97). Here we have two ERCs in tableau format. ERC (a) tells us unambiguously that CONSTRAINT1 dominates CONSTRAINT3, since CONSTRAINT3's L has to be dominated by some W, and CONSTRAINT1 is the only W-assigning constraint in the ERC. On the other hand, ERC (b), with two Ws, only tells us that CONSTRAINT1 *or* CONSTRAINT2 dominates CONSTRAINT3. ERC (b) is therefore less informative than ERC (a), just as the proposition *I weigh 155 pounds or I can lift 155 pounds with one hand* is less informative than the proposition *I weigh 155 pounds*. ERC (a) entails ERC (b). In general, if two ERCs are identical except that blank cells in the first are replaced by Ws in the second, then the first entails the second.

(97)   Entailment I: ERC (a) entails ERC (b)

	Winners	Losers	CONSTRAINT1	CONSTRAINT2	CONSTRAINT3
a.	*winner1*	*loser1*	W		L
b.	*winner2*	*loser2*	W	W	L

Another entailment situation is shown in (98). Since every L must be dominated by some W, ERC (a) tells us that CONSTRAINT1 dominates both CONSTRAINT2 and CONSTRAINT3. ERC (b) tells us only that CONSTRAINT1 dominates CONSTRAINT3, so ERC (a) is more informative. ERC (a) entails ERC (b). In general, if two ERCs are identical except that Ls in the first are replaced by blank cells in the second, then the first entails the second.

(98)   Entailment II: ERC (a) entails ERC (b)

	Winners	Losers	CONSTRAINT1	CONSTRAINT2	CONSTRAINT3
a.	*winner1*	*loser1*	W	L	L
b.	*winner2*	*loser2*	W		L

Prince (2002b: 5) generalizes these relationships to the two rules of entailment in (99), W-extension and L-retraction. In (97), ERC (a) entails ERC (b) by W-extension: (b) is identical to (a) except for the added W. In the more compact format for ERCs, the ERC (W, e, L) entails the ERC (W, W, L). And in (98), ERC (a) entails ERC (b) by L-retraction: (b) is identical to (a) except for the missing L. In the more compact format, (W, L, L) entails (W, e, L).

(99)   ERC entailment rules
    a.   W-extension
        An ERC entails any other ERC that can be derived from it by replacing an empty cell with a W.
    b.   L-retraction
        An ERC entails any other ERC that can be derived from it by replacing an L with an empty cell.

For a practical application of these ideas, look at (100), which is a slightly reorganized version of summary tableau (33) from the

Yawelmani analysis in §2.3. ERC (e) is (e, e, e, W, L), and ERC (d) is (e, e, W, W, L). Because (d) is identical to (e) except that an empty cell in (e) is replaced by a W in (d), ERC (e) entails ERC (d). ERC (a) is also in an entailment relation with ERC (d). ERC (a) is (e, e, W, L, L). By applying L-retraction to the first L, we get the ERC (e, e, W, e, L). Applying W-extension to the last *e* yields (e, e, W, W, L), which is the same as ERC (d). Therefore, ERC (a) entails ERC (d) as well. In summary, ERC (d) does not provide any information about ranking that isn't already provided by (a) or (e).

(100)   ERCs from /taxaː-k$^?$a/ → [ta.xak$^?$] (≈ (33))

	Winner	Losers	*Comp-Syll	*C^{unsyll}	*V#	Max	Ident(long)
a.	ta.xak$^?$	ta.xaː.k$^?$a			W	L	L
b.	ta.xak$^?$	ta.xaːk$^?$	W				L
c.	ta.xak$^?$	ta.xaː.k$^?$		W			L
d.	ta.xak$^?$	ta.xaː			W	W	L
e.	ta.xak$^?$	tax				W	L

We'll now work through the ordinary-language versions of the entailment relations in (100) to make sure that everything is perfectly clear. ERC (d) tells us that *V# *or* Max dominates Ident(long). ERC (e) tells us that Max dominates Ident(long). The proposition "Max dominates Ident(long)" entails the proposition "*V# *or* Max dominates Ident(long)." In other words, ERC (d) isn't telling us anything more than ERC (e) tells us.

The other entailment relation in (100) involves (a) and (d). ERC (a) tells us that *V# dominates Max *and* Ident(long). ERC (d) tells us that *V# *or* Max dominates Ident(long). The proposition "*V# dominates Max *and* Ident(long)" entails the proposition "*V# dominates Ident(long)," which itself entails the proposition "*V# *or* Max dominates Ident(long)." In other words, ERC (d) isn't telling us anything that ERC (a) doesn't already tell us.

The rather cumbersome explanation in the last two paragraphs helps to emphasize the real usefulness of the ERC entailment rules in (99). It is in principle possible to reason our way through ERC entailments using the familiar logic of *and* and *or*, but it is painful to do so. The rules in (99) make it much simpler. Moreover, (repeated) application of these rules is guaranteed by a formal proof to yield all of the entailments of an ERC (Prince 2002b: 6).

Because ERC entailment shows us which winner~loser comparisons are most informative about ranking, it can be used to determine which candidates are necessary in an analysis. Because (d) in (100) is entailed by another ERC, we could safely omit (d) from the tableau with no loss of ranking information and no effect on the soundness of the ranking argumentation.

Harmonic bounding is a special case of entailment. Tableau (101) is abstracted from tableau (51), which appeared in the earlier discussion of harmonic bounding (§2.6). Candidate (g) is harmonically bounded by (a) and also by (e), since (g) has a proper superset of (a)'s violation marks and of and also of (e)'s violation marks. Thus, (g) cannot win under any ranking of these constraints.

(101) Harmonic bounding in violation format

/taxaː-k^{2}a/	*Comp-Syll	*C^{unsyll}	*V#	Max	Ident(long)
a. ta.xak^2				*	*
e. ta.xaː			*	**	
f. tax				***	
g. ta.xa			*	**	*

We can restate (101) as a comparative tableau, so we get a set of ERCs. The result is shown in (102). When a loser is harmonically bounded by the winner, there are no Ls in the loser's ERC. That's the situation in row (g). Furthermore, (g) is also harmonically bounded by another loser, (e). ERC (e) entails ERC (g) by the L-retraction rule. This is no accident: if one losing candidate harmonically bounds another, then the ERC of the bound*ing* candidate entails the ERC of the bound*ed* candidate (Prince 2002b: section 6). The opposite isn't true, by the way: (f) entails (g) by W-extension and L-retraction, but (f) isn't a harmonic bound on (g), since (f) does not have a proper subset of (g)'s violation marks.

(102) Tableau (101) as ERCs

/taxaː-kʼa/	*Comp-Syll	*Cᵘⁿˢʸˡˡ	*V#	Max	Ident(long)
a. → ta.xakʼ					
e. ta.xaː			W	W	L
f. tax				W	L
g. ta.xa			W	W	

For the good of the analysis and the exposition of it, removing harmonically bounded candidates from tableaux is often the best practice. Candidates that are harmonically bounded by the winner are the easiest to identify, since their characteristic is the L-less ERC. Candidates that are harmonically bounded by another loser will be removed automatically if all losers with entailed ERCs are identified and removed. It's possible by these means to produce a summary tableau that is reduced in size but just as informative about ranking as a tableau with a more generous assortment of candidates. (Harmonically bounded candidates are important in typological research, however. See chapter 5.)

The logic of constraint ranking is also useful in understanding how ranking information from different winner~loser pairs can be combined to draw inferences about the overall constraint hierarchy. Tableau (103) illustrates. The *winner1~loser1* ERC by itself tells us only that Constraint1 or Constraint2 dominates Constraint3. The *winner2~ loser2* ERC by itself tells us only that Constraint1 or Constraint3 dominates Constraint2. In other words, each row taken alone is only enough to support a disjunction: one constraint or another dominates the third. These rows are less informative taken individually than they are taken together. Together, they tell us that Constraint1 must dominate both Constraint2 and Constraint3. No other ranking will work.

(103) Ranking with two disjunctions

Winners	Losers	Constraint1	Constraint2	Constraint3
winner1	*loser1*	W	W	L
winner2	*loser2*	W	L	W

It is very easy to get tangled up in trying to reason one's way through even relatively simple disjunctions like (103), so imagine the problem of figuring out more complex systems of disjunctions involving more than two winner~loser pairs. Fortunately, there is a very simple solution: *ERC fusion*. Prince (2002b: 14) proves that all of the consequences of a set of ERCs can be obtained by fusing them according to the rules in (104). Fusion with an L always yields an L. Fusion with *e* results in no change, as does fusion of identical values. The reason for L's special status is clear when we recall what it takes for the winner to be optimal: *every* L must be dominated by *some* W. If *any* of the ERCs being fused has an L in some position, it's as if they *all* have it, since that L has to be dominated by some W.

(104)   ERC fusion rules (Prince 2002b: 7)
   a.   L dominance
        The result of fusing an L with anything (W, L, or *e*) is an L.
   b.   *e* identity
        The result of fusing an *e* with W is W, *e* with L is L, and *e* with *e* is *e*.
   c.   Self identity
        The result of fusing anything with itself is itself.

Let's go back to (103). When combined, the ERCs (W, W, L) and (W, L, W) should yield the ERC (W, L, L), just as (103) leads to the inference that Constraint1 dominates Constraint2 and Constraint3. Because every L must be dominated by some W, the ERC (W, L, L) unambiguously points to a ranking where Constraint1 dominates Constraint2 and Constraint3. The fusion of the ERCs (W, W, L) and (W, L, W) is illustrated in (105). Two Ws fuse to W by the self-identity rule, whereas the combinations with L fuse to L because of L dominance. When two ERCs are fused according to these rules, then the resulting ERC is reliable information about ranking, as guaranteed by the proof in Prince (2002b: 14).

(105)   Fusion of (W, W, L) and (W, L, W)

winner1~loser1	W	W	L
winner2~loser2	W	L	W
Result of fusion	W	L	L
Fusion rule applied (from (104))	(c)	(a)	(a)

ERC fusion can be used to detect inconsistency (Prince 2002b: 11). In the previous section, we used RCD to show that the support table (93) is inconsistent – there is no ranking of the constraints in (93) that will account for all of its winner~loser pairs. When two or more ERCs are inconsistent, their fusion is an ERC that contains no Ws. That's a solid indication of a problem with the analysis, since no constraint favors the winner. The ERC set in (106) is the same as (94). It's the inconsistent set of ERCs left after RCD has stalled because it cannot find any constraints to rank. It fuses to (L, e, e, L, L, e, L), with no W. This confirms that these ERCs place inconsistent demands on constraint ranking.

(106) = (94), plus ERC fusion

	Winners	Losers	*V#	*COMP-SYLL	*C^{unsyll}	ID(long)	DEP	DEP-C	MAX
a.	lan.hin	laː.ni.hin				L	W		
b.	lan.hin	laː.hin				L			W
c.	ta.xak$^{?}$	ta.xaː.k$^{?}$a	W			L			L
d.	ta.xak$^{?}$	tax				L			W
e.	xat.k$^{?}$a	xat	L						W
f.	xat.k$^{?}$a	xa.tik$^{?}$	L					W	W
g.	?i.lik.hin	?il.hin						L	W
Result of fusion			L			L	L		L

This procedure has confirmed that there's inconsistency but hasn't localized it beyond showing that some subset of the winner~loser pairs in (106) are the problem. Since (106) doesn't contain a huge number of winner~loser pairs, it is reasonable to try checking whether any smaller subset of these ERCs is inconsistent. We start by examining pairs of ERCs, checking what they fuse to:

- Begin with ERC (a). Any ERC that could fuse with (a) to produce a W-less ERC has to match (a)'s W in the DEP column with an L in that column. Only one ERC has an L in the DEP column, ERC (g). The fusion of (a) and (g) is (e, e, e, L, L, e, W), so (a) and (g) are not inconsistent. Therefore, no single ERC fused with (a) produces inconsistency.

- Now go to ERC (b). We look at all ERCs that match (b)'s W in the Max column with an L of their own. Only ERC (c) has this property. The fusion of (b) and (c) is (W, e, e, L, e, e, L), so there is no inconsistency.
- ERC (c) has a W in the *V# column. ERCs (e) and (f) match this with an L. The fusion of (c) and (e) is (L, e, e, L, e, e, L), so we have found a pair of inconsistent ERCs.

To determine whether (c) and (e) are the only source of inconsistency, we can check whether RCD succeeds if they are eliminated from the support. It does.

Knowing that (c) and (e) are the source of inconsistency is a useful hint about where to look for a solution: something about one of these winner~loser pairs is problematic, and the problem has to do with one of the constraints on which they differ, *V# or Max. As we know from our earlier discussion of this example, the problem is with Max.

There are two caveats about using these analytic techniques based on ERC fusion. First, we can't conclude that a set of ERCs is consistent just because they fuse to an ERC that contains W. For example, the ERCs in (93) fuse to (L, W, W, L, L, W, L), but as we've just seen those ERCs contain an inconsistent subset. The inferences run only one way: an ERC set is inconsistent if it fuses to a W-less ERC, but fusion to an ERC that contains W doesn't guarantee consistency. Second, the source of inconsistency in a set of inconsistent ERCs could be a subset of any size. The technique of looking for an inconsistent subset might have to look at three-member, four-member, and larger subsets if none of the two-member subsets is inconsistent. In the worst case, the entire set of ERCs is inconsistent but none of its proper subsets is. Fortunately, the worst case isn't the normal case, so the technique can still be useful.

Linguists aren't always accustomed to the idea of studying the formal foundations of a theory. As we've seen, however, research on the formal foundations of OT has yielded practical tools for analysis as well as insights of a more abstract character.

QUESTION

41 Four-constraint ERCs look like (e, W, W, L), (W, e, e, e), etc. Which four-constraint ERCs, taken individually, contain more ranking information than any other four-constraint ERCs? Which four-constraint ERCs contain no ranking information? Which four-constraint ERCs contain some ranking information, but the minimum amount?

EXERCISES

42 The violation tableau below combines and slightly modifies tableaux appearing in Morris's (2000) analysis of /s/-aspiration in a variety of Spanish "found throughout southern and western Spain." The details of Morris's constraint definitions and representational assumptions aren't important in the current context, so just accept them as-is.

Your tasks are the following:

a. Rewrite it as a comparative tableau.
b. Identify any losing candidates that are harmonically bounded by the winner. Explain how we can determine that they are harmonically bounded in the original violation tableau and in the comparative tableau.
c. Using the violation tableau, identify the losing candidates that are harmonically bounded by other losers. Using the comparative tableau, explain the entailment relations between harmonically bounded candidates and the candidates that harmonically bound them.
d. Rewrite the comparative tableau, removing all harmonically bounded candidates.
e. Determine whether there are any entailment relations among the remaining candidates.
f. Rewrite the comparative tableau, removing all entailed rows. Compare this with the original (much larger) tableau, and explain why no information about ranking has been lost.
g. Using your reduced tableau, determine any constraint rankings.

/susto/ 'fright'	IDENT (–cont)	IDENT (+cont)	IDENT (spread)	*CODA [+cont]	*CODA [spread]	DEP (link)	UNIF
a. → súh.to		*			*		
b. sús.to				*	*		
c. súh.θo	*				*	*	
d. súʰt.to		*			*	*	
e. súθ.θo	*			*	*	*	
f. sút.to		*	*			*	
g. súð.ðo	*		*	*		*	
h. sú.θo	*						*
i. sú.ðo	*		*				*
j. sú.to		*	*				*

43 The tableau below is based on Lombardi's (1999) analysis of voicing in Swedish. (The constraints were defined in (36).) Your tasks are the same as in the previous question.

Inputs		AGREE([VOICE])	*VOICE	ID([voice])	ID$_{Onset}$([voice])
/skuːg/ 'forest'	a. → skuːg		*		
	b.　skuːk			*	
/vigsəl/ 'marriage'	c. → viksəl			*	
	d.　vigsəl	*	*		
	e.　vigzəl		*	*	*
/stekdə/ 'fried'	f. → stektə			*	*
	g.　stekdə	*	*		
	h.　stegdə		**	*	
/ɛgdə/ 'owned'	i. → ɛgdə		**		
	j.　ɛkdə	*	*	*	
	k.　ɛktə			**	*
	l.　ɛgtə	*	*	*	*

Notes

1 The Latin third declension has alternations involving voicing ([urps]~ [urbis] 'city~gen.'), vowel length ([reks]~[reːgis] 'king~gen.'), deletion ([lapis]~[lapidis] 'stone~gen.'), and rhotacism ([oːs]~[oːris] 'mouth~gen.').

2 *Know/acknowledge* is sometimes mentioned as an example. Others are even more dubious, such as *pterodactyl/helicopter* or *pneumonia/apnea*.

3 On how to distinguish deletion from epenthesis when establishing underlying representations, see Kenstowicz and Kisseberth (1979: 86–87) or almost any other phonology textbook.

4 The evidence for the underlying representations comes from alternations that are observed when these numeral words are compounded. An example is /bʤu-bʃi/ → [ʤub.ʃi] 'fourteen' ('ten'-'four').

5 In principle, we might have been able to produce a ranking argument where only MAX favors the loser. For instance, if we had data like hypothetical /pata-kʔa/ → [pa.takʔ], then we would be able to show *V# forcing a

violation of MAX without also forcing a violation of IDENT(long). But with the data we actually have there is no way of doing that.

6   In more formal terms, the question of how to define IDENT(long) is really about the representational and faithfulness status of moras. If IDENT(long) is really MAX(mora), then shortening or deleting a long vowel are both violations.

7   In (35) and (36), the stringency relationships can be determined simply by inspecting the constraint definitions: the set of all traces that aren't lexically governed is a subset of the set of all traces that aren't governed; the set of onset consonants is a subset of the set of consonants. These constraints are in a stringency relationship in every language. But stringency relationships can also be contingent on language-particular patterns (Prince and Tesar 2004: 272ff., Tessier 2006). For instance, Beckman (1998) proposes constraints requiring faithfulness in stressed syllables and faithfulness in initial syllables. These constraints are in a stringency relationship in a language that stresses all initial syllables and also some noninitial syllables. (An example would be a language that places stress on the initial syllable and every other syllable thereafter.) But they aren't in a stringency relationship in any language that has some unstressed initial syllables.

8   The correct expression is "harmonically bounded" and not "harmonically bound." "Bounded" is a form of the verb "to bound," which is derived from the noun "bound," as in "115 years seems to be the upper bound on human longevity." When candidate A harmonically bounds candidate B, A acts as an upper bound on B's aspirations to optimality.

9   A candidate can also be harmonically bounded by a set of other candidates. See Samek-Lodovici and Prince (1999) on *collective harmonic bounding*.

10 MAX$_{stem-final}$ subsumes some of the functions of ALIGN-RIGHT(stem, syllable) in McCarthy and Prince (1993a, 1993b) or ANCHOR-RIGHT in McCarthy and Prince (1995, 1999).

11 The symbol σ stands for a syllable. The symbol ' is the IPA stress mark.

12 In the Arthur Conan Doyle story "Silver Blaze," Holmes draws attention to the "curious incident of the dog in the night-time." When it is pointed out that "the dog did nothing in the night-time" (i.e., it did not bark), Holmes responds "That was the curious incident."

13 "The *base* of the syntactic component is a system of rules that generate a highly restricted (perhaps finite) set of *basic strings*, each with an associated structural description called a *Base phrase-marker*" (Chomsky 1965: 17).

14 As Newman (1944: 27) says, in a remark that is a little obscure but exactly on point, "Protective measures aren't required to preserve the rule demanding an initial consonant in words, for this rule is never endangered by morphological operations."

15 Madurese has nasalized vowels with no preceding nasal in reduplicated and truncated words (Stevens 1968). See McCarthy and Prince (1995) for an analysis.

16 Prince and Smolensky (1993/2004: 225) propose a principle of learning called *lexicon optimization*. It tells learners what to do when there are no alternations and therefore no independent evidence for the underlying representation: assume an underlying representation that is identical to the surface representation. According to this principle, the underlying representation for [kæt] is indeed /kæt/.

Like richness of the base, lexicon optimization has engendered much confusion. Sometimes, authors seem to think that it relieves them of responsibility for dealing with richness of the base: "Since lexicon optimization says that the underlying form of [kæt] is /kæt/, my analysis doesn't need to deal with inputs like /ŋkæt/." That's wrong. The analysis still needs to explain why /ŋkæt/ cannot map faithfully to [ŋkæt] in English, since /ŋkæt/ is a possible input even if it is isn't the underlying representation of any actual word. For further explanation, see McCarthy (2002: 78–80).

Because lexicon optimization is a source of so much misunderstanding, readers of this book are strongly urged not to use it as an analytic tool. Since by its nature it cannot have empirical consequences for any analysis, this is no loss.

17 According to Wikipedia, BLAG is the name of a Linux distribution, an acronym for the Brixton Linux Action Group. Presumably the creators of this acronym accepted [blæg] as a legal phonological word of English.

18 I am ignoring a potential complication: variation or optionality, where more than one candidate from a given input is optimal. See §6.2 for discussion.

19 The candidate [xa.tik$^?$] in (96) is harmonically bounded by [xat.k$^?$a?]. Normally, we wouldn't want to waste our time with harmonically bounded candidates, but I've left it in because it appeared in the original discussion of Yawelmani in chapter 1.

3

How to Write Up an Analysis

3.1 Introduction

After the hard work of analysis has been mostly completed, the time comes to write it up into a paper. This chapter gives advice about how to do that. Some of this advice is specific to OT (§3.3), but a lot of it is just as relevant to writing about other topics. Throughout, there are suggestions about how to make your writing as clear as possible.

Clear writing is important for three reasons. First, we want and need our work to be understood. An instructor reading a term paper misunderstands a student's proposal and wrongly thinks that it won't work. An author complains that a journal has unfairly rejected his or her manuscript because the editors misunderstood it. These problems can be avoided with greater attention to writing clearly. Second, readers are busy. With many papers to read and little time in which to do it, readers want to know quickly whether a paper is relevant to their interests and worth reading. Busy readers become impatient with papers that lack a clear, transparent structure. Third, it's impossible to write clearly without thinking clearly. The desire to write clearly forces habits of thought that lead to a much better grasp of a theory or an analysis. Often, discoveries made during the writing process will lead to significant changes and improvements in the analysis.

The advice in this chapter is just that – advice – and not the law. Because time runs out or exhaustion sets in, we all make compromises in our writing. Readers of this book will undoubtedly find that I have sometimes failed to heed my own advice. All that any of us can do is to try to make our writing better and clearer than it would have been if we didn't try at all.

3.2 How to Organize a Paper

The overall structure of a piece of writing depends on what kind of writing it is: problem set, paper, or dissertation, for example. The recommendations here apply to works of intermediate length, from the 12–20 pages of a term paper or conference paper, through the 40–50 pages of a journal article or a chapter in a book or dissertation. It's also a good idea to try to follow most of this advice when writing up solutions to problem sets in essay form. Writing clear solutions to problem sets is good practice for writing clear papers, chapters, and articles.

Linguistics papers always have numbered sections, just like the chapters of this book. Numbered sections aren't the stuff of elegant prose, but they are a simple way of giving any paper coherent, logical structure, and they greatly reduce the difficulty of writing transitions from one part of the paper to another. If the numbered sections are highlighted in boldface and their titles are informative, then a reader can quickly skim the paper to get an outline of the author's argument. If the reader is pressed for time, he or she can locate and read just the relevant parts.

Section 1 is usually called the introduction, for obvious reasons. It would be more accurate to to call it the *hook*, because it's usually the author's only opportunity to pull the reader into the paper. The introduction needs to grab the reader's attention. But the best way to do this is somewhat counterintuitive.

Works of fiction get the reader's attention by raising questions and creating mysteries. Nonfiction in any field, including linguistics, gets the reader's attention by raising questions and answering them right away. The answers in the introduction don't have to be detailed and highly technical, nor do they need to be fully justified – that is what the rest of the paper is for – but they need to be presented in a way that any professional in the field can immediately understand and appreciate.

There are three common objections to writing an introduction that answers the questions immediately. One objection is that it seems to defy logic: "How can I state a paper's main conclusion without first presenting all of the supporting evidence and argumentation?" A second objection is that it bypasses all previous work on the subject: "How can I propose a solution to a problem without first explaining and critiquing everybody else's solutions?" A third objection is that it gives away the ending: "Why would anyone go on to read my paper if they already know what I'm going to say?"

The source of all of these objections is an inappropriate model of how readers engage with the introduction to a technical article. Readers of an introduction aren't expecting to find the entire argument or a review of the literature. They will be satisfied with seeing the argument's endpoints: a statement of the problem and a summary of the proposal or result. If they are interested in the topic, then that will be enough to capture their attention and persuade them to read the rest of the paper. Readers of the introduction to a technical article certainly don't want to be presented with a mystery. It won't intrigue them and make them read on. Language is full of mysteries, and sophisticated readers want to see solutions to them. If the introduction presents a problem but doesn't give away the solution, it's usually too much trouble for a reader to start searching through the subsequent sections in the hope that the author really does have an interesting solution to propose.

In many linguistics papers, section 2 is a review and critique of previous work on the problem. In my opinion, this is almost always a mistake. Previous scholarship needs to be acknowledged, but it must not distract from the paper's proposal. The new proposal can be compared with previous proposals after the new proposal has been presented. Obviously, the comparison would be meaningless if it came before the new proposal has been explained.

This advice often elicits an objection: "How can anyone be convinced of a new proposal unless they have first seen that all previous proposals fail?" This objection also comes from applying an inappropriate model of what readers are doing. Readers do not have a limited capacity for ideas, so they do not need to eliminate old ideas to create space for new ones. Rather, intelligent readers are accustomed to temporarily entertaining hypotheses that are inconsistent with their prior beliefs. The objection also comes from an inappropriate model of scholarship. Newton said "If I have seen further it is by standing upon the shoulders of giants." Though his work was truly revolutionary, he did not insist on standing on the giants' corpses. Scholarship in linguistics is far more cumulative and incremental than it sometimes seems. Even wrong ideas often contribute to our understanding. Before attacking some idea, then, it's wise to reflect on how your own work is indebted to it.

There is one exception to this advice. Very rarely, a problem may have a universally accepted and virtually unquestioned solution. For any new proposal about this topic to get traction with readers, they need to be disabused of the idea that the universally accepted solution is really as good as they think. In that case alone, the second and even first sections of the paper may need to contain some remarks about the shortcomings of the previous proposal. Even then, however, the work of comparing the old proposal with the new one must come after the sections of the paper that present the new proposal in detail.

Instead of a review of the literature, section 2 is the place to introduce the theoretical content. This includes both essential background assumptions as well as new ideas. If the main goal of the paper is to present an analysis and no new theory is introduced, then this section may be relatively brief: "In this paper, I will assume the version of Optimality Theory developed in Prince and Smolensky (1993/2004). In particular, I will make use of the notion . . ." If the point of the paper is to introduce a new constraint or modify an old one, then section 2 is the place to explain the proposed innovation. This explanation should include a definition of the new constraint, something about its intellectual roots inside and outside OT, and a preliminary sketch of how the argument for this constraint will develop in the course of presenting the analysis. If this is done correctly, it will typically repeat material that was already covered in an even more preliminary way in section 1. That's fine; there is nothing wrong with telling readers the paper's main point several times in several different ways. They will be grateful, not bored or insulted.

By the way, putting the proposal in section 2 does not mean dumping a long list of constraints into the reader's lap. It's unreasonable to expect readers to retain more than, say, three novel constraints for the duration of the paper. If an idea requires seven new constraints, then the idea itself, plus a couple of constraints for illustration, should appear in section 2. If the analysis requires seven new constraints that cannot be subsumed under one or two central ideas, then maybe the whole paper needs some rethinking. Perhaps it's trying to do too much.

The recommendation to explain the proposal in section 2 sometimes elicits another objection: "How can I convince readers of my proposal before they have seen all of the evidence and argumentation that support it?" The answer is that we do not expect section 2 to convince readers. Rather, the goal of section 2 is to tell them what it is that we hope to convince them of as the argument develops. If sections 1 and 2 are written well, readers will know where the argument starts (the problem) and where it ends (the proposal), and they will have some idea of how the intervening steps will go.

By writing sections 1 and 2 in this way, we give readers a framework or mental map into which they can put pieces of the argument as it's built up. They aren't forced to remember several seemingly unrelated points that will be tied together in a concluding section – that sort of writing is typical of mystery novels, but it isn't appropriate in technical works. Nor are readers forced to contrive some sort of mental framework of their own as they try to guess where the author is going with the argument.

The middle sections of the paper are where the argument and analysis are built up. Since this task presents special challenges in OT, it will be addressed separately (§3.3).

There is also a more general problem in writing the middle sections of a paper or the middle chapters of a book or dissertation.[1] Unless the content is relatively simple and straightforward, the order of presentation is always an issue. What aspect of the theory should be explained first, and what should follow it? I struggled with this problem when I wrote this book. People who read the outline or manuscript often gave me advice about how a different organizational scheme would be better. All of this advice was excellent and it was supported by good arguments. But there are also good arguments for the scheme that I finally settled on.

This conundrum is intrinsic to any presentation of complicated technical material. Ideally, we would like to present the argument or proposal in a strictly linear way, building up the elements systematically so that it would never be necessary to give the reader promises like "This will be explained in section 7" or "We will see the reasons for this in chapter 9." Unfortunately, complex material rarely lends itself to a purely linear presentation. Usually, the ideas are so interdependent that a perfect, strictly linear organization scheme is simply impossible. Everybody who had a different view of how to organize this book is correct, and so am I. We all simply had different views of how to optimize its structure, since the perfectly linear structure is elusive.

Knowing that there is no perfect organizational scheme is reassuring and liberating. Give serious thought to the problem of how to organize the middle sections, and review your decisions from time to time as the work progresses. But otherwise don't worry about it, and especially don't worry about the remaining imperfections in the organizational scheme that you decide on. They are inevitable.

The last section of a paper, the conclusion, should contain much of the same material as the introduction. It should restate the problem and the solution, and it should briefly review the highlights of the analysis or argumentation that link the problem with the solution. It's customary in the field of linguistics to use the conclusion to discuss any remaining problems and prospects for further development of the proposal in future research. This is fine, but it must not get out of hand. A conclusion that raises too many questions can make readers think that the paper isn't really finished and more work needs to be done.

EXERCISES

1   Look at the structure of three papers on ROA. Do they conform, more or less, with the guidelines in this section? If not, explain how they differ. Could they be improved?

2   Imagine that you will be writing a paper presenting the argument for a separate MAX-C constraint based on the Yawelmani evidence (see §2.10.3). Write the first two sections of the paper. (A couple of pages should be enough.)

3   The following paragraph is my best effort at doing a *bad* job of writing the introductory paragraph to a paper on *do*-support based on the analysis in §2.9.[2] Explain what is wrong with this introduction and write a better one. Then compare my effort and yours with the introduction to section 3 of Grimshaw's original article (1997: 381). (If that issue of *Linguistic Inquiry* isn't at hand, see pages 8–9 of paper #68 on ROA).

> The problem of English *do* has confounded syntacticians since Chomsky (1957). Where is *do* allowed? Where is it forbidden? These questions have never been answered satisfactorily. In this paper, after all previous analyses starting with Chomsky's have been reviewed and shown to be grossly mistaken, a definitive solution to the mystery of *do* will be proposed. In future work, this solution will shed surprising light on a variety of other problems in the syntax of English and other languages.

4   Write good and intentionally bad first paragraphs for a paper of your own. Do the same for another paper you've recently read.

3.3   How to Present an OT Analysis

Suppose that the analytic work of chapter 2 has been carried as far as possible, and the overall structure of the paper has been established based on the recommendations in §3.2. It's now time to write up the analysis itself in a form that will be maximally comprehensible and persuasive to readers.

The write-up of an OT analysis presents some challenges that don't usually come up in other theories. An OT analysis is rather tightly integrated or cohesive, since any constraint can in principle interact with any other constraint. But, unless the entire analysis consists of just two or three constraints, readers won't be able to grasp it if it's presented all at once. We need to find a way of dividing up the analysis so that it can be presented incrementally. In an OT analysis, a good way of doing this is to first locate the cases where some of the constraints clearly do not interact.

To do this, look at the summary tableaux that were constructed in the course of working out your analysis. In almost every tableau, there are some constraints that favor no winners or losers. Constraints that favor neither winners nor losers can be omitted from a tableau with no effect on the result or the validity of any ranking arguments (§2.7). This means that the tableau can legitimately be discussed before those constraints have been introduced. In other words, by setting aside constraints that favor neither winners nor losers in some tableaux, we have a way of presenting the analysis incrementally.

Tableaux (1)–(4) contain the analysis of Yawelmani, including some refinements that have been introduced since §2.3. As we look them over, we can see that all of the tableaux except (2) include one or more constraints that favor no winners or losers. These constraints are: *V# and Max-V in (1); Ident(long) in (3); and *V#, Ident(long), and Max-V in (4). In each case, there is a good reason why the particular constraints aren't relevant. For instance, because there is no active markedness constraint in Yawelmani that favors long vowels, Ident(long) is relevant only when it opposes vowel shortening. It can be safely ignored when the input contains only short vowels, as in (3) and (4).

(1) /laːnhin/ → [lan.hin]

/laːnhin/	Max-C	*Comp-Syll	*C^unsyll	Dep	*V#	Id(long)	Max-V
a. → lan.hin						*	
b. laːn.hin		*W				L	
c. laː.n.hin			*W			L	
d. laː.ni.hin				*W		L	
e. laː.hin	*W					L	

(2)   /taxaːkʼa/ → [ta.xakʼ]

/taxaːkʼa/	Max-C	*Comp-Syll	*C^unsyll	Dep	*V#	Id(long)	Max-V
a. → ta.xakʼ						*	*
b. ta.xaː.kʼa					*W	L	L
c. ta.xaːkʼ		*W				L	*
d. ta.xaː.kʼ			*W			L	*
e. ta.xaː.kʼaʔ				*W		L	L
f. tax	*W					L	***W

(3)   /xatkʼa/ → [xat.kʼa]

/xatkʼa/	Max-C	*Comp-Syll	*C^unsyll	Dep	*V#	Id(long)	Max-V
a. → xat.kʼa					*		
b. xatkʼ		*W			L		*W
c. xat.kʼ			*W		L		*W
d. xat	*W				L		*W
e. xa.tikʼ				*W	L		*W
f. xat.kʼaʔ				*W	L		

(4)   /ʔilkhin/ → [ʔi.lik.hin]

/ʔilkhin/	Max-C	*Comp-Syll	*C^unsyll	Dep	*V#	Id(long)	Max-V
a. → ʔi.lik.hin							
b. ʔilk.hin		*W		L			
c. ʔil.k.hin			*W	L			
d. ʔil.hin	*W			L			

To be perfectly clear, (1)–(4) are the product of all the work of doing the analysis, but they aren't the place to start explaining the analysis to someone else. It isn't uncommon in the OT literature to find one or more big tableaux plopped down at the beginning of a paper, with subsequent text explaining or justifying them in a somewhat haphazard way. Similarly, far too many papers begin by asserting some constraint ranking – often a total ordering for which there is no justification (see §2.2). This mode of exposition does not help readers to understand the analysis, nor is it likely to convince them that the analysis is correct. In fact, analyses that are presented in this way are often riddled with errors. If an author presents his or her analysis by pure assertion rather than careful argumentation, then it's likely that very little argumentation went into creating the analysis in the first place. When that occurs, mistakes are almost unavoidable.

The expository goal is to present the analysis in a way that is both incremental and responsible to its interactive character. That is why we first try to identify tableaux with constraints that favor neither winners nor losers. Since tableau (4) has the most such constraints, it's probably the best place to begin when presenting the analysis. Therefore, the first data and descriptive generalization introduced to readers should be the evidence for [i] epenthesis in triconsonantal clusters.

Begin by laying out the data (as in example (2) in chapter 1) and the descriptive generalization that the data support. After that, the exposition needs to get across two points. First, the various possible ways of faithfully parsing a triconsonantal cluster are ruled out by *COMPLEX-SYLLABLE and *C^{unsyll}. Even at this early stage, it's helpful to tell readers that neither of these constraints is ever violated in Yawelmani, so they must be undominated. Second, since the language has epenthesis rather than consonant deletion, *COMPLEX-SYLLABLE and *C^{unsyll} compel violation of DEP rather than MAX-C.

The presentation of the analysis must include the formal ranking arguments in tableaux (5)–(7) below. These ranking arguments each compare a winner from the data set under discussion with a single loser. The ranking arguments include all of the constraints that prior analysis (in §2.3) has shown to be relevant to the /ʔilkhin/ → [ʔi.lik.hin] mapping – in other words, these are the constraints that favor the winner or the loser in any of [ʔi.lik.hin]'s competitions with other candidates. (They are the constraints with non-blank columns in (4).) Each tableau should also be accompanied by some explanatory text, to spare readers the burden of trying to figure out the point of analysis that the tableau illustrates.

Here is an example of how this part of the paper could be written up:

> Tableau (5) compares the unfaithful winning candidate [ʔi.lik.hin] with the faithful losing candidate *[ʔilk.hin]. Since [ʔi.lik.hin] has epenthesis, it violates DEP. The faithful candidate obeys DEP, of course, but at the expense of parsing the sequence [ʔilk] into a single CVCC syllable. This is a violation of the markedness constraint *COMPLEX-SYLLABLE. For winning [ʔi.lik.hin] to be more harmonic, *COMPLEX-SYLLABLE must dominate DEP.

(5) *COMPLEX-SYLLABLE >> DEP

/ʔilkhin/	MAX-C	*COMP-SYLL	*C^{unsyll}	DEP
a. → ʔi.lik.hin				
b. ʔilk.hin		*W		L

> The losing candidate in (6) is also faithful, but with a different syllabic analysis. The [k] of *[ʔil.k.hin] is parsed as an appendix – it's a consonant that is an immediate constituent of a phonological word node. Since appendices violate *C^{unsyll}, that constraint must also dominate DEP.

(6) *C^{unsyll} >> DEP

/ʔilkhin/	MAX-C	*COMP-SYLL	*C^{unsyll}	DEP
a. → ʔi.lik.hin				
b. ʔil.k.hin			*W	L

Together, tableaux (5) and (6) show why there is no way of faithfully parsing an input triconsonantal cluster into syllables. The faithful parses require a syllable that is too big or a consonant that remains unsyllabified. Neither of these outcomes is ever observed in Yawelmani, so *COMPLEX-SYLLABLE and *C^{unsyll} must be undominated. Since vowel epenthesis occurs instead of violating one of these constraints, both must dominate DEP.

Tableau (7) presents a different sort of losing candidate. The form *[ʔil.hin] satisfies both of the high-ranking markedness constraints by deletion rather than epenthesis. Consonant deletion is ruled out by MAX-C, also ranked above DEP.

(7)   MAX-C >> DEP

/ʔilkhin/	MAX-C	*COMP-SYLL	*C^{unsyll}	DEP
a. → ʔi.lik.hin				
b. ʔil.hin	*W			L

We are now ready to move on to another data set. Ideally, the exposition will continue by presenting constraints one at a time, if possible. Tableau (1) is perfect, since it requires us to introduce just one additional constraint to the exposition, IDENT(long). The next step, then, is to introduce the data and descriptive generalization for vowel shortening in closed syllables. This is a very logical way to develop the argument after the discussion of [i] epenthesis, since the two phenomena are connected: both occur when the faithful candidates violate one of the undominated syllable markedness constraints *COMPLEX-SYLLABLE and *C^{unsyll}. The most important comparison – and the one that should be discussed first – is the relationship between IDENT(long) and the faithfulness constraint that dominates it, DEP. That ranking argument, which is given in (8), should be the main focus of the exposition at this point in the paper. Although MAX-C, *COMPLEX-SYLLABLE, and *C^{unsyll} are inactive in (8), it's best to keep these constraints in the tableau because all of them are active in other candidate comparisons involving the same winner, [lan.hin]. This makes it easier for readers to compare (8) with other tableaux where that winner will appear.

(8)   DEP >> IDENT(long)

/laːnhin/	MAX-C	*COMP-SYLL	*C^{unsyll}	DEP	ID(long)
a. → lan.hin					*
b. laː.ni.hin				*W	L

The ranking argument in (8) is perfectly valid and consistent with the entire analysis, even though the exposition will later show that *V# intervenes in the ranking between DEP and IDENT(long). We can be confident of this because, before showing readers this tableau with *V# omitted, we made sure that *V# isn't relevant to the /laːnhin/ → [lan.hin] mapping.

After presenting (8) and the evidence for it, we would do well to account for the remaining candidates in (1). Although ranking arguments should usually be presented with one loser at a time, it's probably OK at this point to give readers the multi-loser tableau (9). Since (9) offers no new information about ranking and is completely expected given what the reader has already seen, we aren't in danger of creating confusion by dealing with several losers at once.

(9)   /laːnhin/ → [lan.hin] summary

/laːnhin/	MAX-C	*COMP-SYLL	*C^{unsyll}	DEP	ID(long)
a. → lan.hin					*
b. laːn.hin		*W			L
c. laː.n.hin			*W		L
d. laː.ni.hin				*W	L
e. laː.hin	*W				L

Only two constraints remain to be discussed, *V# and MAX-V. There is no way of introducing these constraints one at a time, since both favor winners or losers in the two remaining tableaux. The question, then, is which mapping to discuss first: /taxaːkʼa/ → [ta.xakʼ] in (2) or /xatkʼa/ → [xat.kʼa] in (3). We can answer this question by applying some ranking logic (see §2.12). In (10), I've taken tableau (2) and scrambled the constraint ordering to force us to look at which rankings this tableau could be used to prove. (I've also omitted the violation marks, since they aren't relevant to questions of ranking logic.) In (11), I've done the same thing with tableau (3). I've drawn boxes around the loser rows in (10) and (11) so I can refer to them as what they are, sets of ERCs (Prince 2002b).

(10)   Ranking information in (2)

/taxaːkʼa/	*V#	Max-C	*Comp-Syll	*Cᵘⁿˢʸˡˡ	Dep	Max-V	Id(long)
a. → ta.xakʼ							
b. ta.xaː.kʼa	W					L	L
c. taːxaːkʼ			W				L
d. ta.xaː.kʼ				W			L
e. ta.xaː.kʼaʔ					W	L	L
f. tax		W				W	L

(11)   Ranking information in (3)

/xatkʼa/	*V#	Max-C	*Comp-Syll	*Cᵘⁿˢʸˡˡ	Dep	Max-V	Id(long)
a. → xat.kʼa							
b. xatkʼ	L		W			W	
c. xat.kʼ	L			W		W	
d. xat	L	W				W	
e. xa.tikʼ	L				W	W	
f. xat.kʼaʔ	L				W		

What novel information about ranking could each of these ERC sets contribute? Recall the discussion of entailment in §2.12. An ERC with two Ws and one L like (W, W, L) can only tell us that one of the two winner-favoring constraints dominates the loser-favoring constraint. It is entailed by the ERCs (W, e, L) and (e, W, L), each of which has only one W. All of the rows in (11) except for the last one contain two Ws and one L. Therefore, the ranking information that (11) offers us consists of one certainty (Dep dominates *V#) and a disjunction of con-junctions: *V# is dominated by Max-V or by all of Max-C, *Complex-Syllable, and *Cᵘⁿˢʸˡˡ. To the reader, who has not previously seen *V# in the analysis, neither branch of this disjunction has any greater claim to being true. So, if we were to present the /xatkʼa/ → [xat.kʼa] mapping first, readers would be in the uncomfortable position of having to remember this disjunction of conjunctions until it was resolved by evidence presented later. That isn't a sound expositional strategy, since it unnecessarily taxes the reader's memory.

On the other hand, the ERC set in (10) offers much less ambiguous information about ranking. Rows (b) and (e) each contain only one W, and they present three pieces of solid ranking data that readers won't have seen yet: *V# dominates Max-V; *V# dominates Ident(long); and Dep dominates Max-V. It's true that row (f) in (10) has two Ws and an L, so taken in isolation it tells us only that Max-C *or* Max-V dominates Ident(long), but that disjunction has already been resolved in favor of high-ranking Max-C by a ranking argument presented earlier in the exposition (see (9)).

The correct expositional strategy, then, is to present readers with the ranking arguments supported by the more informative /taxaːkʔa/ → [ta.xakʔ] ERC set (10). After readers have seen this, they will be in a much better position to grasp the ranking consequences of the /xatkʔa/ → [xat.kʔa] mapping. Therefore, the next step in presenting the analysis is to show the evidence and descriptive generalization for the /taxaːkʔa/ → [ta.xakʔ] mapping, leading readers to the ranking arguments in (12) and (13). After explaining these ranking arguments, it would then be appropriate to show readers the multi-loser tableau in (2), to demonstrate that a wider range of candidates has been considered and is accounted for in the analysis.

(12)   *V# >> Ident(long), Max-V

/taxaːkʔa/	Max-C	*Comp-Syll	*C^{unsyll}	Dep	*V#	Id(long)	Max-V
a. → ta.xakʔ						*	*
b. ta.xaː.kʔa					*W	L	L

(13)   Dep >> Max-V

/taxaːkʔa/	Max-C	*Comp-Syll	*C^{unsyll}	Dep	*V#	Id(long)	Max-V
a. → ta.xakʔ						*	*
b. ta.xaː.kʔaʔ				*W		L	L

At this point in the paper, readers are ready to see the evidence and descriptive generalization for the /xatk^{7}a/ → [xat.k^{7}a] mapping. As I just showed, this mapping taken in isolation gives us a disjunction: *V# is dominated by Max-V or by all of Max-C, *Complex-Syllable, *C^{unsyll}, and Dep. But, since readers will have already seen the ranking argument in (12), they will know that *V# cannot be dominated by Max-V, so it must be dominated by the other four constraints. It would be appropriate to present readers with the multi-loser tableau in (3), explaining that it compresses four ranking arguments into a single display.

Let us review these recommendations about how to present an analysis. Look over the summary tableaux that were produced as part of the process of analysis. Locate the tableau with the most constraints that favor neither the winner nor the loser, since all of the ranking information in this tableau can be presented before those constraints have been introduced. The discussion of this tableau should include presentation of the data and descriptive generalization that it accounts for, the ranking arguments in the form of tableaux that include only one loser but all of the constraints that have been introduced so far, and a summary tableau with all constraints discussed and all of the potentially relevant losers. Proceed in the same fashion, adding one constraint at a time whenever possible. When there is doubt about what to present next, look at the information content of the tableaux, giving priority to tableaux that are more informative about ranking.

Obviously, these suggestions are no substitute for doing some hard thinking about the best order in which to present an analysis. But they have the advantage of enforcing a standard that any exposition should strive for. The presentation of the analysis is incremental: readers are given new information in pieces that aren't too large to absorb at once. At every point, the readers' knowledge of the total analysis is accurate but incomplete: they always see all of the constraints that are known to have the potential to affect a particular mapping. They will never be put in the awkward position of having to radically revise their mental picture of the analysis because some constraint introduced later on undermines a previous ranking argument or alters the explanation for why a particular candidate loses. They will never be led to doubt the good faith of an author who seems to be withholding crucial information.

One of the expositional recommendations made here might be somewhat controversial. (I am grateful to Alan Prince for convincing me of the wisdom of this move.) Much previous work in OT develops the analysis through a series of small tableaux that contain a winner, a single loser, and only two constraints. These 2 × 2 tableaux, as they are known, have been the de facto standard for the presentation of ranking arguments. The advantage of the 2 × 2 tableau is that it focuses sharply on a single interaction. This is also its main disadvantage: it relies on the fiction that the rest of the constraint hierarchy is always irrelevant to establishing the validity of the ranking argument. The recommendation here is that ranking arguments should be made with tableaux that still contain a single loser, but they should include *all* of the constraints that favor the winner or the loser. If this seems too much, then at least all of the winner-favoring constraints should be included, since they are the ones with the potential to undermine the validity of the ranking argument. Then other loser-favoring constraints could be dealt with in a separate tableau. The important point is that readers are always presented with all of the information they need to assess the validity of a ranking argument. In general, a 2 × 2 tableau can't do that.

Before Prince (2002a) devised comparative tableau format, another reason for the 2 × 2 tableau was the difficulty of picking ranking arguments out of larger violation tableaux. But the comparative tableau makes ranking arguments much easier to spot, so the restriction to two constraints per tableau is no longer necessary to ensure intelligibility.

EXERCISE

5 Following the recommendations here, write up one or more of the following analyses:

a. English *do*-support (§2.9).
b. Maori consonant deletion (exercise 8 in chapter 2).
c. Palauan vowel reduction (exercise 9 in chapter 2).
d. Diola Fogny (exercise 21 in chapter 2).
e. Axininca Campa (exercise 34 in chapter 2).

3.4 The Responsibilities of Good Scholarship

Good scholarship requires prompt citation of the original source for any observation, constraint, theory, or idea that isn't one's own. This simple principle has a few ramifications in OT that need sorting out. The advice here is intended primarily for papers destined for publication, where the citational standards are high, but it's good to work toward these standards in term papers as well.

First, although correct citation is essential, excessive citation can seem naïve. Certain ideas reach a point where they are known and accepted so universally that they are no longer accorded a citation. An example is the Chomsky and Halle (1968) (*SPE*) theory of distinctive features. Professionals in the field do not cite *SPE* every time they use one of those features, although they will cite *SPE* if the features themselves are the topic of discussion.

OT has not yet reached the same state of near-universal familiarity and acceptance as the *SPE* feature theory, and it may never do so. Therefore, at least one reference to Prince and Smolensky's seminal work belongs in every paper that uses OT, and fuller reference is required when specific aspects of OT are at issue. Citing Prince and Smolensky is a little complicated because several versions of this work are in existence. (See the title page of ROA-537 for its prepublication history.) The general rule for citation is always to cite the published version when several versions exist, but this can lead to odd anachronisms like "Building on a proposal in Prince and Smolensky (2004), Jones (1997) argues that . . .". It's better to follow the practice in this book: cite Prince and Smolensky (1993/2004), and include something like the following information in the bibliography:

Prince, Alan and Smolensky, Paul (1993/2004) *Optimality Theory: Constraint Interaction in Generative Grammar*. Malden, MA & Oxford, UK: Blackwell. [Revision of 1993 technical report, Rutgers University Center for Cognitive Science. Available on Rutgers Optimality Archive, ROA-537.]

Citations of page numbers should come from the published version. Alternatively, since the numbers assigned to sections, examples, and footnotes have remained constant across all versions of this work, they can be cited for most purposes.

Another citation question that arises in OT is how to cite prior research on a specific constraint. It's important to do this as acknowledgment of an intellectual debt. It's also important because previous work arguing for constraint X or something like it in other languages is independent support for X. Since constraints are claims about universal CON, they need all the independent support they can get. Ideally, if time and space permit, the citation will even offer readers a précis of the evidence for X, such as "Jones (1997) argues for X based on phrase-final [n] epenthesis in Tunica." This is particularly important – and easier to do – if *X* isn't a widely known constraint because the prior literature on it isn't very extensive.

A related question is how far back to go in citing precedents for a constraint. Ideally, all the way. Although faithfulness constraints are unique to OT, many markedness constraints can be traced back to the pre-OT literature of the 1970s and 1980s. This is true of ONSET, for example. In syntax, particularly, markedness constraints often correspond to ideas about structure from other contemporary theories, as in these passages where Grimshaw (1997: 377) explains the extra-OT origins of OPERATOR-IN-SPECIFIER and OBLIGATORY-HEADS:

> OP-SPEC is based on the insight of Rizzi (1996) and Haegeman (1992) that there is a special relationship between the specifier position and a syntactic operator . . .

> This extra projection has no head and thus violates OB-HD, which requires a projection to have a head (either lexically realized or occupied by a trace), much as in Haider 1989.

Obviously, authors aren't expected to trace every constraint mentioned in an analysis all the way back to Pāṇini, but if the constraint is a focus of discussion and especially if publication is planned, then some effort to track the origins and development of that constraint will almost certainly pay off.

Suppose you are writing a paper on topic *T*. What are your obligations to prior work on *T*? To read it, of course, but how should it be cited? In §3.2, I explained why you shouldn't discuss the previous work before presenting your own analysis. But suppose the sections of the paper containing your analysis of *T* are written. What comes next?

All previous work on *T* needs to be *cited*, but it doesn't all need to be *discussed*. When we choose which prior work to discuss, if any, it should be with the goal of further explicating the properties of our own analysis by contrasting it with the alternatives. For example, suppose we were comparing the OT analysis of Yawelmani in §2.3 with Kisseberth's (1970) theory of conspiracies (see §1.1). It would be appropriate to use this comparison to explain how OT obtains both blocking and triggering effects, whereas the earlier theory works only for blocking effects. We would then be using the earlier theory as a foil, rather than seeking to demolish it.

The demolition job is a bad expositional strategy for many reasons. First, it's often unfair. To make the critique seem more impressive, criticisms based on inessential details or irrelevancies are often included. Linguists aren't lawyers with the job of offering up as many arguments as possible, no matter how irrelevant or inconsistent, in the hope that one of them will impress the judge. Second, demolition jobs often backfire. Too often, an author will present a problem for another theory that also turns out to be a problem for his or her own theory. Third, this method of exposition is mostly ineffective. Readers will never be persuaded that a new theory or analysis is right just because the alternatives are wrong. The final reason to stay away from demolition jobs is that they are simply not a very lofty ambition.

When discussion of previous work is appropriate, there are certain forms that should be followed. Begin by depersonalizing the object of criticism. Instead of "Jones's (1997) theory of epenthesis . . . Jones says this . . . Jones is wrong about that . . . ," say "Jones's (1997) theory of epenthesis (hereafter ToE) . . . ToE says this . . . ToE makes a wrong prediction about that . . ." Briefly summarize the main premises of the approach and show how it works for some of the data that it was originally designed to deal with. At that point, comparison with the new theory can begin. Stick to important differences, stay away from insignificant or easily fixable details, and never fault the old theory for problems that the new theory hasn't solved. Never ever impugn the motives, intelligence, scholarship, or parentage of the person whose work you are criticizing. Never presume to know his or her mental state: "X must think . . . X must surely know . . ." Do not fault past work for ignorance of current theory.

Since we have been talking about how to *produce* criticism, this is a good opportunity to talk about how to *receive* it. Criticism comes in many forms. For a student, it starts with the instructor's feedback on a term paper. Next comes feedback from several committee members evaluating a qualifying paper or thesis. This is good preparation for receiving anonymous reviews of conference abstracts or journal submissions. Eventually, one may see one's work being criticized in print.

All of us feel personally invested in our ideas and other professional work, so there is always an emotional component to receiving criticism. Since the investment increases with advancement in the profession, the emotional component typically does not diminish, though it may shift from a battered ego to anger. Dealing with criticism requires rational thought. Since rational thought and strong emotions do not happily coexist, it's best to put the criticism aside for a day or a week until the emotions have subsided. It also helps to remember that ideas, rather than character or intellect, are the object of the criticism (even if the critics might sometimes forget that). Resist the urge to take immediate, irreversible actions, like dropping out of school or sending a furious email.

It helps to remember that good criticism is a valuable learning experience. It makes research and writing much better. When I received the anonymous reviews of the manuscript of this book, both reviewers said that some of the advice in this chapter was too idiosyncratic – that I was sometimes trying to legislate matters of taste. My initial reaction was mildly hostile: "Of course the advice is idiosyncratic and personal. This is a very personal book. If they don't like it, they can write their own book!" (I managed to confine all of this to internal monologue, so I didn't openly embarrass myself.) After I cooled off, I realized that there was some justice to their complaint. I eliminated or muted some of the advice, and I tried to give more reasons for my recommendations so they wouldn't seem like they were just personal preferences. Of course, it helped that both reviewers said the same thing and they were obviously real professionals who took their task very seriously.

Even bad criticism has its uses. The worst criticism is inappropriate because the critic has completely misunderstood the point of the proposal. Because of this misunderstanding, such criticisms are irrelevant and unanswerable; they are criticisms of some theory that the critic has imagined rather than the theory that the author has proposed. But the misunderstanding itself is important information for the author. Evidently, the exposition is so lacking in clarity that an informed reader managed to miss the point entirely. Rule of thumb: if you're misunderstood, you should assume that it's your fault. Following the guidelines in this chapter will help you to avoid such problems.

Sometimes criticism and advice coming from multiple sources will be inconsistent. People often complain that they have been told inconsistent things by the members of a dissertation committee or a journal's reviewers. This would be a reasonable complaint if the ultimate goal of revision were to please everyone, but that's wrong. The goal is to make the work as good as it can be, and of course different people will have different ideas about how that should be done. Think about all of the advice and choose the course that seems best, often in consultation with your dissertation committee chair or the journal's lead editor.

A final point about dealing with journal editors. Editors will often tell an author to "revise and resubmit." Authors sometimes understand this to be a kindly way of rejecting the paper. It's not. It means precisely what it says: the editor expects and even hopes that the author will take the reviewers' comments seriously, make strenuous efforts to improve the paper, and submit it for another round of review at the same journal. Very few papers are accepted on first submission. It's far more common for acceptance to come after one or (at some journals) two resubmissions. The likelihood of acceptance after resubmission is increased if the revised manuscript is accompanied by an explanation of how the reviewers' specific comments have been addressed. If some criticisms have not been answered in the revision, explain why. The likelihood of acceptance after resubmission is also increased if the revision addresses important criticisms in the main text, integrating them into into the overall discussion. Adding a few footnotes that begin "An anonymous reviewer has pointed out" isn't going to do the job of responding to significant objections.

EXERCISES

6   Fodor and Lepore (1998) is a response to a book by James Pustejovsky. (It has nothing to do with OT.) Skim the paper and discuss how they handle the problem of writing criticism. In light of what was said above, would you do this any differently? (If the issue of *Linguistic Inquiry* with this article isn't handy, you can access it online at http://ruccs.rutgers.edu/pub/papers/lexicon27.pdf.)

7   Look at one or two of your own papers. How did you handle the problem of writing criticism? Would you do it differently now? If so, rewrite the passage.

3.5   How to Write Clearly

Everything that I have said so far in this chapter is really about how to write clearly. Writing in linguistics or other technical fields does not have to be elegant and shouldn't be self-consciously artful. But it has to be clear. It has to convey to the reader a fully accurate picture of the author's theory and analysis.

There are plenty of books full of good, general advice about how to write clearly, and it would be pointless for me to repeat what they have to say. Rather, I will focus here on some very specific recommendations for dealing with those enemies of clarity and style that are endemic to the field of linguistics. They are listed in approximate order of importance, starting at the top.

Alternate between the abstract and the concrete. When explanations are unremittingly abstract, readers must struggle to associate the words on the page with something in their knowledge and experience. The following passage from Chomsky (1995: 171) is a good example of this difficulty. ("PLD" stands for primary linguistic data, and "P&P" stands for the principles and parameters model of Chomsky (1981) and other works.)

> In early work, economy considerations entered as part of the evaluation metric, which, as was assumed, selected a particular instantiation of the permitted format for rule systems, given PLD. As inquiry has progressed, the presumed role of an evaluation metric has declined, and within the P&P approach, it's generally assumed to be completely dispensable: the principles are sufficiently restrictive so that PLD suffice in the normal case to set the parameter values that determine a language.
>
> Nevertheless, it seems that economy principles of the kind explored in early work play a significant role in accounting for properties of language. With a proper formulation of such principles, it may be possible to move toward the minimalist design: a theory of language that takes a linguistic expression to be nothing other than a formal object that satisfies the interface conditions in the optimal way. A still further step would be to show that the basic principles of language are formulated in terms of notions drawn from the domain of (virtual) conceptual necessity.

On the other hand, when explanations are unremittingly concrete, as in a lengthy description of some data, readers have no abstract framework to organize the facts as they are presented. They need that conceptual framework before the presentation of the data begins, and they need to be reminded from time to time of how the pieces of data fit into that framework. For example, it would be unwise to devote an early section of a paper to a lengthy description of the facts of Yawelmani prior to presenting any of the analysis. It's asking too much of readers to recall unanalyzed data that were presented 10 or 20 pages earlier.

Help readers to process the data. To continue the previous point, it's hard to grasp the relevance of unfamiliar data, so readers will be grateful for anything that aids them in this task. The grouping of examples and the order in which they are presented should always match the descriptive generalization and the presentation of the analysis. When there is a choice, try to put the simplest or shortest examples first, since they will get the most attention. Every numbered example should have a title like "Evidence for epenthesis." (Use a title like "Evidence for epenthesis in Yawelmani" if multiple languages are discussed in the paper.) Furthermore, the text that precedes the example should tell readers how the data are relevant. Linguistics papers often introduce examples with phrases like "Consider the following data," but that is no help to readers. It's better to introduce data by saying what it proves: "The following data show that Yawelmani epenthesizes [i] between the first two consonants of a three-consonant cluster."

Never mislead readers. An expositional technique that is all too common in the field of linguistics involves giving readers crucially incomplete data, incorrect generalizations, or wrong analyses. The deficiencies are then pointed out and the missing pieces are brought in to save the day. This is a terrible expositional strategy. It's irritating and frustrating to readers, and they can become mistrustful of the author. It does not persuade them of the correctness of the analysis. It often recapitulates the author's process of discovering the analysis, as if such autobiography were of general interest. As Leonard Bloomfield reportedly said about writing up an analysis, "Don't take the guests into the kitchen" (Joos 1967: 13). Of course, this textbook is different because it's more like a cooking class; the whole point of *Doing Optimality Theory* is to show the guests everything that happens in the kitchen from buying the food to washing the dishes.

Use the simplest data that will make the point. As much as possible, try to use data that are free of irrelevant complications. For example, Yawelmani has some complex alternations in vowel quality. For the data in §2.3, I chose words that do not alternate in vowel quality, since vowel quality was not the object of the analysis. The alternative is to tell readers to ignore the vowel quality alternations in the examples put before them. This is more confusing.

By the way, I am not urging complete suppression of complications like the vowel-quality alternations. They have to be dealt with in a more complete analysis of Yawelmani, such as McCarthy (2007a: 109–118). Rather, the point is that the author needs to exercise thoughtful control over when and how additional phenomena are presented to the reader.

Use the first person appropriately. In this book and in much of the linguistics literature, the first person singular is used when the author states an opinion or makes a proposal, and the first person plural is used when the author wishes to engage the reader in the process of analysis. For example, "I think that the first person singular is completely appropriate in linguistics books and journals," but "When we read linguistics books and journals, we should ask ourselves how the writing could have been made clearer." Stay away from editorial *we*, which almost always sound pretentious: "In our writing, we avoid the pronoun *I*." Of course, co-authors can use *we*. Second person is never used in technical writing. Even in this book, I've tried to use it sparingly because it's so jarring.

Use memorable and intelligible constraint names. When constraints have standard names, those names should normally be used, but when introducing novel constraints, try to make their names descriptive of their function. The faithfulness constraints DEP and MAX from McCarthy and Prince (1995, 1999) are good examples of what not to do. Grimshaw's (1997) constraints OPERATOR-IN-SPECIFIER and OBLIGATORY-HEADS are good role models. Relatedly, I recommend giving new constraints two names, a full name like OPERATOR-IN-SPECIFIER and a consistent abbreviated name like OP-SPEC. The full name should be used throughout the text, to reduce the demands on the reader's recall. The abbreviated name can be used in tableaux and other situations where space is tight. Both the full name and the abbreviation should be given when the constraint is first defined.

It's also a good idea to give your constraints pronounceable names. This is helpful if you ever need to present your work in a talk somewhere, and it may make the constraints your propose more popular.

Minimize the use of footnotes. Many linguistics papers contain way too many footnotes, and the footnotes are way too long. I use and recommend the following strategy for reducing footnotes. As I am writing, I allow myself the liberty of writing as many footnotes as I like. But before I consider the work to be complete, I go through it looking only at the footnotes. (Many word processors have a way of jumping from one note directly to the next one.) As I read over each note, I ask myself whether it should or could be promoted to the main text. Major problems and crucial references cannot be relegated to footnotes; they need to be in the main text. Often, just knowing that a problem with the analysis cannot be buried in a footnote is sufficient stimulus to find a way to fix it. Cross-references from the main text to a footnote are another indication that the material in the footnote is important enough to move to the main text.

When the material in the footnote does not deserve to be moved to the main text, I ask myself whether the footnote is needed at all. Sometimes, I find that the only audience for the footnote is me – it's just a note to myself about something to remember. Make a copy of such notes and then delete them from your paper.

Use "notice that" only if you mean it.   The phrases "notice that" or "note that" are very heavily used in the linguistics literature. (In February 2007, I got a Google count of nearly 1,000 instances of these phrases on ROA.) Often, they seem to call attention to something that isn't very notable, so they have become almost meaningless. Try to limit your use of these phrases to important observations.

Segregate long lists of citations.   Since even a single citation will interrupt the flow of a sentence, a long list of citations can be very distracting when it occurs in mid-sentence or even mid-paragraph. Try to shift long lists of citations to sentence-final or paragraph-final position. If the list is extremely long, it might be better off in a footnote, where the citations could also be arranged into natural groupings and explained.

Never begin a sentence with an example number.   Instead of "(7) contains the data", write "Example (7) contains the data." Sentences that begin with example numbers are confusing because they look like examples instead of text.

Translate quotations.   The days when any linguist could be expected to understand quotations in French, German, Latin, or Greek are long over.

Use cf. appropriately.   The abbreviation *cf.* is from Latin *confer*, meaning 'compare!'. In linguistics papers, it's often used where no comparison is intended: "The stress evidence (cf. (7)) shows that . . ." or "Optimality Theory (cf. Prince and Smolensky 1993/2004)." Except when making an actual comparison, omit *cf.* or replace it with *see*.

EXERCISES

8   Enter the following search string into Google: *"consider the following"* *site:roa.rutgers.edu*. Pick five cases where this phrase is used to introduce data and rewrite the sentence so that it's clearer and more helpful to readers.

9   Do a similar Google search on ROA for "notice that" or "note that." Pick five examples and evaluate whether the reader's attention is being drawn to something truly notable. Could the phrase be removed without affecting the sense?

10   Rewrite the quotation from Chomsky at the beginning of §3.5 to make it clearer. If the material Chomsky is talking about is unfamiliar, pick a difficult passage by some other author and rewrite that instead.

11   Look at some of the constraint names in this book. Are there any that you find obscure? How would you rename them to be more clear?

12   Look at all of the footnotes in this book. Can you find any that should be eliminated or moved to the text? Look at five of the footnotes in Prince and Smolensky (1993/2004; available as #537 on ROA) and ask the same question. Explain your reasoning.

3.6   General Advice about Research Topics

Choosing good research topics is very important, since even a well-written, competently argued paper on a bad topic can be a disappointment. The material in this section supplements the OT-specific advice about research topics in §2.1.1. The advice here is mostly independent of OT and applies to bigger projects as well as term papers. A warning: The material in this section reflects my personal opinions, and some of them might not be widely shared.

In choosing a research topic, there is an inevitable tension between the novel and the familiar. The topic should offer opportunities for new discoveries, but at the same time it needs to build on previous work. Successful research often depends on getting the right balance between these two competing factors.

It is best to avoid topics that are already extremely well studied, since they offer fewer opportunities for novel insights of the sort that can get a successful career started. For instance, my doctoral dissertation had two parts, one on metrical phonology and the other on Arabic nonconcatenative morphology. Various people were working on metrical phonology at the time, but nobody was working on nonconcatenative morphology. It was the part about nonconcatenative morphology that ended up getting nearly all the attention, particularly because I was able to connect it with then-current discoveries about autosegmental phonology, thereby balancing the novel with the more familiar.

Often, a good way to balance novelty and familiarity is to look for problems in some recent article or manuscript on an interesting topic. Pay particular attention to the footnotes and the conclusion. Footnotes often disclose holes in the analysis, and conclusions are where authors often concede the limitations of their analysis. Phrases like "this is a topic for future research" or "this is a problem for any theory" are beacons guiding you toward potential research topics. You will be building on previous work, but at the same time you will have something new to say. A warning: Don't be satisfied with just raising objections. Better work couples the negative argument with a positive proposal.

Another successful strategy for achieving this balance is to try applying someone else's analysis to a language where it hasn't been previously applied. In OT especially, this is an important research technique, since differences between languages are crucial for understanding the contents of CON. See chapter 5 for more about this kind of research.

There are also more abstract methods of finding a good research topic. These methods are applicable to theories other than OT and to fields other than linguistics. Some ideas:

Invert the conventional wisdom. The sociologist Howard Becker (1998: 1–2) describes how his adviser, Everett C. Hughes, approached the problem of defining the term "ethnic group." The conventional wisdom defined it in top-down terms: "it is a group distinguishable from others by one, or some combination of the following: physical characteristics, language, religion, customs, institutions, or 'cultural traits'" (Hughes 1984: 153). Hughes instead proposed a bottom-up definition, turning the conventional wisdom on its head: "it is an ethnic group because the people in and the people out of it know that it is one; because both the *ins* and the *outs* talk, feel, and act as if it were a separate group" (Hughes 1984: 153–154). There are plenty of similar examples in linguistics: Liberman and Prince (1977) took metrical trees as primary and metrical grids as derivative from trees, but Prince (1983) argued for the primacy of the grid; GB changed case from a superficial property of noun phrases to something much deeper; in underspecification theory, contrast is a property of the lexicon, but in OT, contrast is a property of surface forms (§2.8).

Discard a basic assumption. Chomsky and Lasnik's (1977) filters model dispensed with the distinction between obligatory and optional transformations, and GB went even further. Prince and Smolensky (1993/2004) did something similar, getting rid of phonological rules. The change needn't be earth-shaking to be worth studying. It can be as simple as, say, asking whether DEP constraints are really necessary (Gouskova 2007, Urbanczyk 2006). The basic assumption might turn out to be necessary after all. But even this result can be significant, particularly if the question has not been examined before.

Confront the unrecognized (or unmentioned) problem.   It is often helpful to think through what everyone takes for granted, to discover the implicit assumptions and make them explicit, or to confront the problem that almost everyone else is in denial about. Prince and Smolensky did all these things when they addressed the "conceptual crisis at the center of phonological thought" (§1.1). How constraints can affect rule application was the Medusa that almost everyone else refused to look at.

Make explicit that which is implicit.   One way of doing this is to give a rigorous formal definition to some idea that occasionally appears in analyses but has never been worked out in detail. For example, Kurisu (2001) did this with morpheme-realization constraints, which previously had a rather nebulous status at the fringes of various analyses.

Accomplish the same or more with less.   Sometimes, it can seem as if the goal of every paper is to propose some new mechanism. See how far you can go after eliminating some device or restricting its scope. For example, you might ask whether alignment constraints are really necessary. What work do they do, and what other ways are there of doing that work?

Synthesize.   Many interesting ideas are the result of blending two or more preexisting notions. For example, Wilson (2000, 2001) proposes something called "targeted constraints," which combine some of the properties of phonological rules and normal OT markedness constraints. Guard against the temptation to simply combine all of the resources of two theories to make a third, even more powerful theory. Synthesis isn't the same as set-union.

Give up.   If something is very hard, it might be impossible, and that might be where the real insight is to be found. For example, Pater (1999) introduced a markedness constraint that is violated by clusters of a nasal + voiceless obstruent like [mp]. The effort to construct a formal explanation for this constraint went nowhere. Pater's insight was that this constraint cannot be explained formally but it can be explained in terms of articulation and perception.

A final piece of advice. It's better to be wrong than to be trivial. Ideas that are interesting but wrong are the main engine of progress in this field. This is another reason to be careful in how you frame criticisms.

Notes

1 My views of the organization problem have been strongly influenced by Becker (1986).
2 I am grateful to Kathryn Flack for her help in making this paragraph even worse.

4

Developing New Constraints

4.1 Introduction

OT is a theory of constraint interaction, not a theory of constraints. OT itself doesn't say much about about constraints except that they're universal and limited to markedness and faithfulness. Doing OT requires a theory of constraints, CON, but OT itself offers only minimal guidance about that theory.

For this reason, the process of doing analysis in OT is sometimes hard to separate from the process of theorizing about CON. In the course of doing an analysis, it isn't unusual to find that previously proposed constraints are inadequate. This means that the analyst must occasionally be a theorizer about CON as well. There are responsibilities that go with the role of theorizer, and the goal of this chapter is to explain how those responsibilities can be most effectively discharged.

A clarification is in order before we move on to the details. In this chapter, I am describing how to develop a serious proposal for modifying CON. This task is different from introducing an ad hoc constraint to avoid distractions from the main point of an analysis or to temporarily fill a gap in the analyst's knowledge of the literature. Even ad hoc constraints should be defined properly, but it doesn't make sense to require them to be justified on formal, functional, or typological grounds. Of course, any ad hoc constraints that persist into the final write-up of an analysis should be identified as such to the reader.

4.2 When Is It Necessary to Modify CON?

Suppose we are given some data and a set of constraints – a mini-CON, if you like. If the analysis produces a loser that ties with the winner or if it requires inconsistent ranking, then our mini-CON is insufficient for this data set. We discussed ties in §2.4. We've also looked at inconsistent ranking arguments before, first as ranking paradoxes (§2.10.3) and then in connection with the inconsistency-detection abilities of RCD (§2.11) and ERC fusion (§2.12).

We saw in §2.10.3 that a constraint set with just unadorned DEP and MAX cannot successfully regulate the deletion and epenthesis phenomena in Yawelmani. The inconsistency of the ranking arguments can be demonstrated very simply by laying them side by side, as I have done in (1) below. (No other constraints favor the winners or losers.) The inconsistency is obvious from inspection, but it could also be shown with RCD or ERC fusion. RCD fails immediately, since it cannot locate any constraints that favor no losers. ERC fusion produces (L, L, L), because Ls in any column are dominant.

(1) Inconsistency in Yawelmani

Inputs	Winners	Losers	ID(long)	DEP	MAX
/taxaː-kʼa/	ta.xakʼ	ta.xaː.kʼaʔ	L	W	L
/ʔilk-hin/	ʔi.lik.hin	ʔil.hin		L	W

In the OT literature, arguments for the insufficiency of a constraint set aren't usually presented like this. Instead, the author typically first establishes one of the rankings and then shows the ranking picking the wrong winner when confronted with new data. For instance, if the prior exposition had used [ʔi.lik.hin] versus *[ʔil.hin] to show that MAX dominates DEP, the ranking paradox would be shown by presenting a tableau like (2). (Other icons, such as anarchist's bombs or a frowning face, have been employed for the same purpose as the Jolly Roger.)

(2)   Presenting a ranking paradox (*not* recommended)

/taxaː-k$^{?}$a/	Max	Dep
a. ☒ ta.xak$^{?}$	*!	
b. ta.xaː.k$^{?}$a?		*

For several reasons, this isn't the best expositional technique for demonstrating a ranking paradox. First, it introduces an unwanted bias toward solving the paradox in a particular way. It misleads the reader (and sometimes the analyst) into thinking that [ta.xak$^{?}$] is the problematic datum, so the solution must involve changing the analysis of [ta.xak$^{?}$] instead of changing the analysis of [ʔi.lik.hin]. In reality, the blame for ranking inconsistency is shared equally by all of the ranking arguments that contribute to the inconsistency. Second, tableau (2) gives the impression that the process of analysis is a maze of blind alleys and false starts, whereas (1) gives the impression of gradually accumulating knowledge of a system. As an expositional device, (1) is more effective, since it does not undermine the reader's confidence in the analysis or the analyst. Third, (2) does not include all of the constraints on which the two candidates differ, and therefore it does not present all of the evidence bearing on the question of whether there is a ranking paradox or not.

No amount of fiddling with the rankings will solve a ranking paradox, since the paradox is an inconsistent set of ranking arguments like (1). Sometimes, running into a ranking paradox is a stimulus to rethink the basic premises of the analysis. Perhaps the assumptions about the underlying representations are wrong, or perhaps a different theory of representations will improve the situation. Although it's beyond this book's scope to offer specific advice about details like these, this general approach to ranking paradoxes should never be dismissed until it has been considered seriously.

The only other way of resolving a ranking paradox is to change the constraint set. How can this be done? We will use (1) as an example. Completely eliminating a constraint – that is, dropping it from Con – is never going to help. If, purely hypothetically, either Dep or Max were eliminated, then (1) would contain a row with no W, and that is no help with the ranking paradox. But adding a constraint will work if the added constraint has the right favoring relations. The new constraint needs to add a W to at least one of the rows, and it must add an L to the other row (see (3)). By favoring the winner in one of the candidate competitions, and not favoring the loser in the other, it breaks the paradox. Of course, the new constraint may interact with other constraints as well, and it may have effects on other winner~loser pairs, so its consequences need to be checked in the context of the whole grammar.

(3)   Three ways of resolving the paradox in (1)

Winners	Losers	Id(long)	Dep	Max	New constraint
ta.xak^ʔ	ta.xaː.kʼaʔ	L	W	L	W
ʔi.lik.hin	ʔil.hin		L	W	

or

Winners	Losers	Id(long)	Dep	Max	New constraint
ta.xak^ʔ	ta.xaː.kʼaʔ	L	W	L	
ʔi.lik.hin	ʔil.hin		L	W	W

or

Winners	Losers	Id(long)	Dep	Max	New constraint
ta.xak^ʔ	ta.xaː.kʼaʔ	L	W	L	W
ʔi.lik.hin	ʔil.hin		L	W	W

Where does this new constraint come from? Sometimes, it isn't new at all, but just previously unknown to the analyst. Consult the list of faithfulness constraints in §4.6 or the list of phonological markedness constraints in §4.8 for some ideas. In those sections and elsewhere in this chapter there are also references to works that discuss particular types of constraints at greater length. If this effort fails, using Google to search ROA may turn up some promising leads. Sometimes, though, a constraint is truly new or modifies an old constraint so much that it might as well be new. In that case, the analyst is responsible for properly defining the constraint, providing some rationale for it, and studying its consequences for language typology. Those tasks take up the balance of this chapter and the next one.

EXERCISES

1   Data representative of a general pattern in Warlpiri are given below (Nash 1979, 1980). Example (a) illustrates that, when the root ends in [i], a vowel harmony process changes /u/ to [i] in the next syllable, and in the syllable after that, and so on. Example (b) shows that /u/ isn't affected by harmony when it's immediately preceded by a labial consonant ([w], [m], [p]). Finally, (c) shows that a preceding labial consonant won't cause a following /i/ to change into [u].

Using the asterisked forms as the losers, construct a tableau like (1) for Warlpiri using IDENT(round) and the two constraints supplied below. Are the required rankings consistent, or is there a ranking paradox? Explain your answer.

	Underlying	Surface	
a.	/maliki-kuḻu-ḻu-lku-cu-lu/	[malikikiḻiḻilkicili] *[malikikuḻuḻulkuculu]	'dog-comitative-ergative-then-me-they'
b.	/ŋali-wuru/	[ŋaliwuru] *[ŋaliwiri]	'we two (inclusive)-emphatic'
	/ŋamiṇi-puṯaci/	[ŋamiṇipuṯaci]	'uncle-you'
c.	/wipi-mi/	[wipimi] *[wupumu]	'radiate out'
	/wapiri-mi/	[wapirimi]	'conceal'

Constraints for Warlpiri:

a.   *iCu (ad hoc – see §4.8 on assimilation)
     Assign one violation mark for every sequence of [i] and [u] in adjacent syllables (e.g., *[malikiku . . .]).
b.   LABIAL-ATTRACTION (LABATT)
     Assign one violation mark for every sequence [Pi], where [P] stands for any of the labial consonants [w], [m], and [p] (e.g., *[wi], *[pi]).

2   Data representative of a general pattern in Makassarese are given below (Aronoff et al. 1987). Example (a) illustrates that final consonants other than [ʔ] and [ŋ] are prohibited, and this requirement is enforced by epenthesis of a vowel followed by [ʔ]. Example (b) shows that [ʔ] isn't epenthesized after underlying vowel-final words.

Using the asterisked forms as the losers, construct a tableau like (1) for Makassarese using the two constraints supplied below and DEP. Are the required rankings consistent, or is there a ranking paradox? Explain your answer.

	Underlying	Surface	
a.	/rantas/	[rantasaʔ]	'dirty'
		*[rantasa]	
		*[rantas]	
	/tetter/	[tettereʔ]	'quick'
	/jamal/	[jamalaʔ]	'naughty'
b.	/lompo/	[lompo]	'big'
		*[lompoʔ]	
	/manara/	[manara]	'tower'
	/balao/	[balao]	'rat'

Constraints for Makassarese:

a. *V#
Assign one violation mark for every word that ends in a vowel.
b. CODA-CONDITION (CODA-COND) (cover constraint)
Assign one violation mark for every word-final consonant other than [ʔ] and [ŋ].

4.3 How to Discover a New Constraint

Suppose the process of analysis has gotten stalled at a ranking paradox and a new constraint is needed. The previous section has explained what favoring relations the constraint will need. But how do we go from the favoring relations to the actual definition of the new constraint? I'll begin with an example and then go on to describe some more general techniques.

In the course of analyzing some alternations in Axininca Campa (see exercise 34 in chapter 2), Alan Prince and I ran into a ranking paradox similar to (4). The form [iŋ.ko.ma.ti] requires NO-DIPHTHONG to be ranked higher than DEP, since it has epenthetic [t] and the loser has a diphthong but no epenthesis. But [i.ʧʰi.kai] requires the opposite ranking, since its diphthong isn't broken up by an epenthetic consonant.

(4)   A ranking paradox in Axininca Campa

Inputs	Winners	Losers	No-Diphthong	Dep
/i-ʧʰik-ai/ 'he cut us'	i.ʧʰi.kai	i.ʧʰi.ka.ti	L	W
/i-N-koma-i/ 'he will paddle'	iŋ.ko.ma.ti	iŋ.ko.mai	W	L

As I emphasized in the previous section, ranking paradoxes are symmetrical, so we shouldn't go into this with a prejudice about which ranking is the "right" one. Instead, we should simply look at all of the ways in which the examples that enter into the paradox differ from one another. One difference is that the diphthong is preceded by [k] in [i.ʧʰi.kai] but not in *[iŋ.ko.mai]. General experience with phonological systems or looking at additional data in Axininca Campa will quickly convince us that this is a dead end. In fact, the only important difference seems to be the morphological composition of the words. In the winner [i.ʧʰi.kai], the vowels of the diphthong are in the same morpheme, but in the loser *[iŋ.ko.mai] they are in separate morphemes. Another way to put it: in the loser *[i.ʧʰi.ka.ti], the epenthetic consonant splits a morpheme, but it lies between two morphemes in the winner [iŋ.ko.ma.ti].

These two ways of describing the difference in (4) lead to two possible additions to Con. In McCarthy and Prince (1993a, 1993b), the additional constraint is Align-Right(stem, syllable). This constraint is defined as "assign one violation mark for every stem-final segment that isn't syllable-final." This constraint favors the winner [iŋ.ko.ma.ti] over the loser *[iŋ.ko.mai]. Align-Right(stem, syllable) is obeyed by [iŋ.ko.ma.ti] because the stem-final [a] of /koma/ is syllable-final. It's violated by *[iŋ.ko.mai] because the stem-final [a] is in the middle of a syllable. Align-Right(stem, syllable) doesn't distinguish between [i.ʧʰi.kai] and *[i.ʧʰi.ka.ti]. The stem-final [k] of /ʧʰik/ can't possibly be syllable-final because [k] isn't a possible coda of this language. Both of these candidates violate Align-Right(stem, syllable) equally.

If Align-Right(stem, syllable) is added to (4), the paradox is resolved (see (5)). Now, the two winner~loser pairs tell us that Align-Right(stem, syllable) dominates Dep and Dep dominates No-Diphthong, so there is no paradox. Furthermore, when we check Align-Right(stem, syllable) with this ranking against the rest of the analysis, it presents no insuperable difficulties, so it appears to be a sound and well-justified addition to the system.

(5) (4) with ALIGN-RIGHT(stem, syllable)

Inputs	Winners	Losers	No-Diphthong	Dep	Align-R
/i-ʧʰik-ai/ 'he cut us'	i.ʧʰi.kai	i.ʧʰi.ka.ti	L	W	
/i-N-koma-i/ 'he will paddle'	iŋ.ko.ma.ti	iŋ.ko.mai	W	L	W

The other way of addressing the paradox in (4) starts from the observation that the epenthetic consonant splits a morpheme in *[i.ʧʰi.ka.ti] but not [iŋ.ko.ma.ti]. Suppose there is a version of the faithfulness constraint DEP that is sensitive to this difference – call it $\text{DEP}_{\text{morpheme}}$, and define it as "assign one violation mark for every morpheme-internal epenthetic segment." Adding this constraint to (4) also resolves the paradox, as (6) shows. Here, the two winner~loser pairs tell us that $\text{DEP}_{\text{morpheme}}$ dominates No-Diphthong and No-Diphthong dominates DEP, so again there is no paradox. Furthermore, when we check $\text{DEP}_{\text{morpheme}}$ with this ranking against the rest of the analysis, it presents no difficulties either.

(6) (4) with $\text{DEP}_{\text{morpheme}}$

Inputs	Winners	Losers	No-Diphthong	Dep	$\text{Dep}_{\text{morph}}$
/i-ʧʰik-ai/	i.ʧʰi.kai	i.ʧʰi.ka.ti	L	W	W
/i-N-koma-i/	iŋ.ko.ma.ti	iŋ.ko.mai	W	L	

To sum up this brief discussion of Axininca Campa, there are two ways of resolving the ranking paradox. By starting with an unbiased view of what the ranking of No-Diphthong and Dep should ultimately be, we come up with two entirely reasonable approaches to the problem. Which of these approaches ultimately turns out to be correct is a matter to be settled by studying language typology (see chapter 5). In fact, both of these possible additions to Con have independent support. ALIGN-RIGHT(stem, syllable) was first introduced in Prince and

Smolensky's (1993/2004) analysis of Lardil, and several other applications of the same basic idea can be found in McCarthy and Prince (1993a). DEP$_{\text{morpheme}}$ is usually known as CONTIGUITY (CONTIG) or OUTPUT-CONTIGUITY (O-CONTIG) in the literature, and it has versions that block word-internal as well as morpheme-internal epenthesis (Gouskova 2003, Kenstowicz 1994, Lamontagne 1996, McCarthy and Prince 1995, 1999, Spencer 1993, Stemberger and Bernhardt 1999).

This example illustrates a workable strategy for identifying or discovering new constraints that resolve ranking paradoxes. First, use winners that are as similar as possible to exemplify the paradox. Because the winners are so similar, any of the few remaining differences between them could be the key to discovering the new constraint. Second, carefully inventory the differences between the winners, bearing in mind that the difference could involve markedness or faithfulness. Any property of linguistic structure that is represented in the outputs of the grammar, and any aspect of input-output identity, is in principle available to a newly proposed constraint that could resolve the ranking paradox. Third, do not assume that one particular way of resolving the paradox has to be the right one. There is a very natural tendency to assume that the ranking that was discovered first is the correct one. This assumption is unjustified. The new constraint could in principle favor any of the winners that make up the ranking paradox.

EXERCISES

3   Propose a way of resolving the ranking paradox in exercise 1. Explain how you arrived at your proposal. (That is, produce something similar to the explanation in this section.)

4   Propose a way of resolving the ranking paradox in exercise 2. Explain how you arrived at your proposal.

4.4   How to Define a New Constraint

Constraints are defined in terms of the violation marks they assign. If a constraint favors *cand1* over *cand2*, then it must assign fewer violation marks to *cand1* than *cand2*. Constraint definitions need to be clear and precise about when to assign violation marks and how many to assign. Nothing else matters nearly as much as this.

In my opinion, every constraint definition should begin with the words "Assign one violation mark for every . . ." These words act as a good reminder of what is needed in a proper constraint definition. They help to avoid the problems that arise when constraints subtly shift their behavior at different points in the analysis. They also make it harder to state constraints that do illegitimate things, such as "constraints" that are really rewrite rules.

An OT constraint has just one job: to assign some number of violation marks to a candidate based on its output structure or how it differs from the input. Any proposed constraint definition that fails to do this – and to do so unambiguously – is obviously problematic. That is why I have been insisting on the "Assign one violation mark for every . . ." rubric.

Here are some things to watch out for in constraint definitions. There is no reason for definitions to include words like "avoid," "should not," "tend to," or "must," such as "avoid onsetless syllables" or "syllables should not exceed CVC." These words are unnecessary, and they can foster confusion about what it is that constraints do and what it is that EVAL does. Constraints do nothing more than assign violation marks to candidates. Violation marks are avoided because of how EVAL treats them.

Constraints should not imitate EVAL by making overt comparisons. No constraint should ever say "[l] is a better syllable nucleus than [n]" or "animate nouns are better subjects than inanimate nouns." Rather, the constraints should be defined so that they simply assign more violation marks to [n] nuclei than [l] nuclei or to inanimate subjects than animate subjects, leaving the "better" part to EVAL. (See §4.5.3 for the details of how to do this.) For the same reason, the appearance of comparative or superlative adjectives in definitions – "larger," "closest" – is a mistake. If the larger or closest thing is best, then the constraint should be defined so that smaller or more distant things receive more violation marks. This too leaves the comparison up to EVAL.

A more subtle danger is the constraint definition that reproduces the effects of constraint interaction. The giveaway is the appearance of phrases like "except when" or "only when" in the definition. Definitions like "onsetless syllables are prohibited (except phrase-initially)" or "the head or specifier of a CP may be deleted only when that CP is a complement" are immediately suspect.[1] The "except when" and "only when" clauses are probably hiding other, higher-ranking constraints. The effects of "except when" and "only when" should be obtained by ranking, as we saw in chapters 1 and 2.

Finally, constraints must never read like rewrite rules – no constraint definition should say "form perfect iambic feet" or "move *wh*." The effects of rewrite rules are approximated in OT by constraint hierarchies where markedness dominates faithfulness.

4.5   Properties of Markedness Constraints

4.5.1   How markedness constraints assign violations

A markedness constraint assigns its violation marks based on the presence of some property in the output form under evaluation. While any aspect of the output could in principle be the target for some markedness constraint, there are also significant limitations on the scope of these constraints. They cannot mention the input or the input-output mapping. For instance, there couldn't be a markedness constraint that is violated by [i]s that are derived from underlying /i/ but not by [i]s that are epenthetic – unless this difference were somehow represented in the output structure (see §4.6.4 on the constraint FILL). Nor can markedness constraints mention properties of the overall system or other outputs. For example, no markedness constraint could say "assign one violation mark for every long vowel in a closed syllable, if vowel length is phonemic," since whether vowel length is phonemic in some language is a deduction about the whole language rather than a fact about the output form being evaluated. A final limitation of markedness constraints is that they cannot be sensitive to any property that isn't included in the theory of representations. For instance, constraints on the absolute duration of segments are only meaningful if output representations include information about absolute duration.

As the phrase "assign one violation mark for every . . ." suggests, a single constraint can assign several violation marks to a candidate. The constraint definition specifies exactly how the number of violations is determined, and sometimes there will be questions about exactly how to do this. For a constraint like ONSET, it doesn't matter whether the definition counts violations from the top down – "assign one violation mark for every syllable that begins with a vowel" – or from the bottom up – "assign one violation mark for every vowel that begins a syllable." The number of violation marks assigned will be the same either way. For other constraints, however, this matters. It makes a difference whether NO-CODA is given a top-down or bottom-up definition. The top-down definition – "assign one violation mark for every syllable that has a coda" – and the bottom-up definition – "assign one violation mark for every consonant in the coda of a syllable" – work differently when a coda contains more than one consonant. Under the top-down formulation, the syllables [pænt] and [pæn] are tied on this constraint, since each receives one violation mark, but [pænt] does worse than [pæn] according to the bottom-up definition.

I have not run across any evidence bearing on this question about No-Coda, but the question arises with other constraints as well. Take $*C^{unsyll}$, for example. It has the effect of prohibiting unsyllabified consonants, but how exactly is it defined? It's one of a family of constraints (see §4.7.2 on this notion) that enforce the requirements of the prosodic hierarchy. The prosodic hierarchy organizes phonological structure into successively smaller constituents, as shown in (7). The prosodic hierarchy's structure is enforced by violable constraints (Ito and Mester 1992/2003, Selkirk 1995), and among these are constraints against skipping levels of the hierarchy. An unsyllabified consonant is one that skips the syllable level and attaches directly to the phonological word, as (8) illustrates for Yawelmani [ʔil.k.hin]. Selkirk refers to these no-level-skipping constraints as Exhaustivity(n), since they require constituents at level $n - 1$ of the hierarchy to be exhaustively parsed into constituents at level n. (For further explanation of the prosodic hierarchy, see the boxed text at the end of this section.)

(7) The prosodic hierarchy (partial)

Phonological Phrase
|
Phonological Word
|
Syllable
|
Segment

(8) Syllable level skipped for [k] in [ʔil.k.hin]
$[(ʔil)_{syllable}\ k\ (hin)_{syllable}]_{word}$

The question of interest here is whether $*C^{unsyll}$, also known as Exhaustivity(syllable) (Exh(syll))), should have a top-down or bottom-up definition. Should it be top-down – "assign a violation mark for every phonological word that immediately dominates a segment" – or bottom-up – "assign a violation mark for every segment that is immediately dominated by a phonological word node"? We can investigate this question by looking at what happens when a single phonological word contains more than one unsyllabified consonant.

In Classical Arabic, a constraint similar to *V# causes deletion of short vowels at the end of a phonological phrase. I'll call this constraint *V]$_{phrase}$. Since Arabic syllables are maximally CVː or CVC, just like Yawelmani, *V]$_{phrase}$ will sometimes force a phrase-final consonant to be unsyllabified, as shown in (9). Therefore, *V]$_{phrase}$ dominates EXHAUSTIVITY(syllable) as well as MAX-V. See (10) for the ranking argument.

(9)   Unsyllabified phrase-final consonants in Classical Arabic

Underlying	Phrase-final	Phrase-medial	
/ʔal-kitaːb-u/	ʔal.ki.taːb	ʔal.ki.taː.bu	'the book (nominative)'
/ʔal-bakr-i/	ʔal.bak.r	ʔal.bak.ri	'the young camel (dative)'
/katab-tu/	ka.tab.t	ka.tab.tu	'I wrote'

(10)   *V]$_{phrase}$ >> EXHAUSTIVITY(syllable), MAX-V

/ʔal-bakr-i/	*V]$_{phrase}$	EXH(syll)	MAX-V
a. → ʔal.bak.r]$_{phrase}$		*	*
b. ʔal.bak.ri]$_{phrase}$	*W	L	L

Outside phrase-final position, consonants that could have ended up unsyllabified are dealt with by epenthesis. For example, /staktab-tu/ 'I asked someone to write' becomes [ʔis.tak.tab.tu], with epenthesis of [ʔi] so the [s] won't be left unsyllabified. This shows that EXHAUSTIVITY(syllable) dominates DEP (11).

(11)   EXHAUSTIVITY(syllable) >> DEP

/staktab-tu/	EXH(syll)	DEP
a. → ʔis.tak.tab.tu		**
b. s.tak.tab.tu	*W	L

If /staktab-tu/ is in phrase-final position, there are two potentially unsyllabified consonants, the initial [s] and the final [t]. If EXHAUSTIVITY(syllable) has a top-down definition, then all phonological words that contain at least one unsyllabified segment are treated equally. The result, shown in (12), is a loser row with L but no W. That's a major problem for this way of defining EXHAUSTIVITY(syllable).

(12) Bad result with top-down definition of EXHAUSTIVITY(syllable)

/staktab-tu/	*V]$_{\text{phrase}}$	EXH(syll)	MAX-V	DEP
a. → ?is.tak.tab.t]$_{\text{phrase}}$		*	*	**
b. s.tak.tab.t]$_{\text{phrase}}$		*	*	L
c. ?is.tak.tab.tu]$_{\text{phrase}}$	*W	L	L	**

On the other hand, if EXHAUSTIVITY(syllable) has a bottom-up definition, then each unsyllabified segment incurs its own violation mark. In this case, the predicted result is the correct one, [?is.tak.tab.t], as shown in (13). This tells us that the bottom-up definition of EXHAUSTIVITY(syllable) is superior. This probably isn't a very surprising result, but it's nice to have established it by careful argumentation.

(13) Correct result with bottom-up definition of EXHAUSTIVITY(syllable)

/staktab-tu/	*V]$_{\text{phrase}}$	EXH(syll)	MAX-V	DEP
a. → ?is.tak.tab.t]$_{\text{phrase}}$		*	*	**
b. s.tak.tab.t]$_{\text{phrase}}$		**W	*	L
c. ?is.tak.tab.tu]$_{\text{phrase}}$	*W	L	L	**

This example offers a general lesson about how to study the definitions of constraints. The question here was not about *when* EXHAUSTIVITY(syllable) is violated, but rather *how much* it's violated. To answer this question, we needed to find a language where EXHAUSTIVITY(syllable) is dominated but still potentially active. It has to be dominated because a language that always syllabifies all of its consonants cannot tell us whether it matters how many unsyllabified consonants a candidate contains. And EXHAUSTIVITY(syllable) has to be potentially active because, as we can see by comparing (12) with (13), our question about the definition of EXHAUSTIVITY(syllable) depends on whether or not it's active over this candidate set. Under one definition, EXHAUSTIVITY(syllable) isn't active in (12), so it leaves the decision up to DEP, which decides wrongly. Under another definition,

EXHAUSTIVITY(syllable) is active in (13): additional unsyllabified consonants do not come "for free" in a word that already contains an unsyllabified consonant. The more discriminating bottom-up definition is evidently the correct one.

By the way, it would be wrong to conclude from this example that the bottom-up formulation of a constraint is correct in every instance. Beckman (1997: 19) argues that markedness constraints evaluate autosegmental structures in a less discriminating fashion. When several segments can share the same distinctive feature bundle (Goldsmith 1976a, 1976b), it makes a difference whether a constraint like *MID is defined as "assign one violation mark for every instance of the feature bundle [−high, −low]" or "assign one violation mark for every vowel that is associated with the feature bundle [−high, −low]." Beckman uses the first definition in her analysis of vowel harmony in Shona.[2]

Explanation: The prosodic hierarchy

The prosodic hierarchy was developed by Selkirk (1980), Nespor and Vogel (1986), Inkelas (1989), and others. The idea is that every phonological representation includes layers of constituent structure consisting of, from top to bottom, utterance, intonation phrase, phonological phrase, phonological word, foot, syllable, and segment. Every utterance contains one or more intonation phrases, every intonation phrase contains one or more phonological phrases, and so on. Going the other way, every segment belongs to some syllable, every syllable belongs to some foot, and so on.

Although the structure of the prosodic hierarchy was originally assumed to be invariant and universal, Selkirk (1995) and Ito and Mester (1992/2003) propose that some aspects of the hierarchy may be enforced by violable constraints.

The text discusses the constraints of the EXHAUSTIVITY family, which prohibit structures that skip levels of the hierarchy, enforcing a so-called strict layering requirement. For example, EXHAUSTIVITY(foot) is violated by syllables that are attached directly to the phonological word node, a situation that is commonly encountered when odd-syllabled words are parsed into binary feet, such as Garawa [('punja)$_{foot}$la]$_{word}$ in (18).

NONRECURSIVITY constraints are violated by structures in which a prosodic category dominates itself. For example, NONRECURSIVITY(word) is violated by a type of structure that is often assumed for English words with suffixes that do not affect stress placement, such as [[kind]$_{word}$ness]$_{word}$ or [[draw]$_{word}$ing]$_{word}$.

> HEADEDNESS constraints are violated when a constituent of type n contains no constituents of type $n - 1$. For example, HEADEDNESS(word) requires every phonological word to contain at least one foot. The evidence that HEADEDNESS is a violable constraint isn't as extensive as the evidence for violability of EXHAUSTIVITY and NONRECURSIVITY.
>
> Other aspects of the prosodic hierarchy – for example, that words contain feet and not vice versa – do not seem to be violable at all, and so they are presumably encoded in GEN.

4.5.2 Constraints that are evaluated gradiently

As we saw in the previous section, constraints can assign multiple violation marks when a candidate contains several instances of the forbidden structure. Starting with the earliest work on OT, it has also been assumed that there is another way for constraints to assign multiple violation marks: *gradient evaluation*. The idea is that a constraint can assign a different number of marks to a structure depending on how far it deviates from some requirement. Although there are several sorts of gradient constraints in the literature, including a few gradient faithfulness constraints (see McCarthy 2003c: 82 for an overview), the most common by far is *linear gradience*.

Constraints that assesses violations by linear gradience are known as *alignment constraints*. Gradient alignment constraints apply to phonological or syntactic structures of the form $[\ldots X \ldots]_Y$. ALIGN-LEFT(X, Y) requires every instance of the constituent X to be initial in some Y, and ALIGN-RIGHT(X, Y) is its mirror image. If alignment constraints are assessed gradiently, then the number of marks assigned by, say, ALIGN-LEFT(X, Y) depends on how much structure intervenes between each X and the beginning of Y.

Prince and Smolensky (1993/2004) introduced these constraints as part of a theory of morphological infixation. The general idea is that every affix is associated with a violable constraint aligning it to initial or final position of the word, depending on whether it's a prefix or a suffix. If some affix's alignment constraint is crucially dominated, then that affix is displaced from its preferred position at the periphery. Constraints on syllable structure, such as ONSET and NO-CODA, are often the impetus for infixation.

For example, the Nakanai nominalizing morpheme /il/ is an infix that goes after the root-initial consonant, if there is one.[3] It is shown in boldface in (14).

(14) Infixation in Nakanai (Johnston 1980)

	Root	*Root with infix*	
	[au]	[ilau]	'steering'
	[ali]	[ilali]	'feast'
	[taga]	[tilaga]	'fear'
	[gogo]	[gilogo]	'sympathetic'
	[peho]	[pileho]	'death'

Because /il/ is infixed, ALIGN-LEFT(*il*, stem) must be crucially dominated. The constraints that dominate it are shown in (15). They include No-CODA as well as the faithfulness constraints DEP and MAX, since epenthesis and deletion offer alternative ways of avoiding codas without infixation.

(15) NO-CODA, DEP, MAX >> ALIGN-LEFT(*il*, stem)

/il-taga/	NO-CODA	DEP	MAX	ALIGN-LEFT(*il*, stem)
a. → ti.la.ga				*
b. il.ta.ga	*W			L
c. i.li.ta.ga		*W		L
d. i.ta.ga			*W	L

The argument that ALIGN-LEFT(*il*, stem) is gradient comes from comparing [ti.la.ga]'s relatively shallow infixation with *[ta.gi.la]'s deeper infixation. These two candidates tie on all the other constraints, so they have to be distinguished by how much they violate ALIGN-LEFT(*il*, stem). The usual assumption is that constraints like ALIGN-LEFT(*il*, stem) measure the severity of violation by counting intervening segments, so [ti.la.ga] receives one mark while *[ta.gi.la] receives three (see (16)). Although ALIGN-LEFT(*il*, stem) is dominated, it's still able to demand minimal depth of infixation when it decides between candidates that tie on all of the higher-ranking constraints.

(16) Gradient ALIGN-LEFT(*il*, stem)

/il-taga/	NO-CODA	DEP	MAX	ALIGN-LEFT(*il*, stem)
a. → ti.la.ga				*
b. ta.gi.la				***W

The recommended formula for defining constraints can be used for ALIGN-LEFT(*il*, stem): "Assign one violation mark for every segment that intervenes between the left edge of the morpheme [il] and the left edge of the stem." It can also be used for syntactic alignment constraints, such as those proposed by Grimshaw (2002). For example, her constraint HEADLEFT is, in alignment terms, ALIGN-LEFT(head(XP), XP). It assigns one violation mark for every constituent that intervenes between an XP's head and its left edge. It therefore assigns the violation marks shown in (17).

(17) Gradient evaluation by ALIGN-LEFT(head(XP), XP)

		ALIGN-LEFT(head(XP), XP)
a.	[Head Comp Spec]$_{XP}$	
b.	[Spec Head Comp]$_{XP}$	*
c.	[Spec Comp Head]$_{XP}$	**

One type of alignment cannot be reconciled with this way of defining constraints, however. McCarthy and Prince (1993a), adopting a proposal made by Robert Kirchner, use ALIGN-LEFT(foot, word) and ALIGN-RIGHT(foot, word) as a way of obtaining the same effects as directional foot parsing in rule-based metrical phonology. (For a brief explanation of metrical phonology, see the boxed text at the end of this section.)

Stress in Garawa (18) is a good example of how this analysis works. In this language, main stress falls on the initial syllable, and secondary stress (marked by ˌ) falls on every even-numbered syllable counting from the right. This stress pattern indicates that the metrical feet in Garawa are strictly disyllabic and trochaic. In rule-based phonology, the first rule assigns a single main-stress foot at the beginning of the word. Then another rule assigns the secondary-stress feet by applying iteratively from the end of the word leftward. This rule groups every pair of syllables into a foot, and it quits when there are fewer than two unfooted syllables remaining. (The Garawa examples appear in the original transcription rather than IPA.)

(18) Garawa stress (Furby 1974)

Example	*Foot parsing*	
'yami	('σ σ)	'eye'
'punjala	('σ σ) σ	'white'
'watjim,paŋu	('σ σ) (,σ σ)	'armpit'
'kamala,řinji	('σ σ) σ (,σ σ)	'wrist'
'yaka,laka,lampa	('σ σ) (,σ σ) (,σ σ)	'loose'
'ŋankiři,kirim,payi	('σ σ) σ (,σ σ) (,σ σ)	'fought with boomerangs'
'ŋampa,laŋin,mukun,jina	('σ σ) (,σ σ) (,σ σ) (,σ σ)	'at our many'
'nařiŋin,mukun,jina,miřa	('σ σ) σ (,σ σ) (,σ σ) (,σ σ)	'at your own many'
'nimpa,laŋin,muku,nanji,miřa	('σ σ) (,σ σ) (,σ σ) (,σ σ) (,σ σ)	'from your own two'

Analyzing these facts in OT requires, among other things, dealing with the different ways of parsing a long, odd-syllable word like 'at your own many' into binary feet. Among the possibilities that need to be considered are those listed in (19). These candidates keep the location of main stress constant, since that is completely consistent in the language. They differ in how the secondary-stress feet parse the odd-syllabled sequence.

(19) Some metrical parses of ['nařiŋin,mukun,jina,miřa]
  a. → ('naři)ŋin(,mukun)(,jina)(,miřa)
  b.   ('naři)(,ŋinmu)kun(,jina)(,miřa)
  c.   ('naři)(,ŋinmu)(,kunji)na(,miřa)
  d.   ('naři)(,ŋinmu)(,kunji)(,nami)řa

The OT analysis of these facts presented by McCarthy and Prince (1993a) crucially relies on the constraint ALIGN-RIGHT(foot, word) to decide among the candidates in (19). This constraint is defined in (20). This definition is unlike any of the other constraints we have seen because it uses universal quantification twice: "For every foot" and "for every syllable." It assesses each foot's alignment gradiently, and then it sums up the violation marks for each foot to determine how the entire word performs.

(20) ALIGN-RIGHT(foot, word)
   For every foot, assign one violation mark for every syllable that intervenes between the right edge of that foot and the right edge of the word.

ALIGN-RIGHT(foot, word) is applied to the Garawa data in (21). (Because there are so many violations, I have represented them with numbers instead of asterisks.) For example, the initial foot in candidate (a) is followed by seven syllables, so it's responsible for seven violation marks. The next foot is misaligned by four syllables, and so on. In general, the secondary-stress feet must be as far to the right as possible if ALIGN-RIGHT(foot, word) is to be maximally satisfied. (There are other candidates that perform even better on ALIGN-RIGHT(foot, word). Exercise 10 asks you to deal with them.)

(21) Evaluation by ALIGN-RIGHT(foot, word)

	foot 1	foot 2	foot 3	foot 4	total
a. → ('naři)ŋin(ˌmukun)(ˌjina)(ˌmiřa)	7	4	2	0	13
b. ('naři)(ˌŋinmu)kun(ˌjina)(ˌmiřa)	7	5	2	0	14W
c. ('naři)(ˌŋinmu)(ˌkunji)na(ˌmiřa)	7	5	3	0	15W
d. ('naři)(ˌŋinmu)(ˌkunji)(ˌnami)řa	7	5	3	1	16W

In their use of double universal quantification, ALIGN-RIGHT(foot, word) and ALIGN-LEFT(foot, word) stand apart from other constraints. Alternatives to ALIGN(foot, word) have been explored and, may be sufficient (see Kager 2001, McCarthy 2003c). It's likely, then, that a single universal quantifier will suffice in any constraint definition, and so the formula "Assign one violation mark for every . . ." can be relied on when defining new constraints.

Explanation: Metrical phonology

Since Liberman and Prince (1977), the properties of word stress have been mostly explained in terms of metrical structure, particularly feet. Typically, a foot consists of two syllables, one of which is designated as the head and the bearer of stress. If the head syllable is initial in the foot, then the foot is trochaic; if the head is final, then the foot is iambic. In general, analyzing a stress system is a matter of determining whether feet are trochaic or iambic and ensuring that the feet appear in the right places in the word.

Many languages, with Garawa among them, categorically prohibit monosyllabic feet. In these languages, then, Foot-Binarity(syllable) is undominated.

In Garawa, all syllables are treated alike for stress purposes. It's therefore said to have a quantity-insensitive stress system. Many other languages have quantity-sensitive stress systems that treat heavy syllables differently from light syllables. A syllable is heavy if if contains a long vowel (in all languages) or has a coda (in some languages). In a quantity-sensitive stress system, the constraint Weight-to-Stress (WSP)[4] is active.

Besides direction of foot parsing, which Garawa illustrates, an important factor in stress systems is the family of Non-Finality constraints. Non-Finality(foot) is violated if the word-final syllable belongs to a foot. Non-Finality('σ) is violated if the word-final syllable is stressed (or perhaps main-stressed).

4.5.3   Constraints derived by harmonic alignment

The word "alignment" is used in a completely different sense in the phrase *harmonic alignment*. Harmonic alignment was introduced by Prince and Smolensky (1993/2004: 161–162) as a way of relating constraints to natural linguistic scales. The constraint systems obtained with harmonic alignment are typically used to explain implicational universals of language (§5.1). Here, we will only be looking at markedness constraints that are related to linguistic scales, but the idea is applicable to faithfulness constraints as well (for which see de Lacy 2002).

There are many natural scales in language. The sonority scale orders segments by their intensity (Parker 2002); vowels are at one end of the scale, then liquids, nasals, fricatives, and plosives (see exercise 7). The animacy hierarchy orders nouns and pronouns by their proximity or similarity to the speaker (Silverstein 1976); first person pronouns are at one end, then second followed by third person pronouns, proper nouns, human nouns, animate nouns, and inanimate nouns. Scales aren't constraints; instead, harmonic alignment establishes a link between a scale and a set of related constraints.

Harmonic alignment requires two things: a natural linguistic scale like sonority or animacy; and a position in linguistic structure that prefers to be occupied by material at one end of the scale over material at the other end of the scale. The nucleus of a syllable is a position in linguistic structure, and it is preferentially filled by a high-sonority segment. The onset of a syllable is another position, and it is preferentially filled by a low-sonority segment. Subject position favors nouns and pronouns that are high on the animacy scale; object position favors low-animacy nouns (Aissen 1999). In each case, harmonic alignment combines a position and a scale to create a family of constraints that disfavor candidates in proportion to how poorly they match the position with its preferred end of the scale.

There are two ways of doing this formally. In Prince and Smolensky's original work, harmonic alignment produces a *universally fixed hierarchy* of constraints. For example, (22) contains the fixed hierarchy of constraints on the sonority of syllable nuclei, assuming a relatively simple version of the sonority scale. Since plosives are the least preferred nuclei, *Nucleus/Plosive (*Nuc/Plo) is the highest-ranking constraint, followed by *Nucleus/Fricative (Nuc/Fric), and so on. (Since vowels are the least marked nuclei, there is no need for a constraint *Nucleus/Vowel.)[5] Because this is a universally fixed hierarchy, these constraints must appear in this order in the grammar of every language. Thus, plosives are the most marked nuclei universally.

(22)   Fixed hierarchy of constraints on sonority of nuclei
     *Nuc/Plosive >> *Nuc/Fricative >> *Nuc/Nasal >> *Nuc/Liquid

Alternatively, harmonic alignment could be used to create a set of constraints in stringency form (§2.4). The idea is that plosives violate every constraint in the set, fricatives violate all but one constraint, and so on (see (23)). For instance, *Nucleus/Plosive–Nasal (read as "star nucleus plosive through nasal") is violated once by every syllable nucleus consisting of a plosive, fricative, or nasal. Each constraint refers to a range of contiguous positions on the sonority scale that always includes the least sonorous class, the plosives.

(23)   Constraints on sonority of nuclei in stringency form
     *Nucleus/Plosive–Liquid (*Nuc/Plo-Liq)
     *Nucleus/Plosive–Nasal (*Nuc/Plo-Nas)
     *Nucleus/Plosive–Fricative (*Nuc/Plo-Fric)
     *Nucleus/Plosive (*Nuc/Plo)

Either of these constraint systems can account for the implicational universal relating a segment's sonority to its ability to fill a syllable nucleus. The evidence for this implicational universal comes from observations like the following. All languages have vowel nuclei, but some languages (e.g., Spanish or Arabic) forbid all consonantal nuclei. Some languages allow vowels and liquids (Slovak) or vowels, liquids, and nasals (German or English) to function as syllable nuclei. Some varieties of Berber allow any segment type, including plosives, to fill the nucleus under the right conditions (Dell and Elmedlaoui 1985, 1988). From observations like these, we can conclude that, if a language allows segments of type X to be nuclei, then it must also allow all segment types that are more sonorous than X to be nuclei.

To see how the fixed hierarchy in (22) accounts for this implicational universal, look at (24). In this tableau, DEP is ranked below *NUCLEUS/ LIQUID. (Assume that MAX dominates DEP.) *NUCLEUS/LIQUID and all higher-ranking constraints will therefore compel epenthesis when the alternative is a syllabic plosive, fricative, nasal, or liquid. This is the case in Classical Arabic, a language that allows no syllabic consonants whatsoever. If DEP were ranked higher, then some syllabic consonants would be permitted, always including those that are most sonorous. English, for example, violates *NUCLEUS/LIQUID in *bottle* and *NUCLEUS/ NASAL in *button*. In sum, the placement of DEP, MAX, or some other relevant faithfulness constraint in the fixed hierarchy sets a minimum sonority threshold for syllable nuclei in a language.

(24) Epenthesis versus syllabic consonants in Classical Arabic

Inputs	Winners	Losers	*Nuc/Plo	*Nuc/Fric	*Nuc/Nas	*Nuc/Liq	Dep
/ktub/ 'write!'	ʔuk.tub	k̟.tub	W				L
/ftaħ/ 'open!'	ʔif.taħ	f̟.taħ		W			L
/mlik/ 'possess!'	ʔim.lik	m̟.lik			W		L
/rkab/ 'ride!'	ʔir.kab	r̟.kab				W	L

If the constraints are in stringency form like (23), the minimum sonority threshold is also set by the choice of which constraint dominates faithfulness, but the ranking of the other constraints doesn't matter. (For the reason why constraints in a stringency relation aren't directly rankable, see §2.4.) Tableau (25) illustrates. The constraints other than *NUCLEUS/PLOSIVE–LIQUID are segregated because they do not contribute to deciding which candidate is optimal, and so they are unrankable. The last winner~loser pair is the one that proves the ranking *Nucleus/Plosive–Liquid* >> Dep, since no other *Nucleus* constraint can account for why [ʔir.kab] is more harmonic than [r̩.kab].

(25) Epenthesis versus syllabic consonants – stringency form

Winners	Losers	*Nuc/Plo– Liq	Dep	*Nuc/Plo	*Nuc/Plo– Fric	*Nuc/Plo– Nas
ʔuk.tub	k̩.tub	W	L	W	W	W
ʔif.taħ	f̩.taħ	W	L		W	W
ʔim.lik	m̩.lik	W	L			W
ʔir.kab	r̩.kab	W	L			

To sum up, harmonic alignment takes a linguistic scale *s*, a structural position *p*, and a dispreference for elements at one end of *s* to fill *p*. Depending on one's theoretical inclinations, it can combine these elements to produce a fixed hierarchy or a set of constraints in stringency form. The fixed hierarchy consists of constraints against each step in *s* occurring in position *p*. The constraint that is ranked highest is the one referring to the least preferred end of *s*, and so on from there. The constraints in stringency form prohibit elements drawn from a range of steps on *s* from occurring in position *p*. The ranges that these constraints refer to must be continuous and they must all include the dispreferred end of *s*. These concepts have important applications in phonology and syntax, wherever linguistic scales are involved in implicational universals.

The remainder of this section deals with a more advanced topic: the difference between fixed hierarchies and stringency. It can be skipped on first reading and looked at later.

There is no reason to think that we need harmonic alignment to produce both fixed hierarchies and stringency systems, so which is correct? It's sometimes suggested that stringency systems are a better idea because they avoid the need to stipulate a fixed ranking. But both approaches require some sort of stipulation, fixed ranking in one approach and continuous ranges anchored at one end of scale in the other. A more substantial difference is that stringency systems predict a wider variety of possible languages than do fixed hierarchies, keeping all else equal.

This difference appears only when the constraints of a stringency system are in an *anti-Paninian ranking* (Prince 1997b). Since Paːɳini discussed situations where the specific takes precedence over the general, an anti-Paninian ranking is one where a more general constraint in a stringency system is crucially ranked over a more specific constraint, as proven by an argument from transitivity of domination. There are real-life examples of this (such as Nganasan in de Lacy 2002: 62–63), but to keep things simple I will use a hypothetical example. The issue in this invented language is how to syllabify an input like /pmr/ as a single syllable without epenthesis or deletion. Should it be [pmr̩] with syllabic [r̩] and a complex onset or [pm̩r] with syllabic [m̩] and a simple onset? This is a choice between [pmr̩]'s better nucleus and [pm̩r]'s simple onset.

The "facts" of this hypothetical language are given in (26). The comparison of [pmr̩] and *[pm̩r] in (a) shows that the language tolerates a complex onset if the alternative requires a syllable nucleus with sonority lower than that of a liquid. (The comparison in (b) and (c) is similar.) The choice between [pṣm] and *[psm̩] in (d) involves comparing a candidate with a nucleus that's less sonorous than a nasal against a candidate with a complex onset. The sonority advantage of the nucleus [m̩] over the nucleus [ṣ] is insufficient to override the dispreference for complex onsets. (The comparison in (e) is similar.) Finally, the comparison of [pts] and *[ptṣ] in (f) follows the same pattern established in (d) and (e): the sonority advantage of a fricative nucleus over a stop nucleus won't override *COMPLEX-ONSET.

(26)   Hypothetical example to illustrate anti-Paninian ranking

	Input	Winner	Loser	Comparison
a.	/pmr/	pmr̩	*pm̩r	Complex onset vs. nucleus < liquid.
b.	/psr/	psr̩	*pṣr	Complex onset vs. nucleus < liquid.
c.	/ptr/	ptr̩	*ptr̩	Complex onset vs. nucleus < liquid.
d.	/psm/	pṣm	*psm̩	Nucleus < nasal vs. complex onset.
e.	/ptm/	ptm	*ptm̩	Nucleus < nasal vs. complex onset.
f.	/pts/	ptṣ	*ptṣ	Nucleus < fricative vs. complex onset.

We'll begin the analysis with the [ptṣ]~*[ptṣ] comparison. Both candidates equally violate *NUCLEUS/PLOSIVE–LIQUID, *NUCLEUS/PLOSIVE–NASAL, and *NUCLEUS/PLOSIVE–FRICATIVE, so none of these constraints is relevant. They differ on *NUCLEUS/PLOSIVE, however: [ptṣ]

violates it and *[ptʂ] obeys it. They also differ on *COMPLEX-ONSET, which favors [pʈs]. Since [pʈs] is optimal, *COMPLEX-ONSET must dominate *NUCLEUS/PLOSIVE (see (27)). None of the other *NUCLEUS constraints favors the winner or the loser in this competition, so we can omit them from the tableau.

(27) *COMPLEX-ONSET >> *NUCLEUS/PLOSIVE

/pts/	*COMP-ONS	*NUC/PLO
a. → pʈs		*
b. ptʂ	*W	L

The comparison between [pʂm] and *[psm̩] is similar. *COMPLEX-ONSET favors the winner, whereas the loser is favored by *NUCLEUS/PLOSIVE–FRICATIVE. This leads to the ranking argument in (28). None of the other *NUCLEUS constraints favors the winner or the loser in this competition, so we can omit them from the tableau.

(28) *COMPLEX-ONSET >> *NUCLEUS/PLOSIVE–FRICATIVE

/psm/	*COMP-ONS	*NUC/PLO–FRIC
a. → pʂm		*
b. psm̩	*W	L

Finally, for [pmr̩] to beat *[pm̩r], *NUCLEUS/PLOSIVE–NASAL has to dominate *COMPLEX-ONSET (see (29)). Again, since none of the other *NUCLEUS constraints favors the winner or the loser in this competition, we can omit them from the tableau.

(29) *NUCLEUS/PLOSIVE–NASAL >> *COMPLEX-ONSET

/pmr/	*NUC/PLO–NAS	*COMPLEX-ONSET
a. → pmr̩		*
b. pm̩r	*W	L

Putting together all of the ranking information in tableaux (27)–(29), we get the hierarchy in (30). This is an anti-Paninian hierarchy because the general constraint in a stringency relation, *Nucleus/Plosive–Nasal, dominates the more specific constraints *Nucleus/Plosive–Fricative and *Nucleus/Plosive. Because constraints in a stringency relation are never directly rankable (§2.4), this demonstration necessarily involves transitivity of constraint domination via *Complex-Onset.

(30) An anti-Paninian constraint hierarchy
   *Nuc/Plo–Nas >> *Comp-Ons >> *Nuc/Plo–Fric, *Nuc/Plo

This system could not be analyzed with constraints in a fixed hierarchy (see exercise 14). In general, when the constraints are in stringency form, an anti-Paninian ranking treats the elements at the high-markedness end of the scale alike. Thus, (30) treats plosives, fricatives, and nasals as if they had identical sonority, since all violate top-ranked *Nucleus/Plosive–Nasal. A Paninian ranking (specific over general) treats the elements at the low-markedness end of the scale alike. Fixed hierarchies and Paninian rankings give the same results, but the fixed hierarchy has no way of reproducing the effect of the anti-Paninian ranking. If real languages work like this, then the formulation of constraints in stringency rather than fixed-ranking form is supported.

EXERCISES

5 Add the following candidates to the Classical Arabic tableau (13): ?is.tak.ta.bit]$_{phrase}$, si.tak.tab.t]$_{phrase}$, and si.tak.ta.bit]$_{phrase}$. Do any of them present any difficulties for the analysis illustrated in that tableau? If so, how would you resolve these difficulties? (Be sure to explain your answers using the tools introduced in this chapter.)

6 Some languages appear to tolerate unsyllabified consonants in word-final position while forbidding them elsewhere. Suppose, then, that there is a constraint that is violated once by any unsyllabified consonant that is not word-final. Would the existence of this constraint affect the argument for the bottom-up formulation of Exhaustivity(syllable) based on comparing (12) and (13)? Explain your answer.

7 Prince and Smolensky (1993/2004) propose a constraint HNuc that assesses syllable nuclei according to their place on the sonority scale. The less

sonorous a segment is, the worse it is as a syllable nucleus, and so the more marks it gets. For instance, the syllable [pş] gets more marks from HNuc than the syllable [pl]. Using the "Assign one violation mark for every . . ." rubric, define HNuc. You can assume that the sonority hierarchy consists of the following scale:

Step	Segments
4	liquids
3	nasals
2	fricatives
1	plosives

8   From the data below, it's clear that the Tagalog morpheme [um] is infixed after a root-initial consonant or consonant cluster.[6] (The morpheme is in boldface to make it easier to locate.) Your task is to analyze the location of the infix along the same general lines as the analysis of Nakanai /il/ in the text. Pay particular attention to the losers provided. Do not consider the additional data in exercise 9 at this point.

Root	Root with infix	Losers	
[su.lat]	[su.**mu**.lat]	*[**um**.su.lat]	'write'
		*[**ʔum**.su.lat]	
		*[su.**lu**.mat]	
		*[su.la.**tum**]	
[grad.wet]	[gru.**ma**d.wet]	*[**um**.grad.wet]	'graduate'
		*[**ʔum**.grad.wet]	
		*[**gum**.rad.wet]	
		*[gra.**dum**.wet]	
		*[grad.**wu**.met]	
		*[grad.we.**tum**]	

9   In fact, the location of the Tagalog infix [um] actually varies with cluster-initial roots, as the data below show. Since we haven't discussed variation yet, you should treat the variants as coming from different grammars – that is, you should produce a different ranking for this exercise than for the previous one. (You may prefer to read ahead in §6.2 for a specific proposal about how to analyze variation in OT.)

Root	Root with infix	Losers	
[grad.wet]	[**gum**.rad.wet]	*[**um**.grad.wet]	'graduate'
		*[**ʔum**.grad.wet]	
		*[gru.**ma**d.wet]	
		*[gra.**dum**.wet]	
		*[grad.**wu**.met]	
		*[grad.we.**tum**]	

10 Add to the analysis of Garawa by dealing with the following losing candidates. You will need the additional constraints listed below the losers to do this.

*[('naři)ŋinmukun(ˌjina)(ˌmiřa)]
*[('naři)ŋinmukunjina(ˌmiřa)]
*[('naři)ŋinmukunjinamiřa]
*[na('řiŋin)(ˌmukun)(ˌjina)(ˌmiřa)]
*[nařiŋin('mukun)(ˌjina)(ˌmiřa)]
*[nařiŋinmukun('jina)(ˌmiřa)]
*[nařiŋinmukunjina('miřa)]
*[('naři)(ˌŋin)(ˌmukun)(ˌjina)(ˌmiřa)]

Additional stress constraints:

a. EXHAUSTIVITY(foot) (usually called PARSE-SYLLABLE)
   Assign one violation mark for every syllable that does not belong to any foot.
b. ALIGN-LEFT(word, head(word))
   Assign one violation mark for every word that does not begin with its head foot (i.e., the foot with main stress).
c. FOOT-BINARITY(syllable) (FT-BIN(syll))
   Assign one violation mark for every monosyllabic foot.

11 Produce the harmonic alignment, in both fixed-hierarchy and stringency form, of the following scale and preference combinations:

a. the sonority scale (as given in exercise 7) and the preference for low sonority in onsets;
b. the animacy scale (as given in the text) and the preference for high animacy in subjects;
c. the animacy scale and the preference for low animacy in objects.

12 The following data come from a child of about 2 years old acquiring American English (Gnanadesikan 1995/2004). Explain what determines the choice of which consonant to delete and which to preserve in initial clusters.[7]

Adult	Child
clean	[kin]
friend	[fɛn]
please	[piz]
skin	[gɪn]
sky	[gɑj]

sleep	[sip]
slip	[sɪp]
snookie	[sʊki]
snow	[so]
spill	[bɪw]
spoon	[bun]
star	[dɑː]

13   Develop analyses similar to (24) and (25) for a language that, like English, allows liquid and nasal nuclei but not plosive or fricative nuclei. Your analysis should be able to handle all of the winner~loser pairs listed below.

	Input	*Winner*	*Loser*
a.	/mitr/	[mit̩r]	*[mitrə]
b.	/batn/	[bat̩n]	*[batnə]
c.	/ups/	[upsə]	*[upṣ]
d.	/mutk/	[mutkə]	*[mut̚k]

14   If you have read the advanced material on anti-Paninian ranking, complete the argument in the text by showing that the hypothetical language in (26) cannot be obtained using the fixed hierarchy in (22).

4.6   Properties of Faithfulness Constraints

4.6.1   Correspondence theory

So far, this chapter has focused on markedness constraints, since most newly proposed constraints are of the markedness type. Still, it's sometimes necessary to introduce a new faithfulness constraint. A faithfulness constraint assigns its violation marks based on disparities between the input and the output. In principle, any input-output difference could elicit a faithfulness violation. Although many of the faithfulness constraints in common use do not refer to the context in which the unfaithful mapping occurs, we will see that faithfulness constraints can also be limited to certain environments.

Correspondence theory provides a general framework for defining faithfulness constraints (McCarthy and Prince 1995, 1999). The idea is that each candidate supplied by GEN includes an output representation and a relation between the input and that output. This is called the correspondence relation, and it's conventionally denoted by ℜ. The relation ℜ associates some or all of the linguistic elements in the input with some or all of the linguistic elements in the output.

Some candidates for the input /kal/ are listed with their correspondence relations in (31). Because I'm being extremely explicit here, the correspondence relations are shown with somewhat more detail than you will usually see in the literature. The segments or other elements of the input and output are given numerical indices to avoid ambiguity, and each candidate's correspondence relation is defined as a set of ordered pairs (i, o), where i is an element of the input and o is an element of the output.[8]

(31)   Some candidates for input $/k_1a_2l_3/$

	Candidate	Correspondence relation	Remarks
a.	$[k_1a_2l_3]$	$\{(k_1, k_1), (a_2, a_2), (l_3, l_3)\}$	Faithful candidate
b.	$[k_1a_2]$	$\{(k_1, k_1), (a_2, a_2)\}$	Input /l/ deleted
c.	$[k_1a_2l_3ə_4]$	$\{(k_1, k_1), (a_2, a_2), (l_3, l_3)\}$	Output [ə] epenthesized
d.	$[k_1a_2r_3]$	$\{(k_1, k_1), (a_2, a_2), (l_3, r_3)\}$	/l/ changed to [r]
e.	$[k_1l_3a_2]$	$\{(k_1, k_1), (a_2, a_2), (l_3, l_3)\}$	Metathesis of /a/ and /l/

In the faithful candidate (a), every input segment has an identical output correspondent. In the candidate with deletion (b), the input /l/ has no output correspondent – it is missing from the set of ordered pairs. In the candidate with epenthesis (c), the output [ə] has no input correspondent, so it too is missing from the set of ordered pairs. Candidate (d) shows one way of implementing changes in feature values: input /l/ has the nonidentical output correspondent [r]. (More about this in §4.6.2.) Finally, (e) is an example of metathesis: the corresponding segments are in a different order in input and output.

Candidate (b) in (31) violates the constraint MAX, which is defined in (32). This definition, like the others that we'll see, begins by identifying the strings of elements that constitute the input and output. Since it requires preservation of input elements, it quantifies universally over the elements of the input, requiring each of them to have an output correspondent. Of the candidates in (31), only (b) violates MAX, and it violates it only once. The definition of MAX is the same as assigning one violation mark for every input element that isn't in the domain of the correspondence relation.

(32)   MAX (No deletion)
Let $input = i_1i_2i_3 \ldots i_n$ and $output = o_1o_2o_3 \ldots o_m$.
Assign one violation mark for every i_x
    if there is no o_y where $i_x \, \Re \, o_y$.

Candidate (c) in (31) violates DEP, which is defined in (33). DEP is just the mirror-image of MAX, quantifying universally over the elements of the output and demanding that each has an input correspondent. The definition of DEP is the same as assigning one violation mark for every output element that isn't in the range of the correspondence relation.

(33)   DEP (No epenthesis)
   Let *input* = $i_1 i_2 i_3 \ldots i_n$ and *output* = $o_1 o_2 o_3 \ldots o_m$.
   Assign one violation mark for every o_y
      if there is no i_x where $i_x \mathcal{R} o_y$.

In addition to these basic constraints, there are versions of MAX and DEP whose scope is limited to word- or morpheme-internal position. INPUT-CONTIGUITY (I-CONTIG) is violated when medial segments delete, and OUTPUT-CONTIGUITY (O-CONTIG) is violated when a segment is epenthesized medially. (OUTPUT-CONTIGUITY made an appearance in the analysis of Axininca Campa in §4.3.) Versions of MAX and DEP whose scope is limited to initial position have been proposed under the rubric of positional faithfulness, which will be discussed in §4.6.3.

Correspondence theory also recognizes the possibility of two input segments fusing into a single output segment. This phenomenon is called segmental coalescence, and Sanskrit (34) is an example. In this language, the sequences /ai/ and /au/ merge into [ē] and [ō], respectively. Both input segments are in correspondence with the single output segment. This relationship is indicated formally by giving the output segment two indices: $/a_1 i_2/ \rightarrow [\bar{e}_{1,2}]$. Coalescence violates the constraint UNIFORMITY, which is defined in (35). Furthermore, because the output segment is featurally distinct from both its input correspondents, coalescence processes also violate the IDENT(feature) or MAX(feature) constraints discussed below.

(34)   Sanskrit vowel coalescence (Whitney 1889)

Underlying	*Surface*	
/tava$_1$ i$_2$ndra/	[tavē$_{1,2}$ndra]	'for you, Indra (vocative)'
/hita$_1$ u$_2$pda$_3$i$_4$ʃah/	[hitō$_{1,2}$padē$_{3,4}$ʃah]	'friendly advice'

(35)   UNIFORMITY (UNIF) (No coalescence)
   Let *input* = $i_1 i_2 i_3 \ldots i_n$ and *output* = $o_1 o_2 o_3 \ldots o_m$.
   Assign one violation mark for every pair i_x and i_y
      if $i_x \mathcal{R} o_z$ and $i_y \mathcal{R} o_z$.

UNIFORMITY has a symmetric counterpart called INTEGRITY; the task of defining it is left for exercise 15.

The constraint LINEARITY in (36) requires the output to preserve the order of input elements. It's violated by phonological metathesis, as in (e) of (31), and perhaps also by syntactic movement (though see §2.9 for an alternative view). Exercise 21 asks you to use this constraint in an analysis.

(36) LINEARITY (LIN) (No metathesis, no movement)
   Let $input = i_1 i_2 i_3 \ldots i_n$ and $output = o_1 o_2 o_3 \ldots o_m$.
   Assign one violation mark for every pair i_w and i_y
      if $i_w \, \mathfrak{R} \, o_x$ and $i_y \, \mathfrak{R} \, o_z$,
      i_w precedes i_y,
      and o_z precedes o_x.

Because LINEARITY has a more complicated definition than the other faithfulness constraints seen so far, it's a good object lesson in how to define a faithfulness constraint. As usual with faithfulness, the definition begins by setting up a way of referring to the segments or other structural elements in the input and output: "Let $input = i_1 i_2 i_3 \ldots i_n$ and $output = o_1 o_2 o_3 \ldots o$." It then describes a way of assigning violations: "for every pair i_w and i_y." This is followed by several conditions, the first of which is "if $i_w \, \mathfrak{R} \, o_x$ and $i_y \, \mathfrak{R} \, o_z$." In other words, this is a constraint on pairs of input segments, each of which has an output correspondent. The last two conditions in the definition describe metathesis in correspondence-theoretic terms.

Why does the definition need the condition "if $i_w \, \mathfrak{R} \, o_x$ and $i_y \, \mathfrak{R} \, o_z$"? Because it's the only way we can talk about metathesis in terms of correspondence. As (37) shows, there are two different ways that the input /kəl/ could map to the output [klə]: by metathesis or by a combination of deletion and epenthesis. These are distinct candidates because a candidate consists of an output form *and* its correspondence relation. The condition "if $i_w \, \mathfrak{R} \, o_x$ and $i_y \, \mathfrak{R} \, o_z$" in the definition of LINEARITY tells us that candidate (a) violates this constraint but (b) doesn't. Instead, (b) violates MAX and DEP, which (a) obeys.

(37) Metathesis compared with deletion and epenthesis – input /$k_1 ə_2 l_3$/

	Candidate	Correspondence relation	Remarks
a.	[$k_1 l_3 ə_2$]	{(k_1, k_1), ($ə_2$, $ə_2$), (l_3, l_3)}	Metathesis of /ə/ and /l/.
b.	[$k_1 l_3 ə_4$]	{(k_1, k_1), (l_3, l_3)}	Input /ə/ deleted and output [ə] epenthesized.

To avoid problems when defining faithfulness constraints, try to distinguish between the conditions that have to be met for the faithfulness constraint to even be relevant and the conditions that produce an actual violation. LINEARITY isn't relevant to segments that have been deleted or epenthesized, and so we build a correspondence requirement into the antecedent of the definition. It's violated when segments are reordered, and so that is what we say in the rest of the definition. To be safe, a newly defined faithfulness constraint should be tested against various hypothetical unfaithful mappings, to make sure that the definition does what is intended. When testing newly proposed faithfulness constraints, write out the correspondence relations using indices and check that the conditions in the definition are correctly applied. This will avoid trouble and unintended consequences later on.

4.6.2 Faithfulness to features

IDENT(feature) constraints have appeared at various places in this book. These constraints require corresponding segments to have identical feature values. For example, IDENT(round) is defined in (38). It says that segments in input-output correspondence have to have identical values for the feature [round]. Vowel harmony in Warlpiri (exercise 1) is a phenomenon that involves violating this constraint. For instance, the mapping $/m_1a_2l_3i_4k_5i_6\text{-}k_7u_8l_9u_{10}\text{-}l_{11}u_{12}\text{-}l_{13}k_{14}u_{15}\text{-}c_{16}u_{17}\text{-}l_{18}u_{19}/$ $\rightarrow [m_1a_2l_3i_4k_5i_6k_7i_8l_9i_{10}l_{11}i_{12}l_{13}k_{14}i_{15}c_{16}i_{17}l_{18}i_{19}]$ incurs six violation marks from this constraint.

(38) IDENT(round)
Let *input segments* $= i_1i_2i_3 \ldots i_n$ and *output segments* $= o_1o_2o_3 \ldots o_m$.
Assign one violation mark for every pair (i_x, o_y), where $i_x \, \Re \, o_y$ and i_x and o_y have different values for the feature [round].

A variation on IDENT(feature), originally proposed by Pater (1999), treats plus and minus values of features with separate constraints. IDENT(+round) is violated when a segment that is [+round] in the input has a [−round] output correspondent. That's what happens in Warlpiri. IDENT(−round) is violated when a [−round] input segment has a [+round] output correspondent. As you will see in exercise 16, this slightly more elaborate IDENT(feature) approach is useful for analyzing coalescence phenomena.

IDENT(feature) constraints treat distinctive feature values as attributes of segments. Attributes describe things and have no existence apart from the things they describe. This is how features were thought of in *SPE* (Chomsky and Halle 1968). IDENT(feature) constraints are based on the idea that segments are in correspondence and featural identity is always mediated by segmental correspondence. The approach with IDENT(feature) constraints can be referred to as the *segmental theory of featural faithfulness.*

Features-as-attributes is not the only way of thinking about distinctive features. In autosegmental phonology (Goldsmith 1976a, 1976b), segments are more like molecules with features as the atoms that make them up. Featural atoms can exist independently of the segmental molecules, and they can be transferred from one segmental molecule to another.

The autosegmental idea can be carried over to correspondence theory. Features themselves are in correspondence, so there are MAX(feature) and DEP(feature) constraints specific to each autosegmental tier. These constraints are exemplified in (39). They are the basis for an *autosegmental theory of featural faithfulness.*

(39) MAX(round)
Let *input [round] tier* = $r_1r_2r_3 \ldots r_n$ and *output [round] tier* = $R_1R_2R_3 \ldots R_m$.
Assign one violation mark for every r_x if there is no R_y where r_x $\Re$ R_y.

DEP(round)
Let *input [round] tier* = $r_1r_2r_3 \ldots r_n$ and *output [round] tier* = $R_1R_2R_3 \ldots R_m$.
Assign one violation mark for every R_y if there is no r_x where r_x $\Re$ R_y.

There is some evidence to indicate that the segmental theory of featural faithfulness is inadequate and the autosegmental theory is required instead. One example involves the distribution of glottalization (and aspiration) contrasts in Cuzco Quechua (Parker 1997, Parker and Weber 1996). The situation, somewhat simplified, is this. Glottalization can only appear on plosive consonants ([p], [t], [ʧ], [k], and [q], but not [m], [r], [s], etc.). Furthermore, glottalization is limited to the leftmost plosive in the root. These restrictions are illustrated in (40).

(40) Laryngeal restrictions in Cuzco Quechua

Some possible words		*Some impossible words*
[pʔataj]	'to bite'	*[patʔaj]
[miʧʔu]	'mixed'	*[mʔiʧu]

There are many languages that, like Cuzco Quechua, limit glottalization to plosives. The constraint in (41) accounts for this common restriction. The positional restriction on glottalization is less common. It looks like a job for an alignment constraint like the one in (42).

(41) Glottal/Plosive (Gl/Pl)
Assign one violation mark for every consonant that is glottalized (i.e., [+constricted glottis]) and not a plosive (i.e., not [−continuant, −sonorant]).

(42) Align-Left(+constricted glottis, root) (Align-L(+cg, rt))
Assign one violation mark for every segment intervening between a consonant that is specified as [+constricted glottis] and the left edge of the root.

There is no way to rank these two markedness constraints and the Ident(constricted glottis) faithfulness constraint so as to reproduce the restrictions observed in Cuzco Quechua. The inputs /pʔataj/ and /mitʃʔu/ need to be mapped faithfully to [pʔataj] and [mitʃʔu], since those are both possible words of the language. Because of richness of the base (§2.8), the grammar also needs to deal with the inputs /patʔaj/ and /mʔitʃu/, and it needs to map them *un*faithfully to possible words of some sort, perhaps [pataj] and [mitʃu]. The winner~loser pairs in (43) reveal an inconsistency: the faithful mapping /mitʃʔu/ → [mitʃʔu] requires Ident(+constricted glottis) to dominate Align-Left(+constricted glottis, root), whereas the unfaithful mapping /patʔaj/ → [pataj] requires the opposite ranking of these two constraints.

(43) A problem with the segmental theory of featural faithfulness

Inputs	Winners	Losers	Gl/Pl	Align-L(+cg, root)	Ident(+cg)
/pʔataj/	pʔataj	pataj			W
/mitʃʔu/	mitʃʔu	mitʃu		L	W
/patʔaj/	pataj	patʔaj		W	L
/mʔitʃu/	mitʃu	mʔitʃu	W		W

To solve this problem, we should first reconsider the two mappings that lead to the ranking paradox. The /mitʃʔu/ → [mitʃʔu] mapping looks unimpeachable. Since Cuzco Quechua has words like [mitʃʔu], they have to come from some input, and it's hard to imagine any input other than /mitʃʔu/ as the source. (For example, [mitʃʔu] couldn't be derived from nonglottalized /mitʃu/, since there is no general process of glottalization and [mitʃu] is also a possible word.) On the other hand, the /patʔaj/ → [pataj] mapping is just an assumption. Richness of the base requires that the grammar deal with an input like /patʔaj/ by mapping it to something. The faithful mapping *[patʔaj] isn't a possible word, so we assumed that /patʔaj/ simply loses its glottalization, yielding [pataj]. Perhaps this assumption is wrong. (See §2.10.4 on dealing with richness of the base.)

Suppose instead that the correct mapping is /patʔaj/ → [pʔataj], with transfer of glottalization from the medial plosive to the initial one. For a feature to be able move like this, features must be represented autosegmentally. In our terms, this means that IDENT(+constricted glottis) is replaced by MAX(+constricted glottis). In the mapping /patʔaj/ → [pʔataj], the input token of [+constricted glottis] is in correspondence with an output token of [+constricted glottis], even though they are associated with different segments. I've shown this in (44) by writing [+constricted glottis] tokens as *cg* on a separate autosegmental tier and by coindexing their input and output correspondents. MAX(+constricted glottis) is violated whenever one of the input *cg* tokens has no output correspondent.

(44)   Autosegmental theory of featural faithfulness

Inputs	Winners	Losers	ALIGN-L(+cg, root)	MAX(+cg)
/pʔataj/ | cg_1	pʔataj | cg_1	pataj		W
/mitʃʔu/ | cg_1	mitʃʔu | cg_1	mitʃu	L	W
/patʔaj/ | cg_1	pʔataj | cg_1	patʔaj | cg_1	W	

Changing the assumptions has definitely improved the ranking situation. The winner~loser pairs in (44) support a consistent ranking where Max(+constricted glottis) dominates Align-Left(+constricted glottis, root). Why is it that the autosegmental theory of featural faithfulness works in this case but the segmental theory doesn't? In the segmental theory, there is only one way of dealing with the input /pat$^?$aj/: mapping it to [pataj]. Mapping it to [p$^?$ataj] wouldn't make any sense because this would incur an additional Ident(+constricted glottis) violation beyond the one that [pataj] has. Under the autosegmental theory of featural faithfulness, however, mapping /pat$^?$aj/ to [p$^?$ataj] makes perfect sense, since it preserves a token of the feature value [+constricted glottis] by moving it to another segment and thereby improving its alignment. (See exercises 18 and 19 for more about this analysis and Cuzco Quechua generally.)

Both Ident(feature) and Max(feature) constraints are widely used in the literature. There is a tendency for authors to use the Ident(feature) constraints except when the Max(feature) constraints are absolutely necessary, as they seem to be in Quechua. In fact, some authors use Ident(feature) and Max(feature) constraints together in the same analysis (e.g., Lombardi 1995/2001). The attraction of Ident(feature) constraints is that they're easier to use, even if Max(feature) constraints are necessary in some cases. Eventually, this issue needs to be sorted out, since presumably phonological theory doesn't need both constraints for every distinctive feature.[9]

4.6.3 Positional faithfulness

Positional faithfulness constraints are based on the general idea that faithfulness constraints can be relativized to certain contexts that have greater prominence (Beckman 1997, 1998, Casali 1996, 1997). These include phonological contexts like word-initial or onset position, as well as morphological contexts like root or lexical morpheme (McCarthy and Prince 1995). Some alternations in the Benue-Congo language Emai illustrate positional faithfulness at work (Casali 1996: 62–68, Schaefer 1987).

In Emai, Onset is satisfied at V_1#V_2 word junctures by deleting either V_1 or V_2. (Under some conditions, V_1 changes into a glide – see exercise 20.) As (45) shows, the choice among these options depends on whether the morphemes that contain V_1 and V_2 are lexical or functional. (The to-be-deleted vowels are highlighted in boldface in the underlying representations.)

(45) Emai descriptive generalization (partial)
   Onsetless syllables are forbidden at $V_1\#V_2$ word juncture. This
   requirement is enforced by:
   a. Deletion of the vowel in the functional morpheme, if one of
       the morphemes is lexical and the other is functional.

/ɔli ebe/	[ɔlebe]	'the$_{func}$ book$_{lex}$'
/uk͡pode ɔna/	[uk͡podena]	'road$_{lex}$ this$_{func}$'

   b. Deletion of the word-final vowel V_1, if both morphemes are
       lexical or both are functional.

/kɔ ema/	[kema]	'plant$_{lex}$ yam$_{lex}$'
/fa edi/	[fedi]	'pluck$_{lex}$ palm-nut$_{lex}$'

The main issue in analyzing Emai is accounting for the choice of which
vowel to delete. There is a preference for not deleting a vowel that
belongs to a lexical morpheme and there is also a preference for not
deleting a vowel that is morpheme-initial. As I noted above, initial position and association with a lexical morpheme are two of the factors
that can lead to greater faithfulness. We therefore require the two
constraints defined in (46).

(46) Positional MAX constraints
   Let input = $i_1i_2i_3 \ldots i_n$ and output = $o_1o_2o_3 \ldots o_m$.
   a. MAX$_{initial}$
       Assign one violation mark for every i_x if i_x is morpheme-
       initial and there is no o_y where $i_x \; \Re \; o_y$.
   b. MAX$_{lexical}$
       Assign one violation mark for every i_x if i_x is in a lexical
       morpheme and there is no o_y where $i_x \; \Re \; o_y$.

In the mapping /uk͡pode$_{lex}$ ɔna$_{func}$/ → [uk͡podena], ONSET compels
deletion of [ɔ], which is initial in a functional morpheme. This shows
that ONSET dominates MAX and MAX$_{initial}$ (47).

(47) ONSET >> MAX and MAX$_{initial}$

/uk͡pode$_{lex}$ ɔna$_{func}$/	ONSET	MAX	MAX$_{initial}$	MAX$_{lexical}$
a. → u.k͡po.de.na	*	*	*	
b. u.k͡po.de.ɔ.na	**W	L	L	

In the mapping $/k\mathfrak{I}_{lex}$ ema$_{lex}/ \rightarrow$ [kema], ONSET compels deletion of a vowel that is final in a lexical morpheme. This shows that ONSET also dominates MAX$_{lexical}$ (48).[10]

(48) ONSET >> MAX and MAX$_{lexical}$

$/k\mathfrak{I}_{lex}$ ema$_{lex}/$	ONSET	MAX	MAX$_{initial}$	MAX$_{lexical}$
a. → ke.ma		*		*
b. k$\mathfrak{I}$.e.ma	*W	L		L

The ranking arguments in (47) and (48) show that ONSET dominates the three MAX constraints, but they tell us nothing about how the MAX constraints are ranked with respect to one another. Because MAX is more stringent than MAX$_{initial}$ and MAX$_{lexical}$, it isn't possible to construct any direct argument for ranking MAX in relation to the two positional faithfulness constraints (see §2.4). But the two positional constraints aren't in a stringency relationship with one another – it is not the case that every segment in a lexical morpheme is also morpheme-initial, nor is it the case that every morpheme-initial segment is also in a lexical morpheme. Therefore, MAX$_{initial}$ and MAX$_{lexical}$ can conflict under the right circumstances. To see the conflict, we need an example where the choice is between deleting the final vowel of a lexical morpheme and the initial vowel of a functional morpheme. The example $/uk\widehat{po}de_{lex}$ $\mathfrak{I}na_{func}/$ has exactly the right properties. The initial vowel of the functional morpheme $/\mathfrak{I}na_{func}/$ deletes, thereby violating MAX$_{initial}$ rather than MAX$_{lexical}$. This shows that MAX$_{lexical}$ is ranked higher.

(49) MAX$_{lexical}$ >> MAX$_{initial}$

$/uk\widehat{po}de_{lex}$ $\mathfrak{I}na_{func}/$	ONSET	MAX	MAX$_{lexical}$	MAX$_{initial}$
a. → u.k̂po.de.na	*	*		*
b. u.k̂po.d$\mathfrak{I}$.na	*	*	*W	L

In OT, a constraint can still be active even when it's crucially dominated. Tableau (49) shows that MAX$_{lexical}$ is active even though it's dominated by ONSET. MAX$_{initial}$ is also crucially dominated, and it too is active under the right conditions, when V_1 and V_2 are both in lexical morphemes. Tableau (50) shows a case of this sort. $MAX_{initial}$ protects the morpheme-initial vowel, so the candidates tie on $MAX_{lexical}$.

(50) Need for $MAX_{initial}$

$/kɔ_{lex}\ ema_{lex}/$	ONSET	MAX	$MAX_{lexical}$	$MAX_{initial}$
a. → ke.ma		*	*	
b. kɔ.ma		*	*	*W

One of the general issues in the theory of positional faithfulness concerns the problem of identifying all of the factors that can define a position of special faithfulness. MAX_{root}, $MAX_{lexical}$ and $MAX_{initial}$ are sensitive to contexts that are defined on morphological or phonological grounds. Ito and Mester (1999) argue that Japanese phonology requires faithfulness constraints to be differentiated by lexical classes. Although the classes have names that refer to etymology, the membership of a morpheme in a particular class can be established by using morphological as well as phonological, orthographic, and etymological criteria. The classes, which they call *strata*, are listed in (51).

(51) Japanese lexical strata (Ito and Mester 1999)
    a. Yamato – consists mostly of native Japanese morphemes.
        Examples: [kotoba] 'word, language', [oto] 'sound'.
    b. Sino-Japanese – includes ancient loans from Chinese.
        Example: [geŋ-go-gaku] 'speak-word-study'='linguistics'.
    c. Mimetic or onomatopoeic
        Examples: [peɾa-peɾa] '(speak) fluently', [mota-mota] 'slowly, inefficiently'.
    d. Foreign – consists of relatively recent loans
        Example: [ɾaŋgeːʤi ɾaboɾatoɾiː] 'language laboratory'.

The evidence that faithfulness constraints are relativized to strata comes partly from differences in the surface sound sequences that each stratum allows. For example, the foreign stratum permits voiced geminate obstruents ([bb], [dd], and [gg]): [webbu] 'web', [kiddo] 'kid', [suɾaggaː] 'slugger'. But the other three strata prohibit them. For example, in the Yamato stratum, although the prefixal root /ow/

'chase' normally causes gemination of a following consonant, it becomes [oN] when the following consonant is a voiced obstruent: /ow-kake-ɾu/ → [okkakeɾu] 'run after' vs. /ow-das-u/ → [ondasu], *[oddasu] 'drive out'. These observations and others like them show the need to differentiate between IDENT$_{foreign}$ and IDENT$_{Yamato}$ constraints; the first is ranked above the markedness constraint against voiced geminates, and the latter is ranked below it.

Another general issue in the theory of positional faithfulness concerns the problem of identifying the appropriate level of representation for the position of special faithfulness. Is the position defined on the input or the output? An example of a positional faithfulness constraint that is sensitive to an input position is MAX(Vː) (Gouskova 2003, McCarthy 2005). This constraint prevents deletion of underlying long vowels. For example, Cairene Arabic has syncope of medial short /i/: /ʃirib-u/ → ['ʃirbu] 'they drank'. It also shortens long vowels in unstressed syllables: /maːsik-hum/ → [ma'sikhum] 'holding them'. When unstressed medial short [i] is derived from /iː/, it's prevented from deleting by MAX(Vː): /ji-ʃiːl-uː-na/ → [jiʃi'luːna], *[jiʃ'luːna] 'they ask us'. So MAX(Vː) protects underlying long vowels from deleting, even when they are shortened in the output.

On the other hand, some faithfulness constraints must be sensitive to a position that is defined on the output. Beckman (1998: chapter 3) proposes a class of IDENT$_{σ}$(feature) positional faithfulness constraints that require vowels that are stressed in the output to have the same feature values as their input correspondents. She uses these constraints to analyze reduction of vowels in unstressed syllables. We previously saw this phenomenon in the Palauan exercise 9 in chapter 2, and the data are repeated in (52).

(52)   Vowel reduction in Palauan

Underlying	Noun	Noun-'my'	Noun-'our'	
/ʔabu/	[ʔáb]	[ʔəbúk]	[ʔəbəmám]	'ashes'
/mada/	[mád]	[mədák]	[mədəmám]	'eyes'
/keri/	[kér]	[kərík]	[kərəmám]	'question'
/ʔuri/	[ʔúr]	[ʔərík]	[ʔərəmám]	'laughter'
/ʔara/	[ʔár]	[ʔərák]	[ʔərəmám]	'price'
/buʔi/	[búʔ]	[bəʔík]	[bəʔəmám]	'spouse'
/duʔa/	[dúʔ]	[dəʔák]	[dəʔəmám]	'skill'
/badu/	[bád]	[bədúk]	[bədəmám]	'rock'

This phenomenon is analyzed by ranking markedness constraints against the peripheral vowels [i], [e], [a], [o], and [u] above IDENT(high), IDENT(low), and IDENT(back). Crucially, these same markedness constraints are dominated by IDENT$_\sigma$(high), IDENT$_\sigma$(low), and IDENT$_\sigma$(back), all of which protect the features of stressed vowels.[11] Since the location of stress is determined by the grammar, this approach only works if IDENT$_\sigma$(feature) constraints are sensitive to the placement of stress in the output. The same goes for constraints like IDENT$_{onset}$(voice) (see exercise 17): because syllabification is determined by the grammar, a consonant's status as an onset can only be known for sure by looking at the output.

As yet, there is no general proposal about which positional faithfulness constraints should be sensitive to input structure and which should be sensitive to output structure. Anyone who proposes a positional faithfulness constraint needs to be attentive to this question and specify the appropriate level of representation in the definition of the constraint.

4.6.4 Faithfulness constraints in the early OT literature

When reading Prince and Smolensky (1993/2004) and other works written in the early days of OT, you will encounter an implementation of faithfulness that looks very different from correspondence theory. Although it's no longer used very much, some acquaintance with it is necessary to make the earlier OT literature accessible.

Prince and Smolensky assume a restriction on GEN called *containment*. Containment says that all of the phonological material in the underlying representation must be preserved ("contained") in every candidate output form. The main difference between containment and correspondence is that there are no literal deletion processes under containment. Instead, the effects of deletion are obtained from the joint action of the three additional assumptions in (53), all of which have pre-OT precedents.

(53)   Assumptions in the containment model of faithfulness
   a.   Underlying representations lack syllable structure.
   b.   Segments may remain unincorporated into syllable structure in the output.
   c.   If a segment is not incorporated into syllable structure in the output, it receives no phonetic interpretation.

Under these assumptions, a deleted segment like the final /g/ of English *long* (cf. *longer*) is literally present in the output of the grammar but syllabically unparsed – [lɔŋ<g>], in their notation. The unsyllabified [g] violates the constraint PARSE, as does any other segment that isn't incorporated into syllable structure. Since remaining unincorporated into syllable structure is effectively the same as deletion in this theory, PARSE is the anti-deletion faithfulness constraint, even though it has the form of a markedness constraint, since it evaluates only the output and not the input–output relation.

Prince and Smolensky make a related assumption about epenthesis. The idea, which also has pre-OT precedents, is that epenthesis isn't literal segmental insertion but rather syllabic overparsing. In overparsing, syllables are created with empty structural positions. (See the box in §1.2.) The phonetic content of these empty positions is determined after the phonological grammar has completed its work. Syllabic positions that are devoid of segmental content violate faithfulness constraints from the FILL family, which militate against such mismatches between segmental and prosodic structure. For example, the phonological output corresponding to Classical Arabic [ʔuktub] (from /ktub/) is [ONktub], where O and N stand for an unfilled onset and nucleus, respectively. The spell-out of O as [ʔ] and N as [u] happens in a separate grammatical module that interprets the output structures derived by the OT phonological grammar.

Correspondence theory has mostly supplanted this earlier implementation of faithfulness. There are several reasons for this. Correspondence theory is more flexible, since it works for processes other than segment deletion and epenthesis. Correspondence theory also avoids some empirical problems with the earlier approach.

For example, containment has trouble with assimilation across deleted segments. In Maltese Arabic, consonant clusters assimilate in voicing (Borg 1997). The language also has vowel deletion in some environments. Clusters created by vowel deletion undergo voicing assimilation: /ni-ktib-u/ → ['nigdbu] 'we write'. If Containment is assumed, however, there is a problem: in ['nigd<i>bu], the consonants that assimilate are separated by an unparsed vowel. Since voicing assimilation never proceeds across a parsed vowel in this or any other language, something needs to be said about why the unparsed vowel is invisible to voicing assimilation despite its presence in the output.

Epenthesis by prosodic overparsing is also problematic. If the output of the phonology is [ONktub], then phonological principles cannot be called on to explain why the O is filled with [ʔ] and N with [u]. But it seems clear that the phonology should have a role in determining the choice of these and other epenthetic segments. Phonology tells us why Classical Arabic, like many other languages, epenthesizes unmarked [ʔ] rather than highly marked [ʕ]. And phonology explains why the epenthetic vowel must agree in [round] with the next vowel: [ʔuktub] has epenthetic [u], but [ʔifʕal] 'do!' and [ʔidʕrib] 'hit!' have epenthetic [i]. (For more on the quality of epenthetic segments, see Lombardi (1997/2002, 2003).)

EXERCISES

15   Define the constraint INTEGRITY, using the definition of UNIFORMITY in (35) as a model. INTEGRITY is violated in the phenomena known as diphthongization or breaking. For example, long /ē/ diphthongizes to [ie] in Slovak (Rubach 1993). (The long vowels /ō/ and /æ/ are also affected, becoming [uo] and [iæ], respectively.) Show the correspondence relations for the segments in the example /ʒēn/ → [ʒien] 'women (gen.)' and explain how your constraint is violated.

16   Finish the analysis of Sanskrit coalescence. Be sure that your analysis answers the following questions: (a) Why is UNIFORMITY violated? (Hint: Consider the alternatives.) (b) What determines the height and backness/rounding of the resulting vowel? (Hint: Consider the ranking of IDENT(+feature) and IDENT(−feature) constraints.)

17   In Lombardi's (1999) analysis of coda devoicing in German (see (39) in chapter 2), there is a positional faithfulness constraint IDENT$_{onset}$(voice) that is violated whenever a segment that is in onset position in the output differs in voicing from its input correspondent. Provide formal definitions for IDENT$_{onset}$(voice) and MAX$_{onset}$(voice). (The latter is much harder.) For the reason given in the text, it's crucial for your constraints to be sensitive to a segment's status as an onset *in the output*.

18   The MAX(+constricted glottis) analysis of Cuzco Quechua is incomplete in certain respects. Answer the following questions that deal with some of the ways in which it's incomplete:

a.   For input /miʧʔu/, why does the winner [miʧʔu] beat the loser *[mʔiʧu]?
b.   What does the input /mʔiʧu/ map to?
c.   In the last row of (44), an unfaithful candidate wins, and that row has W but no L. Why is this a matter for concern? (Hint: Think about language typology.)

d. Solve the problem raised in question (c) by using one or both of the following constraints, which are necessary in Max(feature)/Dep(feature) approaches to faithfulness (McCarthy 2000).

No-Delink(+constricted glottis)
  Let *input segmental tier* $= i_1 i_2 i_3 \ldots i_n$ and *output segmental tier* $= o_1 o_2 o_3 \ldots o_m$.
  Let *input [cg] tier* $= g_1 g_2 g_3 \ldots g_p$ and *output [cg] tier* $= G_1 G_2 G_3 \ldots G_q$.
  Assign one violation mark for every g_w if g_w is autosegmentally associated with i_x, $g_w \, \Re \, G_y$, $i_x \, \Re \, o_z$, and G_y is not associated with o_z.

No-Link(+constricted glottis)
  Let *input segmental tier* $= i_1 i_2 i_3 \ldots i_n$ and *output segmental tier* $= o_1 o_2 o_3 \ldots o_m$.
  Let *input [cg] tier* $= g_1 g_2 g_3 \ldots g_p$ and *output [cg] tier* $= G_1 G_2 G_3 \ldots G_q$.
  Assign one violation mark for every G_y if G_y is autosegmentally associated with o_z, $g_w \, \Re \, G_y$, $i_x \, \Re \, o_z$, and g_w is not associated with i_x.

19 Below, you are given some further facts about Cuzco Quechua. Integrate them into the analysis.

a. If a root contains no plosives, then none of its consonants can be glottalized: hypothetical /m^{ʔ}aru/, /mar^{ʔ}u/, and /m^{ʔ}ar^{ʔ}u/ all map to [maru] rather than their faithful candidates *[m^{ʔ}aru], *[mar^{ʔ}u], and *[m^{ʔ}ar^{ʔ}u].
b. Glottalized consonants are prohibited in syllable codas. Glottalization is therefore limited to the leftmost onset plosive in the word: *[rak^{ʔ}ta] vs. [rakt^{ʔ}a] 'thick'.
c. Glottalization is prohibited in suffixes, and no suffix causes glottalization of the preceding root. Therefore, hypothetical /tanta$_{root}$-k^{ʔ}una$_{suffix}$/ maps to [tantakuna] and not *[tantak^{ʔ}una], *[t^{ʔ}antakuna], or *[tant^{ʔ}akuna].

20 Below, you are given some additional information about the phonology of $V_1 \# V_2$ juncture in Emai. Integrate this into the analysis given in the text. You may assume that mapping an underlying vowel to a surface glide violates the constraint Ident(syllabic). When the vowel and glide differ in height, as they would in a mapping like /e/ → [j], Ident(high) is also violated. You should also assume that Emai has an undominated markedness constraint against falling diphthongs (that is, diphthongs in which the glide follows the vowel, such as [aw] or [aj]).

If V_1 and V_2 are both contained in lexical morphemes and V_1 is a high vowel [i] or [u], then V_1 changes into the homorganic glide [j] or [w]:

/ku ame/   [kwame]   'throw$_{lex}$ water$_{lex}$'
/fi ɔpia/   [fjɔpia]   'throw$_{lex}$ cutlass$_{lex}$'

21 The following Bedouin Arabic data illustrate a process that affects sequences of [a] plus one of the so-called guttural consonants ([ʔ], [h], [ʕ], [ħ], [ʁ], [χ]) when they occur in the same syllable (Al-Mozainy 1981). Analyze this process.

Underlying	Surface	
/baʁθa/	[bʁa.θa]	'gray'
/dahma/	[dha.ma]	'dark red'
/ja-χdim/	[jχa.dim]	'he serves'
/ʔistaʕʒal/	[ʔist.ʕa.ʒal]	'he hurried'
/maχsˤuːr/	[mχa.sˤuːr]	'neglected (masculine singular)'
/maħzuːm-ah/	[mħa.zuː.mah]	'tied (feminine singular)'

Then integrate the following data into your analysis.

Underlying	Surface	
/balah/	[ba.lah]	'dates'
/balah-kin/	[ba.lah.kin]	'your (feminine plural) dates'
/manaʕ/	[ma.naʕ]	'he prohibited'
/manaʕ-na/	[ma.naʕ.na]	'we prohibited'

4.7 Justifying Constraints

4.7.1 The three ways of justifying a constraint

Because OT constraints are claims about the universal constraint component Con, they need to be justified on grounds that go beyond the immediate needs of some analysis. Similarly, when we evaluate the work of others, we should ask how well their constraints are justified. Without such justification, a constraint is really nothing more than a temporary, ad hoc expedient.

There are three types of constraint justification: formal, functional, and typological. Typological justification is the ultimate test of a constraint, but it's also the most time consuming. It's the topic of chapter 5. Formal or functional justification can be quicker, but ultimately they are somewhat less compelling than typological justification. In the best work, typological justification is often buttressed by formal or functional justification. In time-limited exercises like term papers, of course, typological justification for new constraints may be sparse or absent entirely.

4.7.2 Justifying constraints formally

Con is more than just a list of constraints. There is a theory of Con. This theory is as yet incomplete and often only implicit, but it can nevertheless be used to help justify a novel constraint. (For an overview of the theory of Con and references to some of the relevant literature, see McCarthy 2002: 11–22, 43–44.)

The organization of constraints into *families* can often be used to help justify a constraint. Families are sets of formally similar constraints. If a newly proposed constraint fits into a known family, that constraint gains in plausibility. Furthermore, the shared formal properties of constraints in a family can lead to predictions about what other constraints should exist in order to fill out the expected membership of the family. A newly proposed constraint that fulfills one of these expectations gains even more plausibility.

All constraints belong to either the markedness or faithfulness families. Obviously, being able to say that a novel constraint is a member of one of these families contributes only very modestly to its plausibility, since these families (especially markedness) are so large and diverse. On the other hand, if a novel constraint cannot be assigned to either the markedness or the faithfulness family, then it's immediately cast into doubt. It will need to be impeccably and robustly justified on other grounds, and its broader implications for the theory of Con and for OT in general will need to be considered seriously.

Smaller constraint families are composed of constraints with similar definitions. The constraints derived from a single linguistic scale by harmonic alignment constitute a family of constraints. The various Ident(feature) or Max(feature) constraints may be said to constitute a family, and likewise the positional faithfulness constraints are a family. Since some of these featural constraints are also positional faithfulness constraints, the "family" metaphor is obviously being used a bit loosely. A constraint can belong to several families at the same time.

The family of alignment constraints is the best known and currently most populous family of constraints defined by a shared *constraint schema*. A schema is a formula for defining constraints of a particular type. In McCarthy and Prince (1993a), a schema for defining alignment constraints is proposed. This schema, which is given in (54), provides a general means of defining constraints that require matching the edges of grammatical and/or prosodic constituents. In the definition, *GCat* stands for the set of grammatical categories {root, stem, syntactic word, XP, . . . }, and *PCat* stands for the set of prosodic categories {syllable, foot, phonological word, phonological phrase, . . . }.

(54) Alignment constraint schema (McCarthy and Prince 1993a: 80)
  ALIGN(Cat1, Edge1, Cat2, Edge2) $=_{def}$
    ∀ Cat1 ∃ Cat2 such that Edge1 of Cat1 and Edge2 of Cat2 coincide,
    where Cat1, Cat2 ∈ PCat ∪ GCat and Edge1, Edge2 ∈ {Right, Left}.

Any constraint that can be defined according to the alignment schema may be said to belong to the alignment family and to receive some formal justification on that basis.

The alignment schema in (54) has a couple of problematic properties that shouldn't go unmentioned. The most conspicuous is that it does not specify how violations are to be counted. (The issue is raised, but left "open for future exploration," in McCarthy and Prince (1993a: 135–136).) This led to inconsistency in subsequent work, and that is one reason why I am now recommending that constraints be defined using the "Assign one violation for every . . ." formula. Another issue turns on the claim implicit in (54) that same-edge and different-edge alignment belong to the same constraint family. All of the examples of alignment constraints in this book have been same-edge constraints: ALIGN(Cat1, Left, Cat2, Left), which we have been writing as ALIGN-LEFT(Cat1, Cat2); and ALIGN(Cat1, Right, Cat2, Right), which we have been writing as ALIGN-RIGHT(Cat1, Cat2). Different-edge alignment constraints seem to be much less common and more idiosyncratic in character, so perhaps they don't belong in the alignment family and the schema should be restated to allow reference to only a single edge.[12]

Local conjunction is another schema for defining new constraints (Smolensky 1995, 1997, 2006). Local conjunction provides a rationale for constraints that rule out "the worst of the worst." For example, we have various reasons for thinking that CON includes a constraint against voiced obstruents like [bdg]: *VOICED-OBSTRUENT (*VOI). We also think there is a constraint NO-CODA. By conjoining *VOICED-OBSTRUENT and NO-CODA, we get a third constraint that is violated by voiced obstruents in coda position. Intuitively, if voiced obstruents are marked and codas are marked, then perhaps voiced obstruent codas are even more marked. They are the worst of the worst. This combined constraint could be responsible for coda devoicing processes in German and other languages. German allows codas and it allows voiced obstruents, but it does not allow codas that are also voiced obstruents. That is the "conjunction" part of local conjunction.

Formally, the local conjunction of two different constraints CONST1 and CONST2 in the domain δ, written [CONST1 & CONST2]$_δ$, is a constraint that is violated once by any instance of δ that contains violations of CONST1 and CONST2.[13] In the example just discussed, the conjoined constraint is [*VOICED-OBSTRUENT & NO-CODA]$_{segment}$. As tableau (55) shows, this conjoined constraint dominates IDENT(voice) in German, and IDENT(voice) itself dominates one of the constraints in the conjunction, *VOICED-OBSTRUENT. (For a different approach to German voicing alternations, see examples (38) and (39) in chapter 2.)

(55) [*VOICED-OBSTRUENT & NO-CODA]$_{segment}$ in German

/bad/	[*VOI & NO-CODA]$_{segment}$	ID(voice)	*VOI
a. → bat		*	*
b. bad	*W	L	**W
c. pat		**W	L

The "local" part of local conjunction has to do with the proximity of the two constraint violations to one another. Tableau (55) shows a potential use for a constraint against voiced obstruents that are also codas. In that case, one could say that the same *segment* is violating both *VOICED-OBSTRUENT and NO-CODA, so the domain of the conjunction is "segment." But we probably have no use for a constraint that would prohibit any *syllable* that contained violations of both *VOICED-OBSTRUENT and NO-CODA: *[VOICED-OBSTRUENT & NO-CODA]$_{syllable}$. That is, we don't seem to find languages that prohibit *[bad], *[bat], and *[pad] but allow [ba] and [pat]. Likewise, we don't have much use for a constraint that bans having a voiced obstruent and a coda in the same word: [*VOICED-OBSTRUENT & NO-CODA]$_{word}$. This constraint would rule out *[batak] while still allowing [bata] and [patak]. In other words, it makes sense to conjoin *VOICED-OBSTRUENT and NO-CODA when we are looking at a single segment, but not when we are looking at a syllable or a word. It's important to specify the domain whenever a conjoined constraint is proposed. In the literature, one sometimes sees conjunction without a domain, but that's an oversight.

Pharyngealization harmony in Palestinian Arabic supplies a nice example where local conjunction can be used to justify a constraint (Davis 1995, McCarthy 1997). First, a bit of background. Pharyngealization is represented by the feature [retracted tongue root], or [RTR] for short. For articulatory reasons (see §4.7.3), there are markedness constraints against simultaneously retracting the tongue root and raising or fronting the tongue body (Archangeli and Pulleyblank 1994). Those constraints are defined in (56). Because of these constraints, front or high segments tend to resist becoming [+RTR], which means they can block pharyngealization harmony.

(56) Constraints on [RTR]
   a. *RTR/FRONT
      Assign one violation mark for every segment that is [+RTR, −back].
   b. *RTR/HIGH
      Assign one violation mark for every segment that is [+RTR, +high].

The interesting case is a southern Palestinian dialect where rightward pharyngealization harmony is blocked only by [i], [j], [ʃ], or [ʤ] (see (57)). This is exactly the class of segments that are both front *and* high. Harmony isn't blocked by segments that are front but not high like [e] or segments that are high but not front like [u] (see (58)).

(57) Blocking of pharyngealization harmony by [+high, −back]

Underlying	Surface	
/tˤiːn-ak/	[tˤiːnak]	'your mud'
/sˤajjaːd/	[sˤaˤjjaːd]	'hunter'
/ðˤajj-aːt/	[ðˤaˤjjaːt]	type of noise (plural)

(58) No blocking of harmony by [−high, −back] or [+high, +back]

Underlying	Surface	
/sˤeːf-ak/	[sˤeˤːfˤaˤkˤ]	'your sword'
/tˤuːb-ak/	[tˤuˤːbˤaˤkˤ]	'your blocks'

We'll assume that rightward harmony of [+RTR] is demanded by the constraint ALIGN-RIGHT(+RTR, word). (See §4.8 on alignment and assimilation processes.) Tableau (59) summarizes the evidence for ranking these constraints. The winner~loser pair in (b) requires ALIGN-RIGHT(+RTR, word) to dominate *RTR/FRONT. The pair in (c) requires ALIGN-RIGHT(+RTR, word) to dominate *RTR/HIGH. But the pair in (a) says that *RTR/FRONT or *RTR/HIGH dominates ALIGN-RIGHT(+RTR, word) – a contradiction.

(59)   Insufficiency of the constraint set without local conjunction

	Inputs	Winners	Losers	*RTR/Front	*RTR/High	Align-R
a.	/tˤiːn-ak/	tˤiːnak	tˤiˤːnˤaˤkˤ	W	W	L
b.	/sˤeːf-ak/	sˤeˤːfˤaˤkˤ	sˤeːfak	L		W
c.	/tˤuːb-ak/	tˤuˤːbˤaˤkˤ	tˤuːbak		L	W

Although the constraint system in (59) is inadequate, local conjunction offers a nice way of extending this system to make it adequate. Rightward assimilation of [+RTR] is only blocked by segments that are front *and* high, so we need the conjoined constraint [*RTR/Front & *RTR/High]$_{segment}$. As shown in (60), it's ranked above Align-Right(+RTR, word). The individual constraints that make up the conjunction are both ranked below this alignment constraint. In this way, the conjoined constraint rules out the worst of the worst; a segment that is [+RTR], front, and high is categorically worse than a segment that is just [+RTR] and front or just [+RTR] and high.

(60)   [*RTR/Fr & *RTR/Hi]$_{segment}$ >> Align-R(+RTR, word) >>
         *RTR/Fr, *RTR/Hi

Winners	Losers	[*RTR/Fr & *RTR/Hi]$_{seg}$	Align-R	*RTR/Fr	*RTR/Hi
tˤiːnak	tˤiˤːnˤaˤkˤ	W	L	W	W
sˤeˤːfˤaˤkˤ	sˤeːfak		W	L	
tˤuˤːbˤaˤkˤ	tˤuːbak		W		L

The local conjunction of two markedness constraints is another markedness constraint, as in this example. The local conjunction of two faithfulness constraints is likewise another faithfulness constraint. For instance, if a low vowel becomes high – for example, /æ/ → [i] – then both [low] and [high] change their feature values. This is a violation of the conjoined faithfulness constraint [Ident(low) & Ident(high)]$_{segment}$. (On conjoining markedness with faithfulness, see Łubowicz (2002) and Ito and Mester (2003b).) Constraints can be conjoined with constraints that are themselves the products of conjunction, thereby singling out the worst of the worst of the worst, etc.[14]

Self-conjunction of constraints is a somewhat different notion. The conjunction of constraint C with itself in the domain δ, usually written as C_δ^2, is violated once by any instance of δ that contains at least (in some versions, exactly) two distinct violations of C (Smolensky 1997, 2006). In phonology, self-conjunction of markedness constraints has been used as the basis for a theory of sonority (in Smolensky's work) and for a theory of dissimilation (Alderete 1997, Ito and Mester 1998, 2003a).[15] In syntax, it has been used as the basis for a theory of barriers (Legendre, Smolensky, and Wilson 1998).

We can look at dissimilation as an example of self-conjunction. In Seri and Classical Arabic, [ʔVʔ] syllables are prohibited; the second glottal stop is deleted instead (see (61)). Glottal stops are characterized by the feature value [+constricted glottis]. Since there are languages without any [+constricted glottis] segments, there must be a markedness constraint against this feature value: *[+constricted glottis]. The conjunction of this constraint with itself in the domain of the syllable, *[+constricted glottis]$_\sigma^2$, dominates MAX in Seri and Arabic. The same constraint conjunction, but with a larger domain, is responsible for a similar restriction on entire words in Cuzco Quechua.

(61)   [ʔ] dissimilation in Seri and Arabic
    a.   Seri (Marlett and Stemberger 1983: 628)

Underlying	*Surface*	
/ʔa-aːʔ-sanx/	[ʔaː.sanx]	'who was carried'
	*[ʔaːʔ.sanx]	
/ʔi-ʔ-aːʔ-kaʃni/	[ʔi.ʔaː.ka.ʃni]	'my being bitten'
	*[ʔi.ʔaːʔ.ka.ʃni]	

    b.   Arabic (Wright 1971: 18)

Underlying	*Surface*	
/ʔa-ʔman-a/	[ʔaː.ma.na]	'he believed'
	*[ʔaʔ.ma.na]	
/ʔ-u-ʔmin-u/	[ʔuː.mi.nu]	'I believe'
	*[ʔuʔ.mi.nu]	
/ʔi-ʔman-u-n/	[ʔiː.maː.nun]	'belief'
	*[ʔiʔ.maː.nun]	

Constraint schemas or local conjunction are useful for justifying constraints that seem to be needed on other grounds. But can they be used to predict the existence of constraints? That is, should we expect to find alignment constraints for all combinations of prosodic and grammatical categories? Can every markedness constraint be conjoined with every other markedness constraint, in every possible domain? Can constraint conjunction apply recursively, without limit? With our present level of understanding, the answer to all of these questions probably has to be no. The literature includes some work proposing restrictions on alignment (McCarthy and Prince 1994b) and local conjunction (Fukazawa 1999, Fukazawa and Miglio 1998, Ito and Mester 1998, 2003b, Łubowicz 2005, 2006), but matters are far from settled. The theory of CON is progressing, but it isn't yet fully predictive.

EXERCISES

22   There are two restrictions on voicing in the native or Yamato vocabulary of Japanese (§4.6):

(i)   Voiced geminate obstruents are prohibited: *[bb], *[dd], *[gg], etc.).
(ii) No root can contain more than one voiced obstruent: *[gotoba], *[kodoba], *[godoba], etc.

Analyze these observations. Your analysis should map hypothetical /kadda/ to [katta] and not *[kadda], and it should map hypothetical /gada/ to [gata] and not *[gada].

23   Once you are confident of your analysis of these aspects of the phonology of the Yamato vocabulary, extend your analysis to account for the observations below about the foreign vocabulary stratum (Kawahara 2006). When dealing with the variation, do the same thing as you did in exercises 8 and 9.

Words containing geminate voiced obstruents are allowed

[sunobbu]	'snob'
[habbuɾu]	'Hubble'
[ɾeddo]	'red'
[heddo]	'head'
[eggu]	'egg'
[fuɾaggu]	'flag'

Words containing two voiced obstruents are allowed

[bagiː]	'buggy'
[bobu]	'Bob'
[dagu]	'Doug'
[giga]	'giga-'

But in words containing two voiced obstruents, one of which is also geminate, the geminate optionally devoices

[gebbuɾusu] ~ [geppuɾusu]	'Göbbels'
[guddo] ~ [gutto]	'good'
[beddo] ~ [betto]	'bed'
[deibiddo] ~ [deibitto]	'David'
[doɾaggu] ~ [doɾakku]	'drug'

4.7.3   Justifying constraints functionally

Functionalist approaches to linguistic phenomena look for explanations that go beyond the properties of formal grammar. In the limit, a radically functionalist view would see formal grammar as completely superfluous, but a much more widely held position is that analyses and explanations should combine formal and functional properties. OT has recently emerged as a significant force in shaping these developments.

Prior to OT, the study of formal grammar and the study of functional explanations were conducted almost entirely separately. We can use the situation in phonology to illustrate this, though syntax would do almost as well. Phonological theory in the tradition of *SPE* was purely formal; the causes of phonological processes were "placed entirely outside grammar, beyond the purview of formal or theoretical analysis, inert but admired" (Prince and Smolensky 1993/2004: 234). The following quotation nicely summarizes that position:

> Any adequate theory of phonology must contain postulates that will define natural sound changes. Although many of these can be expressed by appeal to the notion of assimilation defined over the features of a feature system, it is clear that not all natural sound changes fit into this mold. For example, many languages have a rule converting consonants to ʔ or *h* in preconsonantal and final position. Such a process is clearly not assimilatory in nature. Nevertheless phonological theory must have some apparatus for expressing the fact that neutralization to a glottal stop in these positions is a natural rule as opposed to, say, neutralization to *l*. (Kenstowicz and Kisseberth 1979: 251)

These "postulates" were usually expressed as tendencies: stressed vowels tend to be long, geminates tend to be voiceless, languages tend to have triangular vowel systems (*i-a-u* or *i-e-a-o-u*), and so on. The postulates are functional, since they aid articulation (geminates are voiceless) or perception (vowel systems are triangular).

Functional tendencies are clearly an important force in shaping phonological systems. But at that time the tendencies stood outside the formal grammar. For a theory based on applying rules, a tendency was a fairly useless concept. Furthermore, the tendencies were often contradictory. Easy articulation is often purchased at the expense of perceptual distinctness, and maintaining perceptual distinctness often requires more careful and therefore more difficult articulation. The existence of contradictory tendencies led to considerable skepticism of functionalism in formalist circles, as if functionalism couldn't offer anything better than just-so stories.

OT's relevance to this issue should now be apparent. In OT, there is no need to have an apparatus of formal rules and a separate apparatus of functional tendencies to explain the rules. Instead, violable constraints model the tendencies, and those constraints themselves make up the formal grammar, with ranking to settle conflicts between constraints. The formal grammar and the functional explanation can in principle be united in an OT constraint hierarchy.

Functional justification for constraints is an important idea in both phonology and syntax, so I will say a bit about each. In phonology, as was already noted, ease of articulation and ease of perception are the standard modes of explanation. For example, Japanese and other languages show the need for a constraint against voiced geminate obstruents (§4.6.3). The functional explanation for this constraint is aerodynamic (Ohala 1983). To maintain voicing, air has to flow through the glottis, so subglottal pressure has to remain higher than supraglottal pressure. If there is closure or a narrow constriction at the lips or tongue, then supraglottal pressure increases, threatening to exceed subglottal pressure. Some passive expansion of the tissues helps to absorb the additional supraglottal pressure, but if the closure is maintained for a long time, then the task of maintaining voicing becomes more difficult. Thus, voiced geminates present an articulatory problem that isn't shared by voiced singletons or voiceless geminates. Voiced geminates aren't impossible – Arabic has them, for example – but they are hard, and a constraint against voiced geminates is the formal instantiation in an OT grammar of this articulatory difficulty.

Other constraints have perceptual explanations. As we saw in Emai (§4.6), initial position in a root or morpheme is often a location where greater faithfulness is maintained, requiring constraints like $\text{MAX}_{\text{initial}}$. Why initial position and not some other position in the word? Beckman (1998: chapter 2) proposes that greater faithfulness in initial position facilitates lexical access, since there is considerable evidence from the psycholinguistic literature that initial syllables are particularly important in lexical access and word recognition.

There is by now quite a large body of work on functional explanations for phonological constraints in OT. Hayes, Kirchner, and Steriade (2004) is a recent anthology; Paul Boersma's postings on ROA and on his home page (www.fon.hum.uva.nl/paul/) are another resource. A list of earlier references can be found in McCarthy (2002: 233); another early reference is Archangeli and Pulleyblank (1994).

As we have seen, the functional explanations for constraints in OT phonology generally involve reducing the burden on the speaker or hearer. Similar explanations have also been proposed in OT syntax. For example, Haspelmath (1999: 185) proposes a speaker- and hearer-oriented explanation for the constraint STAY (§2.9): "Leaving material in canonical positions helps the hearer to identify grammatical relationships and reduces processing costs for the speaker." Aissen (2003) develops a theory of why some languages have overt case marking on objects only if they are relatively marked (e.g., because they are of high animacy – see §4.5 and exercise 11). "[I]t is those direct objects which most resemble typical subjects that get overtly case-marked . . . Functionally, the overt marking of atypical objects facilitates comprehension where it's most needed, but not elsewhere" (pp. 437–438). Bresnan and Aissen (2002) is an excellent explanation of a functional approach to OT syntax. It's also a response to Newmeyer (2002), which is a critique of this kind of research.

Some phonologists would probably insist that no constraint is legitimate unless it has a functional motivation. Some others aren't so strict, though they would regard a functional explanation as powerful justification for a constraint. Still others would place functional factors alongside formal factors as equally valid ways of justifying a constraint, and a few would deny any role for functional considerations. A concern with providing functional motivation for constraints isn't as widespread in the OT syntax literature, though that may change.

Although functional explanations are common, especially in phonology, they sometimes overlook an important question: How are functionally motivated constraints connected with their explanations? How do functional factors account for or explain the existence of a constraint? There are three different approaches to answering these questions:

(i) *Phylogeny* Constraints are innate. They developed during human evolution in conjunction with the development of the human brain, vocal tract, and perceptual system, and that is when functional factors entered the picture. Chomsky and Lasnik (1977: 437) entertain such an explanation for their *[$_{NP}$ NP tense VP] filter, which appears to be grounded in processing considerations. A worry: Is natural selection sufficient to account for the emergence of an innate prohibition on voiced geminates or other constraints? (See Bresnan and Aissen 2002: 89 for relevant discussion.)

(ii) *Ontogeny* Constraints aren't innate. Learners discover the aerodynamic difficulties with voiced geminates in their early experience of trying to produce these sounds. As a result, they set up a constraint against them (Hayes 1999). An objection: Even if the ambient language has no voiced geminates, the learner still needs to learn the constraint, since there is abundant evidence that speakers know constraints that couldn't have been acquired from the ambient language (see Bresnan and Aissen 2002: 87–89 for a summary). Since the ambient language isn't stimulating the learner to attempt voiced geminates, he or she has to learn about their aerodynamic problems during a prelinguistic babbling phase. That would be fine if we could believe in the myth "that appear[s] to have originated with Roman Jakobson: that at the height of babbling, infants produce the sounds of all the world's languages with ease" (Salzmann 2001: 605). But that myth has been thoroughly debunked. For one thing, babbling is strongly influenced by the ambient language (Vihman 1996: 18). And for another, babbling shows "an essential absence of many rare sounds of languages such as ejectives, implosives, lingual trills, and lateral clicks, sounds that are well-documented as occurring in certain languages around the world" (Oller 2000: 52).

(iii) *Diachrony* Constraints aren't innate. They are induced by learners from the ambient language. Functional factors enter the picture in historical change, and constraints only seem to be functionally motivated because they have to deal with the results of earlier changes (Blevins 2004, Hale and Reiss 2000, Myers and Hansen 2005, Newmeyer 2002). The worry is the same as with the previous explanation: speakers know constraints that they couldn't have learned from the ambient language.

4.8 A Classified List of Common Phonological Markedness Constraints

This list is by no means exhaustive, but it's complete enough to be useful. Since a synopsis like this cannot delve into complex issues, I often refer to the relevant literature rather than try to resolve questions here.

Authors will sometimes use a *cover constraint* when they suspect that some phenomenon requires two or more constraints but the details of those constraints aren't known yet or don't seem relevant. The cover constraint substitutes for ("covers") the unknown or less relevant constraints. Commonly used cover constraints from the early OT literature are identified below, and whenever possible I cite research on the details of the constraint family that they cover.

Syllable constraints (mostly from Prince and Smolensky 1993/2004)

Also see §4.5 on sonority and its role in defining constraints.

Name	*Assign one violation mark for every . . .*
*[μμμ]$_\sigma$	. . . superheavy (=trimoraic) syllable. (In chapter 2, this constraint was referred to as *Complex-Syllable*.) For other constraints governing the weight of syllables and related matters, see Morén (1999), Rosenthall (1994), and Sherer (1994).
*Complex-Onset (*Comp-Ons) *Complex-Coda (*Comp-Coda)	. . . tautosyllabic cluster in the specified position. Sometimes combined into the cover constraint *Complex.
*C^{unsyll} *or* *Appendix (*App)	. . . unsyllabified segment. Same as Exhaustivity(syllable) or Prince and Smolensky's faithfulness constraint Parse.
*Nucleus/X (*Nuc/X)	. . . segment in a syllable nucleus that belongs to sonority class X. Sometimes called *Peak/X. Replaces the HNuc constraint in Prince and Smolensky (1993/2004).
*Onset/X *Coda/X	. . . segment in the specified position that belongs to the sonority class X. Sometimes combined into the cover constraint *Margin/X.

Name	Assign one violation mark for every...
CODA-CONDITION (CODA-COND)	...consonant place specification that is not linked with an onset consonant (Ito 1989). Sometimes used as a cover constraint for a collection of restrictions on consonant clusters that includes the CODA-CONDITION proper.
NO-CODA	...coda consonant.
NO-VOICED-CODA	...voiced obstruent in coda position (or perhaps voiced obstruent not licensed by association with an onset). Disputed – see §6.6.
NUCLEUS (NUC) *or* HAVE-NUCLEUS (HAVE-NUC)	...syllable without a nucleus. Same as HEADEDNESS(syllable).
ONSET	...onsetless syllable.
SONORITY-SEQUENCING (SON-SEQ)	...onset or coda cluster with inappropriate sonority profile, such as Russian [rta] 'mouth'. This is a common cover constraint for a family of constraints on the sonority profiles of tautosyllabic clusters. See Baertsch (1998, 2002) for a proposal.

Prosodic hierarchy constraints (mostly from Selkirk 1995)

Name	Assign one violation mark for every...
EXHAUSTIVITY(X) (EXH(X))	...constituent of type $X - 1$ that is not dominated by some constituent of type X. (See §4.5.1.)
HEADEDNESS(X) (HEAD(X))	...constituent of type X that lacks a head. (See §4.5.1.)
NONRECURSIVITY(X) (NONREC(X))	...constituent of type X that is dominated by a constituent of type X. (See §4.5.1.)
WRAP(X, Y)	...constituent of type X that is not contained in a constituent of type Y (Truckenbrodt 1995).

Prosody–morphology interface constraints

Name	Assign one violation mark for every ...
ALIGN-LEFT/ RIGHT(MCat, PCat)	... instance of the morphological category MCat whose left/right edge does not coincide with the left/right edge of some instance of the prosodic category PCat (McCarthy and Prince 1993a). Possible values for MCat include root, stem, syntactic word, and XP. Possible values for PCat include syllable, foot, phonological word, and phonological phrase. The definition here is categorical; on whether such constraints are assessed gradiently, see McCarthy (2003c).
Lx≈Pr	... lexical (=morphosyntactic) word that is not parsed as a prosodic (=phonological) word (after Prince and Smolensky 1993/2004: 51). Usually, this constraint is assumed to be inherent in GEN.

Stress-related constraints (mostly from Prince and Smolensky 1993/2004)

Name	Assign one violation mark for every ...
*CLASH	... pair of adjacent stressed syllables.
*LAPSE	... pair of adjacent unstressed syllables.
FOOT-BINARITY (FT-BIN)	... foot that does not contain at least two moras or syllables (McCarthy and Prince 1986/1996, Prince 1983). Often split into FOOT-BINARITY(mora) and FOOT-BINARITY(syllable). Sometimes also split into FOOT-BINARITY-MAX and FOOT-BINARITY-MIN, requiring no more than/no fewer than two moras or syllables.
FOOT-FORM (FT-FORM)	Cover constraint frequently used for FOOT-BINARITY, GROUPINGHARMONY, and RHYTHMTYPE.

Name	*Assign one violation mark for every . . .*
GROUPINGHARMONY (GRPHARM)	. . . (HL) foot. (H and L stand for heavy and light syllables, respectively.) After Prince (1990).
I/TL	. . . disyllabic trochaic foot with unequal weight ('HL) or ('LH), or disyllabic iambic foot with equal weight (L'L). Abbreviation for the Iambic/Trochaic Law of Hayes (1995).
NON-FINALITY (NON-FIN)	Usually refers to one of the following three constraints, which are more precise. Should not be used, since the greater precision is needed.
NON-FINALITY(foot)	. . . word-final syllable that belongs to a foot.
NON-FINALITY(head(word))	. . . word-final foot bearing main stress.
NON-FINALITY('σ)	. . . stressed word-final syllable.
PARSE-SYLLABLE (PARSE-σ)	. . . unfooted syllable. Same as EXHAUSTIVITY(foot).
PEAK-PROMINENCE (PK-PROM)	. . . stressed syllable with low intrinsic prominence. A cover constraint, it sometimes substitutes for STRESS-TO-WEIGHT, and it has also been applied to stress-resistant vowels like [ə]. See de Lacy (2002: chapters 3, 4) and references there on sonority-driven stress.
RHYTHMTYPE=IAMB (RHTYPE=I *or* IAMB)	. . . foot whose head is not final. Same as ALIGN-RIGHT(head(foot), foot).
RHYTHMTYPE=TROCHEE (RHTYPE=T *or* TROCHEE)	. . . foot whose head is not initial. Same as ALIGN-LEFT(head(foot), foot).
STRESS-TO-WEIGHT (SWP)	. . . stressed light syllable. (Also see PEAK-PROMINENCE.)
WEIGHT-TO-STRESS (WSP)	. . . unstressed heavy syllable. From Prince (1990).

The following alignment constraints are also frequently used when analyzing stress. (See (54) and §4.5 for the definitions and some applications of these constraints.) Some of them may be referred to by other names – e.g., EDGEMOST in Prince and Smolensky (1993/2004) or ALL-FOOT-LEFT/ALL-FOOT-RIGHT in McCarthy and Prince (1993a).

ALIGN-LEFT(foot, word), ALIGN-RIGHT(foot, word)
ALIGN-LEFT(word, foot), ALIGN-RIGHT(word, foot)
ALIGN-LEFT(head(word), word), ALIGN-RIGHT(head(word), word)

Intrasegmental constraints

These are constraints against marked feature values or feature combinations, without regard to the segmental or prosodic context in the which the affected segment occurs. It's not practical to inventory all such constraints that have been proposed, but the overall structure of the system is relatively clear.

Name	*Assign one violation mark for every . . .*
*[+voice] (*or* *VOICE)	. . . segment bearing this feature value. There must be one such constraint for every marked feature value. It's not clear whether all features have a marked value and which value is the marked one.
*[+constricted glottis]	
*[+nasal]	
*[+round]	
etc.	
*BACK/NONROUND	. . . segment with this combination of feature values. This particular combination is likely marked for perceptual reasons: rounding enhances the backness percept by lowering F2 even further than backing alone does. There are presumably many other constraints against feature combinations that are perceptually marked.
etc.	
*DORSAL	. . . consonant bearing this place of articulation feature. On the relative markedness of the different places of articulation, see de Lacy (2002), Gnanadesikan (1995/2004), Lombardi (1997/2002), and Prince and Smolensky (1993/2004: section 9.1.2). De Lacy also discusses greater faithfulness to segments with marked place features.
*LABIAL	
*CORONAL	

Name	Assign one violation mark for every . . .
*RTR/HIGH (or HIGH/ATR) *RTR/FRONT (or FRONT/ATR) etc.	. . . segment that is [+RTR, +high], etc. As we saw in §4.7.2, these particular combinations are marked for articulatory reasons. There are presumably many other constraints against feature combinations that are articulatorily marked.
*V# or FINAL-C	. . . phonological word that ends in a vowel. (See Gafos 1998, McCarthy 1993, McCarthy and Prince 1994a, Orie and Bricker 2000: 299–300, Wiese 2001 for some of the evidence for this constraint.)

Dissimilation constraints

See §4.7.2 on local self-conjunction.

Miscellaneous intersegmental constraints

Many constraints on segment sequences are ad hoc or cover constraints that deal with assimilation, which is discussed below. The table lists a few intersegmental constraints that aren't primarily associated with assimilation processes.

Name	Assign one violation mark for every . . .
*NÇ or *NT	. . . sequence of a nasal consonant followed by a voiceless obstruent (Pater 1999). See §3.6.
NO-DIPHTHONG (NO-DIPH)	. . . diphthong. See §4.3.
NO-GEMINATE (NO-GEM)	. . . geminate consonant.
NO-LONG-VOWEL or *Vː	. . . long vowel.
NO-VOICED-GEMINATE or *DD	. . . voiced geminate obstruent. See §4.6.3, exercise 22, and §4.7.3.
SYLLABLE-CONTACT (SYLL-CON)	. . . heterosyllabic consonant cluster with rising sonority. This is a cover constraint; see Gouskova (2004) for a detailed proposal.

Assimilation constraints

Since assimilation, including long-distance harmony, is such a common phonological process, it may come as a surprise that there are major unresolved questions about the markedness constraints involved.

To illustrate the issues, we can use the example of nasal harmony in Warao in (62). Nasality assimilates rightward from an underlying nasal consonant, affecting vowels and glides (including [h]). Other consonants, such as [k] in 'shadow', block nasal assimilation because they cannot become nasalized and they cannot be skipped by the nasalization process.

(62) Nasal harmony in Warao (Osborn 1966)

Underlying	*Surface*	
/moau/	mõãũ	'give it to him!'
/nao/	nãõ	'come!'
/inawaha/	inãw̃ãh̃ã	'summer'
/mehokohi/	mẽh̃õkohi	'shadow'
/naote/	nãõte	'he will come'
/panapana hae/	panãpanã h̃ãẽ	'it is a porpoise'

Two main approaches to phenomena like this can be found in the literature, and both have significant problems that are discussed by Wilson (2003, 2004, 2006) and McCarthy (2004). One approach involves local constraints that penalize sequences of adjacent or nearby segments that differ in the harmonizing feature. The constraint *NV$_{[-nasal]}$ in example (59) of chapter 2 is an example of such a constraint, since it's violated by any sequence of adjacent segments that are [+nasal][−nasal]. The constraint *iCu in exercise 1 in this chapter is another example. Constraints like these are often used on an ad hoc basis when assimilation is local or when the author is not primarily interested in the details of the assimilation process. They are sometimes referred to as local agreement or AGREE constraints.

Local agreement constraints work fine for examples like /moau/ → [mõãũ]. As tableau (63) shows, only the winning candidate has no [+nasal][−nasal] sequences, so only this candidate obeys *NV$_{[-nasal]}$. (The sequences that violate *NV$_{[-nasal]}$ are in boldface.)

(63) $*NV_{[-nasal]}$ applied to /moau/ → [mõãũ]

/moau/	$*NV_{[-nasal]}$	IDENT(nasal)
a. → mõãũ		***
b. **mo**au	*W	L
c. **mõ**au	*W	*L
d. **mõã**u	*W	**L

Now look at (64). Perfect satisfaction of $*NV_{[-nasal]}$ is impossible because *[nãõt̃ẽ] violates an undominated constraint against nasalizing voiceless plosives. All of the remaining candidates contain a [+nasal][−nasal] sequence, so they tie on $*NV_{[-nasal]}$. This leaves the decision up to the faithfulness constraint, which wrongly favors *[naote]. This is a general problem with using local constraints to compel long-distance assimilation: they predict a "sour grapes" effect, where harmony fails entirely if it cannot make it all the way to the end of the word.[16] This sort of thing never happens. Harmony processes always go as far as they can, and then they stop.

(64) $*NV_{[-nasal]}$ fails with /naote/ → [nãõte]

/naote/	$*NV_{[-nasal]}$	IDENT(nasal)
a. → nãõte	*	**
b. **na**ote	*	L
c. **nã**ote	*	*L

The other approach to assimilation uses alignment constraints. This approach presupposes autosegmental feature representation (Goldsmith 1976a, 1976b), as illustrated in (65). ALIGN-RIGHT(+nasal, word) says that every token of the feature value [+nasal] (*N* in (65)) must be associated with the word-final segment. If it's evaluated like ALIGN-RIGHT(foot, word) (see (21)), then it will produce the desired result. Unlike local agreement, this approach does not predict a sour grapes effect.

(65)   Harmony with ALIGN-RIGHT(+nasal, word) (*N* stands for [+nasal])

N N | | /panapana hae/	ALIGN-R(+nasal, word)	IDENT(nasal)
a. → *N N* panapanahae	7	5

b.   *N   N*
   | |
   panapanahae
	12 W	L

c.   *N   N*
   |
   panapanahae
	8 W	4 L

Approaches to harmony based on alignment have other problems, however. Because ALIGN-RIGHT(+nasal, word) is violated once for every segment intervening between [+nasal] and the end of the word, it could in principle be satisfied by deleting segments if MAX is ranked low enough. As (66) shows, deletion would affect segments that are inaccessible to harmony because of an intervening blocking segment. Since no known language deletes segments for this reason, it's certainly an unwelcome prediction of the alignment approach.

(66)   A bad prediction: better harmony via deletion

N | /naote/	ALIGN-R(+nasal, word)	MAX	IDENT(nasal)
a. → *N* nao		**	**

b.   *N*
   |
   naote
	****W	L	L

c. *N* naote	**W	L	**

My recommendation to readers of this book is to avoid local agreement constraints unless the assimilation process has little relevance to the main point under discussion. Because local agreement constraints do not work when there is blocking, and blocking is very common in harmony, they are likely to cause problems when doing an analysis. Use alignment constraints, but be aware that they make strange predictions when they dominate MAX, DEP, and other faithfulness constraints besides IDENT. The proper treatment of harmony remains an open research question.

Notes

1 These formulations come from Prince and Smolensky (1993/2004: 20) and Pesetsky (1998: 357), respectively. In both cases, it should be noted, the constraints were offered as temporary expedients rather than serious proposals about CON.

2 See Bakovic (2000: chapter 6) for a different view.

3 The Nakanai nominalizer has another allomorph, the suffix /la/, which is used with stems that are longer than two syllables: [sagegela] 'happiness'. See McCarthy (2003c) for an analysis of how the choice between /il/ and /la/ is made.

4 The constraint WEIGHT-TO-STRESS is abbreviated WSP because it is the successor to the Weight-to-Stress Principle of Prince (1990).

5 On why there must not be a constraint against the least marked element on a scale, see Gouskova (2003).

6 Tagalog [um] marks realis aspect and infinitive in so-called actor-focus verbs. There is also an infix [in], with a similar phonological distribution, that marks realis aspect in verbs of other types.

7 Because plosives in [s] clusters are voiceless and unaspirated, they are identical to English "voiced" plosives, which are also usually voiceless and unaspirated word-initially. Thus, there is no actual difference between the adult pronunciation of orthographic *k* in *skin* and the [g] transcription in the child's pronunciation.

8 See Wolf and McCarthy (forthcoming) for a somewhat different formalization of correspondence theory.

9 A further possibility is that some features systematically require IDENT(feature) constraints and others systematically require MAX(feature) constraints. See Davis and Shin (1999: 291) for a proposal.

10 Examples like /oa$_{Lex}$ isi$_{Func}$ ɔi$_{Func}$/ → [oasɔi] show that Emai tolerates vowel sequences word-internally. Although Schaefer (1987) does not say how these sequences are syllabified, presumably at least some are heterosyllabic – [o.a.sɔi], perhaps. Onsetless syllables are therefore tolerated

in word-medial position, though they are eliminated word-intially. This is an indication that the high-ranking markedness constraint in Emai is specific to word-initial syllables. Flack (2007) has identified a number of languages that require onsets word-initially but not medially, and this leads her to distinguish between ONSET$_{word}$ and ONSET$_{syllable}$ constraints. Emai's tolerance for onsetless syllables phrase-initially (e.g., [uk͡podena]) may have a similar etiology.

11 See Crosswhite (2004) for a theory of vowel reduction that does not use positional faithfulness.

12 There is an example of a different-edge alignment constraint in McCarthy and Prince (1993a, 1993b). It is the constraint ALIGN(suffix, left, phonological word, right), which is required in the analysis of Axininca Campa augmentation.

13 Constraint conjunction is equivalent to logical disjunction if obeying a constraint is regarded as T and violating it as F.

14 For additional references on local conjunction, see McCarthy (2002: 43).

15 Suzuki (1998: 96–97) offers a critique of the local-conjunction theory of dissimilation.

16 The phrase "sour grapes" is an allusion to Aesop's fable of the fox and the grapes. When the fox cannot reach the grapes, he declares that they're probably sour anyway. I believe that Jaye Padgett was the first person to use this phrase in a phonological context.

5

Language Typology and Universals

5.1 Factorial Typology

Prince and Smolensky (1993/2004) propose that CON is universal and that constraint ranking is the only difference between grammars. This means that the permutations of CON define the entire range of permitted variation in the grammars of human languages. The claim, then, is that every permutation of CON is a possible grammar, and every existing language has a grammar that is a permutation of CON. Since the study of variation between languages is called typology, and since the number of permutations of n elements is the quantity n factorial ($n! = 1*2*$ ... $*n$), the grammars predicted by some hypothesized CON are referred to as its *factorial typology*.

Having $n!$ possible grammars doesn't mean that there are $n!$ possible languages. Often, it doesn't matter how two constraints are ranked. In §2.4, we saw some of the limits on ranking arguments. The limits involve situations where two constraints could be ranked either way and still produce the same language.

Often, though, changing the ranking of two or more constraints really does change the language that is generated, and therefore studying the effects of ranking permutation is an important aspect of empirical research in OT. A hypothesis about some constraint in CON might start out as an idea about how to analyze a specific language, but it doesn't end there. If a constraint is truly universal, then it can and should have consequences that go beyond solving a specific problem in a specific language. We need to consider what happens when that constraint is ranked differently with respect to other constraints. In other words, we need to explore the effects of any newly proposed constraint on factorial typology. If the new constraint leads to a plausible typology with solid empirical support, then we have the strongest possible justification for that constraint. But if the constraint leads to implausible typological predictions or, worse yet, undermines an appropriately restrictive typology that we already have, then that constraint is highly suspect. Less dramatically, factorial typology can help us to decide among competing definitions of a constraint or to settle questions like whether there are separate faithfulness constraints against vowel and consonant epenthesis. Methods for studying the factorial typology of a constraint set are described in this chapter (§5.3–§5.5).

Factorial typology is important for other reasons as well. If we are studying the properties of some phenomenon or construction across different languages, then factorial typology is how we'll explain our observations (§5.6). And if we have hypotheses about universals of language, then factorial typology is the place to look for explanations for them (§5.2).

5.2 Language Universals and How to Explain Them in OT

A *language universal* is an observation that is believed to hold of all possible human languages and to have significance for linguistic theory. Universals come in three basic flavors: no language has x; every language has x; and every language that has x also has y. Universals of the first two types are called *absolute* or *categorical*, and universals of the last type are called *implicational*.

An example of a proposed absolute universal from phonology is this:

> There are languages lacking syllables with initial vowels and/or syllables with final consonants, but there are no languages devoid of syllables with initial consonants or of syllables with final vowels. (Jakobson 1962: 256)

An example of an implicational universal from phonology: if a language allows consonant clusters syllable-finally, then it also allows single consonants syllable-finally. (Many of the universals in Greenberg (1978) are stated like this.) From syntax: if a language has overt case marking on nonhuman objects, then it also has overt case marking on human objects (Aissen 2003).

The general explanatory strategy for absolute language universals in OT depends on factorial typology. If every language has x, then x must be the optimal candidate for some input under every ranking of

CON. This means that there can be no markedness constraint in CON that assigns a violation mark to every single instance of *x*. (It also means that there can be no collection of markedness constraints in CON that together have this effect.)

Take, for example, the absolute universal that every language has some syllables with onsets. To account for it, we have to say that CON doesn't include a constraint NO-ONSET that is violated by consonant-initial syllables and obeyed by vowel-initial syllables. If NO-ONSET were to exist, then ranking it above ONSET and, say, DEP would produce a language that consistently avoids syllables with onsets (e.g., /panta/ → [əp.an.ət.a]. (The topic of constraints that must not be in CON is revisited in §5.5.)

Richness of the base (§1.7) is an important aspect of this explanation. Because of richness of the base, there is no way of skewing the inputs so as to subvert the universal. For example, there can be no language whose inputs consist entirely of vowels.

Implicational universals involve relative markedness. If the presence of *x* in a language always entails the presence of *y*, and not vice versa, then *x* must be universally more marked than *y*. In OT, "universally more marked" means "more marked regardless of the ranking". To that end, CON must include a markedness constraint that favors *x* over *y* and no markedness constraint that favors *y* over *x*.

For example, if a syllable ends in one or more consonants, it violates the constraint NO-CODA. If it ends in two or more consonants, it also violates *COMPLEX-CODA. Both CVC and CVCC syllables violate NO-CODA, but CVCC syllables also violate *COMPLEX-CODA. CVCC syllables are therefore more marked than CVC syllables, and the presence of CVCC syllables in a language entails the presence of the less marked CVC syllables. No matter where faithfulness is ranked relative to NO-CODA and *COMPLEX-CODA, there is no way of analyzing a language that allows CVCC syllables and prohibits CVC syllables. This is shown by the contradictory ranking requirements in (1). Such a language is predicted not to exist under this theory of CON.

(1) Impossibility of language with CVCC syllables but not CVC

Inputs	Winners	Losers	NO-CODA	*COMPLEX-CODA	DEP
/patka/	pa.tə.ka	pat.ka	W		L
/pantka/	pant.ka	pa.nə.tə.ka	L	L	W

The explanation for this implicational universal, like the explanation for the absolute universal, depends on banning certain hypothetical constraints from CON and on richness of the base. CON cannot contain a markedness constraint that all CVC syllables violate and some CVCC syllables obey. Such a constraint, were it to exist, would subvert the implicational relation. And no language can subvert the implicational relation by preemptively eliminating all inputs like /patka/.

Many implicational universals refer to linguistic scales, such as the sonority scale. An example: in any language that has liquids and allows nasals to be syllable nuclei, then liquids are also possible syllable nuclei. The techniques for relating scales to constraint systems and their typological implications were addressed in §4.5.

It is clear from this discussion that most predictions about language universals in OT depend on having specific hypotheses about the constraints in CON. There are also some universals, however, that follow from OT's inherent properties with only the most meager assumptions about CON. Of these, the most striking is *harmonic improvement* (Moreton 2003, Prince 1997a).

Since CON contains only markedness and faithfulness constraints, a necessary condition for an unfaithful candidate to win is that it be less marked than the faithful candidate. If the input is /bi/, then every faithfulness constraint favors faithful [bi] as the output. For unfaithful [be] to win, then, some markedness constraint M must favor [be] over [bi], and it must be ranked higher than every faithfulness constraint that is violated in the /bi/ → [be] mapping. OT's basic assumptions entail that unfaithfulness is possible only when it improves markedness, where improvement is determined by the universal markedness constraints as they are ranked in the language in question.

Moreton develops a formal proof of this result and explores its empirical consequences. The most important of these is that no OT grammar can analyze a language with a system of mappings like /bi/ → [ba] and /ba/ → [bi]. (This is referred to as a *circular chain shift*.) To understand why, consider the requirements that a grammar would have to satisfy:

- From input /bi/, the candidate [ba] is more harmonic than the candidate *[bi]. Since *[bi] is completely faithful and [ba] is not, the constraint that favors [ba] over *[bi] has to be a markedness constraint. Therefore, the highest-ranking markedness constraint that distinguishes between [ba] and *[bi] has to favor [ba] over *[bi]

- From input /ba/, the output [bi] is more harmonic than the candidate *[ba]. Since *[ba] is completely faithful, the constraint that favors [bi] over *[ba] has to be a markedness constraint. Therefore, the highest-ranking markedness constraint that distinguishes between [bi] and *[ba] has to favor [bi] over *[ba].

There's an obvious contradiction here. No markedness constraint ranking can simultaneously favor [ba] over *[bi] and [bi] over *[ba]. Markedness constraints can't distinguish between identical output forms that happen to come from different inputs, and faithfulness constraints can never favor unfaithful outputs. The circular chain shift is therefore unanalyzeable with OT's standard resources.

5.3 Investigating the Factorial Typology of a Constraint Set

Any investigation of factorial typology in OT starts with a set of constraints, a set of inputs, and a set of candidate outputs from those inputs. Because all and only the permutations of those constraints are possible grammars, the constraints make predictions about what are possible and impossible languages. A language, in the sense employed throughout this discussion, is a system of input–output mappings.

An obvious approach to studying factorial typology uses brute force to evaluate the consequences of all possible constraint rankings. First, list all of the permutations of a set of constraints, and then run some collection of inputs and their candidate sets through each of the rankings. In exercise 1, you are asked to use this method to determine the factorial typology of a set of four constraints, given just two inputs with three candidates each. That is probably the limit of what can reasonably be done by hand. Even with a computer, the brute force method rapidly becomes intractable as the number of constraints increases, since the number of permutations increases very rapidly indeed. (To give a sense of the numbers we're talking about, 13! is approximately equal to the world population.)

There is an alternative way of studying factorial typology. Instead of listing all the grammars and determining what languages they predict, we can list the languages and determine whether there is a grammar that will produce them. In other words, given a set of inputs and their candidates, we can ask which combinations of input–output mappings are consistent with some ranking of the constraints. The consistency check is extremely quick, since it uses RCD (§2.11), which rapidly detects inconsistency by failing to find a ranking. This method, with some additional efficiencies, is how OTSoft does factorial typology (Hayes, Tesar, and Zuraw 2003). (As we'll see later, the logic of OT allows us to improve on this method as well. See Prince (2006a: 4–8) for a lucid introduction to the problem.)

For example, we can apply this method to the constraints and possible input–output mappings in the Yawelmani analysis. When RCD is applied to the set of mappings consisting of /laːn-hin/ → [lan.hin], /taxaː-kʼa/ → [ta.xaː.kʼa], /xat-kʼa/ → [xat.kʼa], and /ʔilk-hin/ → [ʔi.lik.hin], it finds a ranking. Therefore, the factorial typology of those constraints allows a language that produces these outputs from their respective inputs. But when RCD is applied to this same set of mappings except that /taxaː-kʼa/ maps to [ta.xaː.kʼaʔ], it cannot find a ranking. Therefore, the factorial typology does not admit a language that produces this combination of outputs from their respective inputs. This logically possible language is excluded from the factorial typology. (Bear in mind that the term "language" refers to a set of input–output mappings and not just a set of outputs. Many rankings of the given constraints can produce the set of outputs [lan.hin], [ta.xaː.kʼaʔ], [xat.kʼa], and [ʔi.lik.hin], if the inputs are identical to the outputs.)

I submitted the Yawelmani Excel file ((96) in chapter 2) to OTSoft, requesting that it compute the factorial typology over this set of constraints, inputs, and candidates. To keep things manageable, I made one simplification, removing the constraint *C^unsyll and the candidates that violate it on the grounds that they would tell us very little that we don't already get from looking at *Complex-Syllable and its violators. Since six constraints remain, there are 6! = 720 possible rankings. And since the four inputs have 4, 5, 4, and 3 candidates, respectively, there are 4*5*4*3 = 240 logically possible "languages."[1] OTSoft finds rankings for only the 18 combinations in (2).

(2) Factorial typology from OTSoft

	/laːn-hin/	/taxaː-kʼa/	/xat-kʼa/	/ʔilk-hin/
a.	lan.hin	ta.xakʼ	xat.kʼa	ʔi.lik.hin
b.	lan.hin	ta.xakʼ	xat.kʼa	ʔilk.hin
c.	lan.hin	ta.xakʼ	xat.kʼa	ʔil.hin
d.	lan.hin	ta.xakʼ	xatkʼ	ʔilk.hin
e.	lan.hin	ta.xakʼ	xat	ʔil.hin
f.	lan.hin	ta.xakʼ	xat.kʼaʔ	ʔi.lik.hin
g.	lan.hin	ta.xaː.kʼa	xat.kʼa	ʔi.lik.hin
h.	lan.hin	ta.xaː.kʼa	xat.kʼa	ʔilk.hin
i.	lan.hin	ta.xaː.kʼa	xat.kʼa	ʔil.hin
j.	lan.hin	ta.xaː.kʼaʔ	xat.kʼaʔ	ʔi.lik.hin
k.	lan.hin	ta.xaː.kʼaʔ	xat.kʼaʔ	ʔilk.hin
l.	laːn.hin	ta.xaː.kʼa	xat.kʼa	ʔilk.hin
m.	laːn.hin	ta.xaːkʼ	xatkʼ	ʔilk.hin
n.	laːn.hin	ta.xaː.kʼaʔ	xat.kʼaʔ	ʔilk.hin
o.	laː.ni.hin	ta.xaː.kʼa	xat.kʼa	ʔi.lik.hin
p.	laː.ni.hin	ta.xaː.kʼaʔ	xat.kʼaʔ	ʔi.lik.hin
q.	laː.hin	ta.xaː.kʼa	xat.kʼa	ʔil.hin
r.	laː.hin	tax	xat	ʔil.hin

Our goal in studying the factorial typology of a constraint set is to develop predictions about possible and impossible languages, and then test those predictions against the facts. Clearly, the constraint set we have chosen is making lots of predictions – we know that because there are 240 logically possible combinations of outputs, but only the 18 combinations in (2) are predicted to be possible languages. What happened to the other ~92% of the logical possibilities? Why are some languages possible but not others?

We need a way of finding and understanding patterns and predicted universals in complex typologies like (2). I'll explain how to do this by coming at it backwards: I'll start with a pattern in (2), then I'll show why this pattern emerges from the constraint set, and finally I'll discuss the general problem of finding other patterns.

The pattern in (2) that we'll analyze is this: every system that has [ta.xaː.kʼaʔ] also has [xat.kʼaʔ], but not vice versa. (The systems with both of these forms are (j), (k), (n), and (p). The system with only [xat.kʼaʔ] is (f).) In other words, if the epenthetic mapping /taxaːkʼa/ → [ta.xaː.kʼaʔ] is optimal, then the epenthetic mapping /xatkʼa/ → [xat.kʼaʔ] must also be optimal, under this particular constraint set. To make progress studying this factorial typology, we need to understand why the constraint set has this entailment.

Prince (2006a) explains how implicational relationships in factorial typology follow from the logic of OT (§2.12). Here I will summarize some of his ideas, using Yawelmani to illustrate. Example (3) contains the ERCs required for the mapping /taxaːkʼa/ → [ta.xaː.kʼaʔ] to be optimal, and example (4) does the same for /xatkʼa/ → [xat.kʼaʔ]. The ERCs for [xat.kʼaʔ] are a proper subset of the ERCs for [ta.xaː.kʼaʔ]. Since ERCs express ranking requirements, this means that all of the ranking requirements that have to be met for [xat.kʼaʔ] to win also have to be met for [ta.xaː.kʼaʔ] to win. The ERCs for [xat.kʼaʔ] tell us that Max dominates Dep or Max-C and *Complex-Syllable dominate Dep. The ERCs for [ta.xaː.kʼaʔ] say exactly the same thing, plus they also require *V# to dominate Dep. Therefore, any ranking of these constraints that selects [ta.xaː.kʼaʔ] as optimal will also necessarily select [xat.kʼaʔ] as optimal. That is the reason why the computed factorial typology in (2) contains no systems with [ta.xaː.kʼaʔ] and without [xat.kʼaʔ].

(3) /taxaːkʼa/ → [ta.xaː.kʼaʔ] ERCs

Winner	Losers	*V#	*Comp-Syll	Id(long)	Dep	Max-C	Max
ta.xaː.kʼaʔ	ta.xaː.kʼa	W			L		
	ta.xaːkʼ		W		L		W
	ta.xakʼ			W	L		W
	tax				L	W	W

(4) /xatkˀa/ → [xat.kˀaʔ] ERCs

Winner	Losers	*V#	*Comp-Syll	Id(long)	Dep	Max-C	Max
xat.kˀaʔ	xat.kˀa	W			L		
	xatkˀ		W		L		W
	xat				L	W	W

There is a similar relationship between the ERC sets for two mappings with consonant deletion, /laːn-hin/ → [laː.hin] and /ʔilk-hin/ → [ʔil.hin]. The [ʔil.hin] ERCs in (6) are a proper subset of the [laː.hin] ERCs in (5). We therefore expect to find that every system with [laː.hin] also has [ʔil.hin], but not vice versa. That is correct: only (q) and (r) in (2) have [laː.hin], and both also have [ʔil.hin] as well. Systems (c), (e), and (i) have [ʔil.hin] without [laː.hin], however. That is expected, since for [laː.hin] to be optimal Ident(long) must dominate Max-C and Max, whereas this ranking condition isn't necessary for [ʔil.hin] to be optimal. (The ranking condition can be read directly off of (5), since it's the ERC that isn't shared with (6).)

(5) /laːn-hin/ → [laː.hin] ERCs

Winner	Losers	*V#	*Comp-Syll	Id(long)	Dep	Max-C	Max
laː.hin	lan.hin			W		L	L
	laːn.hin		W			L	L
	laː.ni.hin				W	L	L

(6) /ʔilk-hin/ → [ʔil.hin] ERCs

Winner	Losers	*V#	*Comp-Syll	Id(long)	Dep	Max-C	Max
ʔil.hin	ʔilk.hin		W			L	L
	ʔi.lik.hin				W	L	L

We also find a proper subset relationship between the ERC sets for [laː.ni.hin] and [ʔi.lik.hin] in (7) and (8). Therefore, languages with the

/laːn-hin/ → [laː.ni.hin] mapping are a proper subset of languages with the /ʔilk-hin/ → [ʔi.lik.hin] mapping in the predicted typology.

(7)   /laːn-hin/ → [laː.ni.hin] ERCs

Winner	Losers	*V#	*Comp-Syll	Id(long)	Dep	Max-C	Max
laː.ni.hin	lan.hin			W	L		
	laːn.hin	W			L		
	laː.hin				L	W	W

(8)   /ʔilk-hin/ → [ʔi.lik.hin] ERCs

Winner	Losers	*V#	*Comp-Syll	Id(long)	Dep	Max-C	Max
ʔi.lik.hin	ʔilk.hin		W		L		
	ʔil.hin				L	W	W

Another way to approach factorial typology using ERC sets is to look for ERCs that assert inconsistent ranking requirements. For example, the last row of (5) and (6) is the ERC (e, e, e, W, L, L). The last row of (7) and (8) is the ERC (e, e, e, L, W, W). These two ERCs fuse to (e, e, e, L, L, L), which means that they are inconsistent. (ERC fusion is defined in (104) in chapter 2.) Therefore, this constraint set predicts that no language can combine the mapping /laːn-hin/ → [laː.hin] with /ʔilk-hin/ → [ʔi.lik.hin], nor can any language combine /laːn-hin/ → [laː.ni.hin] with /ʔilk-hin/ → [ʔil.hin]. This is equivalent to what we discovered by looking at the subset relations among the ERC sets.

Ultimately, the goal of studying factorial typology is to come up with predictions that can be checked across languages. Therefore, the most useful predictions are those that abstract away from the details of any particular language. For instance, the result of looking at (5) through (8) can be understood more abstractly as a claim about how languages with maximal CVC syllables deal with underlying /CVːC/ and /CVCC/ sequences. Consonant deletion and vowel epenthesis are options in both cases, but the /CVːC/ case has an additional option, vowel shortening, that isn't available to /CVCC/ inputs. This difference is reflected by the fact that (6) is a proper subset of (5), and likewise (8) is a proper subset of (7). In both cases, the mismatch that makes the subset relation proper involves an ERC where IDENT(long) is the only winner-favoring constraint and *[lan.hin] is the loser that it disfavors. The general typological prediction that emerges from this constraint set, then, is that languages with maximal CVC syllables will treat /CV:C/ and /CVCC/ sequences exactly alike, unless the /CV:C/ sequences undergo shortening. This prediction might very well turn out to be wrong, but even that would be progress, since it would tell us that one of our assumptions about CON is wrong.

This example illustrates a point that harks back to chapter 1 as well as to the beginnings of OT. An analysis in OT is more than just a parochial description of some facts. It's implicitly a claim about universal grammar. By virtue of the assumptions that CON is universal and that languages differ in ranking, OT is an *inherently typological theory of language*. Analyses of particular languages are deeply connected with claims about all languages. That is why I have emphasized the importance of studying the typological consequences of newly proposed constraints. See §5.4 on how to do this.

This example also illustrates a general technique for studying factorial typology. Suppose we have already done an analysis of some phenomenon in a particular language and we want to know what this analysis implicitly predicts about other languages. We have a set of constraints that are used in the analysis and, if the techniques recommended in chapter 2 have been followed, we also have a set of inputs and candidates that thoroughly exercise those constraints. In general, to study factorial typology competently, we need candidates with various combinations of favoring and disfavoring relations across the various constraints.

If the number of inputs and candidates isn't too large, the factorial typology can be explored by creating ERC sets like (3) through (8) for each candidate. Do not rank the constraints; instead, maintain a consistent ordering of the constraints to facilitate comparison. Look at the ERC sets for outputs derived from different inputs. If two outputs from different inputs have identical ERC sets, then they will always appear together in the languages predicted by the factorial typology. In other words, the presence of either input-output mapping in a language entails the presence of the other input-output mapping. If there is a subset relation between their ERC sets, then the one with the stricter ranking requirements entails the presence of the other one in the predicted languages. (The W-extension and L-retraction rules in (99) of chapter 2 are also useful for investigating typology; see Prince (2006a: 17) for an example.) Restate any observations in a more abstract way, so that they are meaningful as claims about language in general rather than about some language with these specific output forms.

Another technique for studying factorial typology begins with creating a violation tableau in Excel for all inputs and their candidates. Submit this tableau to OTSoft with a request that it prepare a "compact factorial typology summary file" like (2). Inspect the result for patterns of cooccurrence: Do some winners imply the presence of other winners? Are there some combinations that never cooccur? One trick to help find these patterns is to copy the factorial typology summary file into a spreadsheet or word processor, and then sort the data on different columns (e.g., sort by columns 3, 4, and 1, in that order of priority). There is even a computer program that will help you find these patterns (see Arto Anttila's page www.stanford.edu/~anttila/research/software.html). When patterns are found, construct the ERC sets in order to explain them.

It is important to understand why the constraint set makes certain typological predictions and not others. This isn't just a matter of intellectual curiosity; sometimes, the typological predictions may turn out to be wrong, and we need to know where the constraints have gone wrong. We also need to understand the reasons for success.

EXERCISES

1 List all of the permutations of the constraints ONSET, NO-CODA, MAX, and DEP. Then, for each ranking, determine the winner in each of the following candidate sets. That is, you are to figure out the factorial typology of this constraint set over just these inputs and candidates.

Input	Candidates
/apa/	[a.pa], [ʔa.pa], [pa]
/kat/	[kat], [ka.tə], [ka]

2 In your solution to exercise 1, which rankings produced identical results? What do these rankings have in common?

3   The text illustrates the study of factorial typology starting from the analysis of Yawelmani. Use the same method to study factorial typology starting from one or more of the following analyses:

a.   English *do*-support (§2.9).
b.   Maori consonant deletion (exercise 8 in chapter 2).
c.   Palauan vowel reduction (exercise 9 in chapter 2).
d.   Diola Fogny (exercise 21 in chapter 2).
e.   Axininca Campa (exercise 34 in chapter 2).

5.4   Using Factorial Typology to Test New Constraints

The initial impetus for adding a constraint to Con may be a specific problem in the analysis of some particular language. But that isn't enough. Because Con is universal, the implications of introducing a new constraint cut across languages. We need to understand how the new constraint affects the predicted typology.

For example, the result of epenthesis in Yawelmani /ʔilk-hin/ is [ʔi.lik.hin] and not *[ʔil.ki.hin]. We haven't tried to explain this yet, and so *[ʔil.ki.hin] has been omitted from the set of candidates. A proposed constraint that will distinguish between these two candidates is Align-Right(stem, syllable). This constraint is violated if the final segment /k/ of the stem /ʔilk/ isn't syllable-final in the output. It favors [ʔi.lik.hin] over *[ʔil.ki.hin], since stem-final [k] is syllable-final in the former but not the latter. As originally formulated in Prince and Smolensky (1993/2004) and McCarthy and Prince (1993a, 1993b), Align-Right(stem, syllable) also disfavors deletion of /k/, since a deleted segment is perforce not syllable-final. For the sake of the argument, I assume that formulation here.

What effect does Align-Right(stem, syllable) have on the factorial typology? Adding it to the spreadsheet and using OTSoft shows that there are now 29 predicted languages instead of the 18 languages predicted under the simpler system of constraints. The additional 11 languages are listed in (9).

(9)   Effect of ALIGN-RIGHT(stem, syllable) on factorial typology

	/laːn-hin/	/taxaː-kʔa/	/xat-kʔa/	/ʔilk-hin/
a.	lan.hin	ta.xakʔ	xat	ʔi.lik.hin
b.	lan.hin	ta.xakʔ	xat	ʔilk.hin
c.	lan.hin	tax	xat	ʔi.lik.hin
d.	lan.hin	tax	xat	ʔilk.hin
e.	lan.hin	tax	xat	ʔil.hin
f.	laːn.hin	ta.xaː.kʔa	xat.kʔa	ʔi.lik.hin
g.	laːn.hin	ta.xaː.kʔaʔ	xat.kʔaʔ	ʔi.lik.hin
h.	laːn.hin	tax	xat	ʔi.lik.hin
i.	laːn.hin	tax	xat	ʔilk.hin
j.	laː.hin	ta.xaː.kʔa	xat.kʔa	ʔi.lik.hin
k.	laː.hin	tax	xat	ʔi.lik.hin

Three entailments of the simpler constraint system were discussed in the previous section: [ta.xaː.kʔaʔ] ⇒ [xat.kʔaʔ], [laː.hin] ⇒ [ʔil.hin], and [laː.ni.hin] ⇒ [ʔi.lik.hin]. Clearly, the [laː.hin] ⇒ [ʔil.hin] entailment does not hold under the constraint system that includes ALIGN-RIGHT(stem, syllable), since there are now two predicted languages ((j) and (k) in (9)) that combine [laː.hin] with [ʔi.lik.hin].

What happened to the [laː.hin] ⇒ [ʔil.hin] entailment? What exactly has changed as a result of adding ALIGN-RIGHT(stem, syllable) to the constraint set? Look at the ERC sets. In (10) and (11) I have added ALIGN-RIGHT(stem, syllable) to the ERC sets (5) and (6). For [ʔil.hin] to be optimal, DEP must dominate ALIGN-RIGHT(stem, syllable). But that ranking isn't necessary for [laː.hin] to be optimal. Because of ALIGN-RIGHT(stem, syllable), the [ʔil.hin] ERCs are no longer a subset of the [laː.hin] ERCs, and the [laː.hin] ⇒ [ʔil.hin] entailment no longer holds. Using the simpler constraint system, we arrived at the general typological prediction that languages with maximal CVC syllables will treat /CVːC/ and /CVCC/ sequences exactly alike, unless the /CVːC/ sequences undergo shortening. That prediction no longer follows when the constraint set includes Align-Right(stem, syllable), since it can favor epenthesis over deletion in [ʔi.lik.hin] but not [laː.ni.hin].

(10) ERC set (5) with Align-Right(stem, syllable) added

Winner	Losers	*V#	*Comp-Syll	Id(long)	Dep	Max-C	Max	Align-R
laː.hin	lan.hin			W		L	L	L
	laːn.hin		W			L	L	L
	laː.ni.hin				W	L	L	

(11) ERC set (6) with Align-Right(stem, syllable) added

Winner	Losers	*V#	*Comp-Syll	Id(long)	Dep	Max-C	Max	Align-R
ʔil.hin	ʔilk.hin		W			L	L	L
	ʔi.ilk.hin				W	L	L	L

If we were doing a real research project on typology, now would be a good point to move from theoretical to empirical investigation. We have one constraint system that predicts identical treatment of /CVːC/ and /CVCC/ when there is no shortening, and we have another system that does not make this prediction. We can then look at some languages in an effort to check whether the prediction holds up or not. If it doesn't hold up, then there is no objection from this quarter to including Align-Right(stem, syllable) in Con. If it does hold up, however, then we would want to reconsider Align-Right(stem, syllable). Perhaps it could be redefined so that it does not favor epenthesis over deletion in [ʔi.lik.hin], while still making the necessary distinction between [ʔi.lik.hin] and [ʔil.ki.hin]. Or perhaps we should pursue some entirely different approach to ruling out [ʔil.ki.hin] in Yawelmani.

This illustration of the typological consequences of adding Align-Right(stem, syllable) highlights an important aspect of OT. The potential effects of constraint interaction are complex and not very easy to grasp in advance of actually working through the typology. A seemingly small change – adding one constraint to rule out one problematic candidate, as we did here – can have substantial unanticipated effects on the kinds of languages that are predicted to be possible. It's extremely important to think and work through the typological consquences of decisions about adding some constraint to CON. By using OTSoft and ERC analysis, we can come to a fairly good understanding of the typological consequences of such moves. We are then well situated to begin looking for relevant evidence in other languages.

4   Suppose you change the constraint set in exercise 1 by replacing DEP with separate DEP-V and DEP-C constraints that prohibit vowel and consonant epenthesis, respectively. How does this affect the factorial typology? Use ERC analysis to explain your answer.

5.5   Factorial Typology When CON Isn't Fully Known

We don't know all of the constraints in CON. And in any individual analysis we typically only discuss a rather small set of constraints, omitting some known constraints and of course all of the as-yet unknown constraints. The constraints we omit from discussion could affect the results of ranking permutation. As a practical matter, then, how is it ever possible to study factorial typology in a responsible way?

There is an answer to this conundrum. We can explain what sort of constraint, if it existed, would interfere with the typological prediction. In other words, a desirable typological result for a specific constraint system can be coupled with a claim about constraints that must *not* be in CON for this result to hold. The discussion of hypothetical NO-ONSET in §5.2 briefly illustrated this sort of reasoning, and we'll look at another example in greater depth here.

The example comes from the theory of infixing reduplication in McCarthy and Prince (1993b). The theory starts from the analysis of a specific case, Timugon Murut (12). This language has CV reduplication (in boldface) that is prefixed when the word starts with a consonant but is infixed after the initial syllable when the word starts with a vowel.

(12) Infixing reduplication in Timugon Murut (Prentice 1971)
    a. Copy initial CV

        [bu.lud]   'hill'   [**bu**.bu.lud]   'ridge'

        [li.mo]   'five'   [**li**.li.mo]   'about five'

    b. Skip initial V(C) and copy following CV

        [u.lam.poj]   no gloss   [u.**la**.lam.poj]   no gloss

        [a.ba.lan]   'bathes'   [a.**ba**.ba.lan]   'often bathes'

        [om.po.don]   'flatter'   [om.**po**.po.don]   'always flatter'

First, a bit of preliminary phonotactic business. As we saw in chapter 1, Timugon Murut allows onsetless syllables initially and medially: [am.bi.lu.o] 'soul'. This observation shows that Max and Dep dominate Onset.

(13) Max, Dep >> Onset

/ambiluo/	Max	Mep	Onset
a. → am.bi.lu.o			**
b. ʔam.bi.lu.ʔo		**W	L
c. bi.lu	***W		L

Next, reduplicative infixation. We will adopt the assumption that infixes are minimally misaligned prefixes or suffixes (see §4.5). The alignment constraint is called Align-Left(RED, stem). ("RED" denotes the reduplicative morpheme.) Some other constraint must be compelling violation of it. That constraint is Onset, as shown in tableau (14). This tableau is interesting because it exemplifies emergence of the unmarked, which was explained in chapter 1. The constraint Onset is violated by surface forms of Timugon Murut, since it's crucially dominated by Max and Dep. Nonetheless, Onset is active when satisfaction of Max and Dep isn't at issue – when instead the issue is satisfaction of Align-Left(RED, stem). That is the situation in which Onset emerges in Timugon Murut.

(14)   ONSET >> ALIGN-LEFT(RED, stem)

/RED-ulampoj/	MAX	DEP	ONSET	ALIGN-L
a. → u.**la**.lam.poj			*	*
b. **u**.u.lam.poj			**W	L
c. u.lam.**po**.poj				****W
d. **la**.lam.poj	*W		L	L
e. **ʔu**.ʔu.lam.poj		*W	L	L

With consonant-initial roots, ONSET can be satisfied without infixation. In that case, infixation is harmonically bounded, as (15) shows.

(15)   No infixation with C-initial stem

/RED-balan/	MAX	DEP	ONSET	ALIGN-L
a. → **ba**.ba.lan				
b. ba.**la**.lan				**W

This analysis of Timugon Murut leads us to a hypothesis about language typology. Here and in §4.5, we've seen infixation resulting from grammars where ONSET or NO-CODA dominates ALIGN-LEFT(affix, word). One of the typological questions that this raises is the following: Can a nonreduplicative prefix have the same distribution as the reduplicative prefix does in Timugon Murut? That is, could this constraint system analyze a language with a nonreduplicative prefix /ta/ that is prefixed to consonant-initial roots ([ta.ba.lan]) and infixed after an initial onsetless syllable ([u.ta.lam.poj])? What if the nonreduplicative prefix had some other shape, such as /a/, /an/, or /tan/? Or is the Timugon Murut pattern of infixation limited to reduplicative prefixes?

To answer this question, we try to construct a consistent ERC set where the winners are [ta.ba.lan] and [u.ta.lam.poj]. As (16) shows, this isn't possible with the constraints under discussion. Because the intended winner [u.ta.lam.poj] and its competitor [ta.u.lam.poj] tie on ONSET by violating it once each, [ta.u.lam.poj] must win because it's better aligned. That is why the [u.**ta**.lam.poj]~[**ta**.u.lam.poj] row of (16) has an L but no W. The candidate [u.**ta**.lam.poj] can never win with this constraint set.

(16)   No way to get [**ta**.ba.lan] and [u.**ta**.lam.poj]

Winners	Losers	ONSET	NO-CODA	ALIGN-L
ta.ba.lan	ba.**ta**.lan			W
u.**ta**.lam.poj	**ta**.u.lam.poj			L

This establishes a typological prediction. Given this constraint set, no language can have a nonreduplicative CV prefix like [ta] that is prefixed to words starting with a consonant and infixed after an onsetless initial syllable. The same is true for other logically possible shapes of nonreduplicative prefixes, such as [a], [an], and [tan]. (You will work this out in exercise 5.) This typological prediction is all the more surprising and interesting because, even though reduplicative infixation is rather rare, five other languages are known to follow the Timugon Murut pattern: Pangasinan (Benton 1971: 99, 117), Yareba (Weimer and Weimer 1970, 1975: 685), Orokaiva (Healey, Isoroembo, and Chittleborough 1969: 35–36), Flamingo Bay Asmat (Voorhoeve 1965: 51), and Sanskrit in its aorist and desiderative forms (Janda and Joseph 1986: 89, Kiparsky 1986). To account for the fact that so many cases of reduplicative infixation work like this, but nonreduplicative infixation doesn't, this gap must have a principled basis.

When we have a typological prediction, particularly one that has good empirical support, then we need to know what it presupposes about CON. What sort of constraint, if it existed in CON, would undermine this typological result? The answer: any constraint that favors the winner in the [u.**ta**.lam.poj]~[**ta**.u.lam.poj] row of (16) and does not favor the loser in the [**ta**.ba.lan]~[ba.**ta**.lan] row.

One putative constraint with these favoring relations is known as NO-HIATUS. It's a special case of ONSET that is violated only by [V.V] sequences. This constraint favors [u.**ta**.lam.poj] over [**ta**.u.lam.poj], and it favors neither of [**ta**.ba.lan] and [ba.**ta**.lan]. Its presence in CON would therefore undermine the typological claim, as (17) shows. Our typological result commits us to a theory of CON that does not include NO-HIATUS.

(17)   ERC set (16) with No-Hiatus added

Winners	Losers	Onset	No-Coda	Align-L	No-Hiatus
ta.ba.lan	ba.ta.lan			W	
u.ta.lam.poj	ta.u.lam.poj			L	W

This sort of reasoning is a very valuable tool for working on factorial typology in OT. We cannot know everything about the constraints that are in Con, but we can say something about the constraints that must *not* be in Con lest our typological predictions be subverted. Often, that is nearly as good.

EXERCISES

5   Tableau (16) establishes part of the typological result about infixation, using the nonreduplicative prefix [ta]. Do the same for nonreduplicative prefixes with other shapes: [a], [an], and [tan]. Question (not part of the exercise): What about longer nonreduplicative prefixes like [ata], [sta], [tana], or [tanana]? How is it possible to establish a typological result that holds over inputs of any length?

6   Incorporate the losers *[u.lu.lam.poj] or *[o.mom.po.don] into the analysis of Timugon Murut, introducing and ranking any additional constraint(s) that are necessary.

5.6   How to Proceed from Typology to Constraints

In the discussion so far, I have assumed that we start with an analysis of a specific language, use factorial typology to determine the typological predictions of the analysis, and then do empirical research to test those predictions. Frequently, however, the empirical research on language typology comes first. After collecting examples of some phenomenon in various languages, the analyst has an idea of how languages vary and would like to formalize this insight using factorial typology. What's the best way to proceed in this situation?

The method I recommend is to hypothesize some constraints and then attempt to use them in careful OT analyses of the languages being studied. Do not invest too much effort in formulating and justifying the constraints until they have been tested in the analyses. Too often, in my own work and that of others, I have seen promising ideas for constraints that did not quite work out when embedded in an analysis. That's progress, since it often points the way toward better constraints, but it's also a warning against too long a delay in trying the constraints out.

How does one arrive at an initial hypothesis about the constraints, starting from some sort of cross-language survey of a phenomenon? If the data suggest that some sort of linguistic scale is involved, then use harmonic alignment to construct a constraint set (§4.5). If not, then try to identify the minimal differences between languages and use them to help formulate constraints. This procedure relies on one of OT's basic assumptions: any systematic difference between languages must reflect a difference in constraint ranking.

For example, a typological survey of the effect of vowel height on rounding harmony reveals some interesting differences among languages (Kaun 1995). In Kirgiz (18), vowel height has no effect on rounding harmony – high (a) and nonhigh (b) suffix vowels harmonize with high and nonhigh root vowels.

(18)   Kirgiz (Comrie 1981)
    a. [bir-intʃi]   'first'
        [beʃ-intʃi]   'fifth'
        [altɨ-ntʃɨ]   'sixth'
        [yʧ-ynʧy]   'third'
        [tørt-ynʧy] 'fourth'
        [on-unʧu]   'tenth'

    b. [iʃ-ten]   'work (ablative)'
        [et-ten]   'meat (ablative)'
        [dʒɨl-dan]   'year (ablative)'
        [alma-dan] 'apple (ablative)'
        [køl-døn]   'lake (ablative)'
        [tuz-don]   'salt (ablative)'

In Turkish (19), however, rounding harmony does not affect nonhigh suffix vowels (b), so only high suffix vowels (a) are observed to alternate in rounding.

(19) Turkish
- a. [ip-im]   'my rope'
       [syt-ym]   'my milk'
       [ev-im]   'my house'
       [ʧøp-ym]   'my garbage'
       [kɨz-ɨm]   'my girl'
       [buz-um]   'my ice'
       [at-ɨm]   'my horse'
       [gol-um]   'my (football) goal'

- b. [ip-e]   'rope (dative)'
       [syt-e], *[syt-ø] 'milk (dative)'
       [ev-e]   'house (dative)'
       [ʧøp-e], *[ʧøp-ø] 'garbage (dative)'
       [kɨz-a]   'girl (dative)'
       [buz-a], *[buz-o] 'ice (dative)'
       [at-a]   'horse (dative)'
       [gol-a], *[gol-o] 'goal (dative)'

In Yawelmani (20), the suffix vowel harmonizes in rounding with the root vowel only if they are in the same height class, both high (b) or both nonhigh (b).

(20) Yawelmani
- a. [giʤʔ-hin]   'touch (aorist)'
       [muṭ-hun]   'swear (aorist)'
       [xat-hin]   'eat (aorist)'
       [gop-hin], *[gop-hun] 'take care of an infant (aorist)'

- b. [giʤʔ-taw]   'touch (gerund)'
       [muṭ-taw], *[muṭ-tow] 'swear (gerund)'
       [xat-taw]   'eat (gerund)'
       [gop-tow]   'take care of an infant (gerund)'

For anyone schooled in the *SPE* tradition, the temptation is to say that Kirgiz, Turkish, and Yawelmani simply have three distinct processes of rounding harmony. That isn't the best way to approach this material in OT, however. Start from the assumption that the basic process is exactly the same in all three languages: the constraint Align-Right(+round, word) dominates Ident(round). (See §4.8 on alignment constraints in harmony systems.) The languages differ in the constraints that dominate Align-Right(+round, word).

In Kirgiz, Align-Right(+round, word) is undominated, so [+round] spreads all the way to the final syllable, regardless of the vowels it affects along the way.

The higher-ranking markedness constraint in Turkish has been called *RoLo (Beckman 1997: 24, Kaun 1995: 104). It assigns a violation mark for every vowel that bears the feature specifications [+round, –high]. Ranked above Align-Right(+round, word), as in (21), it prevents harmony when the result would be a nonhigh round vowel.

(21) Blocking of rounding harmony by nonhigh suffix vowel in Turkish[2]

/syt-e/	*RoLo	Align-R(+rnd, wd)	Id(round)
a. → syte		*	
b.　sytø	*W	L	*W

In Yawelmani, the higher-ranking markedness constraint is Round/αHigh, which is violated by any sequence of vowels that share a [+round] specification and not a [high] specification (Archangeli and Suzuki 1997). Ranked above Align-Right(+round, word), as in (22), it prevents harmony when the result would contain a sequence like [oCu].

(22) Blocking of rounding harmony by height mismatch in Yawelmani

/gop-hin/	Round/αHigh	Align-R(+rnd, wd)	Id(round)
a. → gophin		*	
b.　gophon	*W	L	*W

The essence of this approach to the typology of rounding harmony is that differences among languages are the result of which markedness constraints, if any, dominate Align-Right(+round, word), thereby limiting its effects. This naturally raises some questions: Why take this approach to typology? Why not posit several distinct alignment constraints, each of which is sensitive to different properties of the trigger and/or target vowel? In general, why should we prefer to derive language typology from differences in constraint interaction rather than from differences in the constraints themselves?

There are two reasons to prefer the interactional approach. First, abundant past experience suggests that this approach is more likely to lead to good, interesting results in the long run. Therefore, approaches to typology based primarily on ranking permutation and consequent differences in interaction should have first claim on our attention. Second, the interactive approach to typology makes additional, testable claims about typology that go well beyond the original phenomenon. For example, once we have installed *RoLo and Round/αHigh in Con, we are obliged to ask about their effects in matters having nothing to do with harmony. For instance, through ranking permutation, *RoLo can simply ban nonhigh round vowels from a language's segmental inventory. When combined with a positional faithfulness constraint (§4.6.3), *RoLo can have the effect of prohibiting nonhigh round vowels in noninitial or unstressed syllables. These predictions once again emphasize the extent to which any analytic move in OT can have unintended consequences. If those unintended consequences turn out to be right, then the analytic move has powerful support. If not, then revision is called for.

EXERCISES

7   The ranking in (21) includes, by transitivity of domination, *RoLo >> Ident(round). This ranking will wrongly favor *[ʧep-im] over [ʧøp-ym]. Solve this problem.

8   Vowel harmony in Kachin Khakass follows the pattern illustrated by the data below (Korn 1969): (a) if the root vowel and the suffix vowel are both high, then there is rounding harmony; (b) otherwise there isn't. Can the proposal in the text account for this?

a. [kuʃ-tuŋ]   'of the bird'
    [kyn-ny]   'day (accusative)'

b. [ok-tiŋ]   'of the arrow'
    [ʧør-zip]   'having gone'
    [kuzuk-ta]   'in the nut'
    [kyn-gæ]   'to the day'
    [pol-za]   'if he is'
    [ʧør-gæn]   'who went'

Notes

1 I have omitted the candidate [xa.tikʔ], since is it harmonically bounded by [xat.kʔaʔ]. See note 19 in chapter 2.

2 In assigning violation marks for Aʟɪɢɴ-Rɪɢʜᴛ(+round, word), I assume that intervening syllables rather than segments are counted.

6

Some Current Research Questions

6.1 Introduction

This chapter briefly introduces a few areas of current research in OT. The list of topics chosen isn't meant to be exhaustive or even representative – that would require another book. Also, I won't revisit topics that are discussed elsewhere in this book, such as functional grounding of constraints, learnability, and the logic of OT. The five topics in this chapter were chosen because they have broad relevance and are, to a great extent, independent of specific phenomena. Two of the topics are areas where OT has made important new contributions, the study of variation within languages (§6.2) and language acquisition (§6.3). The other topics involve questions about the sufficiency of OT: derivations (§6.4), absolute ungrammaticality (§6.5), and the too-many solutions problem (§6.6). Each section ends with suggestions for further reading.

6.2 How Does a Language Vary?

Linguistic behavior is often inconsistent. Within a speech community, or even in the utterances of an individual speaker, there may be several ways of saying the same thing. Since a lot of this variation is controlled by the grammar, any linguistic theory needs a way for the grammar to occasionally produce different outputs for the same input.

In classic OT, there is really only one way for the grammar to produce multiple outputs from a single input: two or more candidates must receive exactly the same number of violation marks from every constraint in CON, and EVAL must select them both as optimal. If two candidates violate all constraints equally, then the grammar cannot distinguish them. If one is optimal, then both are.

In practice, this isn't how variation has usually been analyzed in OT.[1] In both phonology and syntax, the typical constraint sets are rich enough that candidates with identical violations probably never occur. So analyzing variation requires a modification of classic OT, though perhaps a very slight one.

There are two basic approaches in current use: multiple grammars (Anttila 1997, Boersma 1998, Kiparsky 1993, and many others) and ranked winners (Coetzee 2004). In the multiple-grammars approach, the speaker of a language has access to several different rankings of CON. Each time EVAL operates, it chooses one of those rankings by some random process. In essence, EVAL remains the same as in classic OT, but there is a change in what it means for a speaker to know the grammar of a language. In the ranked-winners approach, the speaker has access to non-optimal candidates in the order that they are ranked by EVAL. EVAL and the grammar remain the same as in classic OT, but there is a change in what we understand to be the output of the grammar. In the discussion here, I will focus on the multiple-grammars approach.

To illustrate this approach, we'll look at what is perhaps the single most famous example of phonological variation, deletion of /t/ and /d/ from word-final clusters in English. Three contexts are relevant: preconsonantal *cost me* ~ *cos' me*; prevocalic *cost us* ~ *cos' us*; and prepausal *cost* ~ *cos'*. In the prevocalic context, candidates with and without syllabification across the word boundary also have to be considered: [kɔs.tʌs] vs. [kɔst.ʌs].

Kiparsky (1993) presents an OT analysis of this phenomenon, which I have simplified for present purposes by omitting the prepausal context. The constraints are given in (1). *COMPLEX is just a cover constraint for *COMPLEX-ONSET and *COMPLEX-CODA, so it's violated by [kɔst.ʌs] and [kɔ.stʌs]. ALIGN-LEFT(syntactic word, syllable) prohibits resyllabification across word boundaries, so it's violated by [kɔs.tʌs] and [kɔ.stʌs].

(1) Constraints in analysis of /t/, /d/ deletion (after Kiparsky 1993)
   a. *COMPLEX
      Assign one violation-mark for every complex onset or complex coda (e.g., [kɔst.ʌs] or [kɔ.stʌs]).

    b. ALIGN-LEFT(syntactic word, syllable)
        Assign one violation mark for every segment that is initial
        in a syntactic word but not initial in some syllable (e.g.,
        [kɔs.tʌs]).
    c. ONSET
    d. MAX

Under the multiple-grammars theory of variation, speakers of English know more than one ranking of these constraints. In fact, they know that these four constraints are completely unranked with respect to one another – or, to put it differently, they know 24 grammars, since there are 24 permutations of these constraints. Since EVAL requires a ranking, each application of EVAL chooses one of the 24 permutations at random. Obviously, speakers aren't required to learn each of the 24 grammars individually, but by allowing these four constraints to remain unranked, speakers have in effect internalized a 24-grammar system.

For example, if the input is /kɔst ʌs/ and EVAL chooses the ranking in (2), then the optimal form will be [kɔs.ʌs], with [t] deleted. Other rankings will also give this output, or they will give [kɔs.tʌs] or [kɔst.ʌs].

(2) [kɔs.ʌs] (*cos' us*) under one ranking

/kɔst ʌs/	*COMPLEX	ALIGN-L	ONSET	MAX
a. → kɔs.ʌs			*	*
b. kɔst.ʌs	*W		*	L
c. kɔs.tʌs		*W	L	L
d. kɔ.sʌs		*W	L	*
e. kɔ.stʌs	*W	*W	L	L

This variation isn't unconstrained. Candidates (d) and (e) in (2), [kɔ.sʌs] and [kɔ.stʌs], are both harmonically bounded within this constraint set by candidate (c), [kɔs.tʌs]. Since harmonically bounded candidates cannot win under any ranking permutation, (d) and (e) are predicted not to be possible variants. Another limit on the range of possible variation comes from constraints that aren't in the unranked block. For example, DEP must be invariably ranked above these four constraints, since epenthetic *[kɔ.sət.miː] isn't an attested variant for *cost me*. The idea, then, is that these four constraints constitute a mutually unranked block somewhere in the overall hierarchy.

Under the assumption that EVAL has an equal likelihood of choosing any of the totally ordered rankings, this theory also makes predictions about the relative frequency of the variants. Since many rankings will produce the same output for a given input, some outputs are going to be more likely than others. The prediction is that the observed frequency of, say, [kɔs.ʌs] should approximate the fraction of the totally ordered rankings that produce [kɔs.ʌs]. For [kɔs.ʌs] to win, *COMPLEX and ALIGN-LEFT(syntactic word, syllable) must dominate MAX, and ALIGN-LEFT(syntactic word, syllable) must also dominate ONSET. Since five total orderings are consistent with these ranking requirements, the predicted frequency of [kɔs.ʌs] is $5/24 = 21\%$. The balance of the probability, 79%, gets assigned to the [t]-retaining candidates [kɔst.ʌs] and [kɔs.tʌs]. The exact percentages are less important than the prediction that, in the prevocalic environment, retention of /t/ should be more common than deletion of /t/. That prediction is correct.

Another version of the multiple grammars theory of variation is based on a continuous ranking scale (Boersma 1998, Boersma and Hayes 2001). In this approach, called *Stochastic OT*, constraints are ranked on a numerical scale. When EVAL applies, normally distributed noise factors are added to each constraint's ranking value. If two constraints are relatively close on the scale, and if the noise factors happen to push the higher-ranking one down and the lower-ranking one up, then their ranking can be reversed. This richer theory of variation is able to reproduce numerical observations with remarkable exactitude. OTSoft includes an option to use the Gradual Learning Algorithm, which is able to learn numerical rankings from data with variation. (The gradual learning algorithm is explained in Boersma and Hayes (2001).)

A key idea in all of this work is that the source of within-language variation is the same as the source of between-language variation: differences in ranking. (See Bresnan, Deo, and Sharma (2007) for recent discussion of this point.) Ranking differences may be permanent fixtures of languages, or they might be ephemeral effects that can change each time EVAL is called. Either way, the theory makes the powerful prediction that language typology and language variation should have the same qualitative characteristics, despite their obvious quantitative differences.

To learn more about OT work on variation, see Anttila (2007) for a brief but useful survey. Fairly comprehensive bibliographies can be found in McCarthy (2002: 230, 233) and Anttila (2006).

1   The sociolinguistics literature emphasizes the role of external social factors in conditioning variable processes like English *t, d*-deletion. Is this problematic for a theory that integrates the analysis of variation into a formal grammar?

2   English *t, d*-deletion is also sensitive to morphological factors (Guy 1991). The process is most likely to affect root *t* or *d*, as in *past ~ pas'*. It's less likely to affect irregular past tense forms like *lost ~ los'*. It's least likely to affect regular past tense forms like *passed ~ pass'*. How would you integrate these additional observations into the analysis?

6.3   How is Language Acquired?

Like language variation, language acquisition mirrors typology in OT. Developing grammars and mature grammars are made out of the same stuff: CON, GEN, and EVAL. This leads to a hypothesis of *continuity* between child grammars and adult grammars. Developing grammars should differ from each other (over time in one child, among different children acquiring the same language, and among children acquiring different languages) in the same way that the adult grammars of different languages differ. Thus, the strongest claim is that every process or restriction at work in acquisition should also be possible in the synchronic grammars of adults, and vice versa. Any universal, systematic differences between children's and adults' language must have extragrammatical explanations – for instance, maturation of motor skills or the perceptual system.

   Jakobson (1941) said that children's language is unmarked in comparison to adult language, and subsequent research has largely confirmed that. For example, Dutch learners acquire simple onsets before they acquire complex ones, and they acquire syllables with onsets before they acquire syllables without them (Levelt and van de Vijver 2004). (Also see exercise 12 in chapter 4.) OT provides a formal explanation for this observation: learners are biased toward ranking markedness constraints over faithfulness constraints.[2] The markedness constraints are ranked above faithfulness unless the learner receives positive evidence that they must be ranked below faithfulness. This evidence comes in the form of exposure to marked structure in the ambient language. For instance, all children initially have *COMPLEX-ONSET ranked above MAX, DEP, and other faithfulness constraints. Thus, their early productions have only simple onsets. If the ambient language has no complex onsets, as is the case with Japanese, then this ranking does not change as the child matures. If the ambient language has complex onsets, as is the case with Dutch or English, then *Complex-Onset is eventually demoted below Max. In general, as markedness constraints are demoted below antagonistic faithfulness constraints, the child's inventory of allowable structures increases, gradually approximating the adult system.

As a result of these insights, research in OT has been successful in making connections among phonological theory, formal learnability theory, and empirical research on language acquisition. With the exception of Natural Phonology (Donegan and Stampe 1979, Stampe 1973), pre-OT generative phonology was confounded by the facts of language acquisition: children's reduced pronunciations required that child phonology have many rules for which there is no evidence in the adult language. In OT, children's reduction processes are a result of satisfying high-ranking universal markedness constraints. The very same markedness constraints that, through ranking, characterize differences between languages are also responsible for differences between children and adults within a single language.

Two recent anthologies will assist anyone wanting to learn more about this topic. Kager, Pater, and Zonneveld (2004) includes work on learnability as well as acquisition. Dinnsen and Gierut (forthcoming) deals with disordered as well as normal acquisition of phonology. In McCarthy (2002: 232), there is a nearly exhaustive list, compiled by Joe Pater, of the OT literature on acquisition before 2002.

QUESTION

3 The bias toward high-ranking markedness explains why learners' early productions are unmarked in comparison with the ambient language. But it's also necessary because of the Subset Principle. The Subset Principle applies to learning from positive evidence, and it says that learners must always stick to more restrictive hypotheses about a grammar until they receive positive evidence that the ambient language is less restrictive (Baker 1979, Berwick 1985, Gold 1967). For example, learners must assume that their language prohibits onset clusters until they get positive evidence that onset clusters are allowed. If learners instead started with the assumption that their language permits onset clusters and the ambient language happened to be Japanese, then no amount of positive evidence in the form of words without onset clusters would help them find the more restrictive grammar. (This view assumes that learners aren't able to discover and use information about gaps in the ambient language.)

How is the Subset Principle relevant to the claim that learners have a bias toward high-ranking markedness constraints?

EXERCISE

4   Many children learning English reduce words to a single trochaic foot
(['σ]_{foot} or ['σσ]_{foot}) by eliminating whole syllables. The data below were collected from several children around age 2 (Pater and Paradis 1996). According
to the continuity hypothesis, this shortening process must be the result of some
markedness constraint or constraints that are also active in adult phonology,
possibly in other languages. What markedness constraint or constraints,
through dominating MAX, could be responsible for these data? Explain your
answer. (Hint: Review the constraints in §4.5.2 and exercise 10 in chapter 4.)

Adult	*Child*
a'gain	['gɛn]
e'nough	['nʌf]
ce'ment	['mɛnt]
po'tato	['teːdo]
spa'ghetti	['geːdi]
to'gether	['geːdɚ]
mu'seum	['ziːʌm]
Mo'desto	['desto]
pa'jamas	['ʤaːməʃ]
to'morrow	['mowo]

6.4   Does OT Need Derivations?

In OT, inputs are mapped to outputs without any intermediate steps.
Many theories of phonology and syntax require derivations with
intermediate steps, however.

For example, to get from Arabic underlying /ktub/ to surface
[ʔuktub] 'write!' in an *SPE*-style analysis requires the two-step derivation in (3). The first step is vowel epenthesis before a cluster. Vowel
epenthesis introduces a syllable-initial vowel, and that is the context
that requires [ʔ] epenthesis. The derivation is necessary because the structural description of the [ʔ] epenthesis rule isn't met until after the vowel
epenthesis rule has applied.

(3)   Arabic /ktub/ → [ʔuktub] with rules
      Underlying   /ktub/
      Vowel epenthesis   uktub
      [ʔ] epenthesis   ʔuktub
      Surface   [ʔuktub]

OT deals with this differently. GEN isn't limited to producing outputs that differ in only one way from the input. Instead, GEN can apply any number of operations to derive a single candidate. This means that [ʔuk.tub] is in the candidate set, where it competes against *[k.tub], *[uk.tub], and other forms. The candidates that EVAL compares are complete surface structures rather than intermediate steps on the way to surface structure.

Why does OT have flat derivations? There are empirical arguments (many of which are summarized in McCarthy 2002: 138–163), but the main reason is theoretical parsimony. Nonflat derivations are often a way of establishing priority relationships among linguistic requirements, and OT already has a way of setting priorities, ranking.

In Yawelmani, for example, the choice between vowel shortening in /laːn-hin/ → [lan.hin] and vowel epenthesis in /ʔilk-hin/ → [ʔi.lik.hin] is a matter of setting priorities. In both cases, the problem is how to deal with an unsyllabified consonant. Vowel epenthesis could in principle work in both cases: *[laː.ni.hin] and [ʔi.lik.hin]. Since /laːn-hin/ undergoes shortening rather than epenthesis, an *SPE*-style analysis has to order the shortening rule first, as shown in (4). With the opposite order, epenthesis would apply to both forms, wrongly yielding *[laː.ni.hin].

(4)   Yawelmani shortening/epenthesis priority with rules

    a. Correct rule order

Underlying	/laːn-hin/	/ʔilk-hin/
Syllabification	laː.n.hin	ʔil.k.hin
Shortening	lan.hin	—
Epenthesis	—	ʔi.lik.hin
Surface	[lan.hin]	[ʔi.lik.hin]

    b. Wrong rule order

Underlying	/laːn-hin/	/ʔilk-hin/
Syllabification	laː.n.hin	ʔil.k.hin
Epenthesis	laː.ni.hin	ʔi.lik.hin
Shortening	—	—
Surface	*[laː.ni.hin]	[ʔi.lik.hin]

In OT, however, the priority relationship between shortening and epenthesis is determined by the ranking of two faithfulness constraints (see (5)). Since the faithful candidate is ruled out by *C^{unsyll}, DEP or IDENT(long) has to be violated. With the input /laːn-hin/, shortening is favored because IDENT(long) is ranked below DEP.

Constraint ranking, rather than rule ordering, decides the competition in favor of [lan.hin]. Since the input /ʔilk-hin/ has no long vowels, shortening isn't an option, so higher-ranking DEP has to be violated anyway.

(5) Yawelmani shortening/epenthesis priority in OT

/laːn-hin/	*C^unsyll	DEP	IDENT(long)
a. → lan.hin			*
b. laː.n.hin	*W		L
c. laː.ni.hin		*W	L

/ʔilk-hin/	*C^unsyll	DEP	IDENT(long)
d. → ʔi.lik.hin		*	
e. ʔil.k.hin	*W	L	

OT's flat derivations are controversial. The literature includes a number of works claiming that derivations are indispensable, in phonology at least. There are also counterproposals that try to remain closer to the classic OT position. Two main arguments for derivations have been put forward.

The first argument is based on transderivational similarities. In Palestinian Arabic, short high vowels normally delete in unstressed open syllables, leading to the alternations illustrated in (6). But the bold-face unstressed high vowels in the initial open syllables of the words in (7) do not delete. The reason: somehow the fact that this vowel is stressed – and therefore undeletable – in the word ['fihim] 'he understood' prevents it from being deleted in derived words like [fi'himna] 'he understood us'. Since ['fihim] has no such effect on ['fhimna] 'we understood', these two words must be related in a different way that does not evoke a transderivational similarity requirement.

(6) Syncope in Palestinian Arabic

Underlying	*Surface*	
/fihim/	['fihim]	'he understood'
/fihim-u_subj/	['fihimu]	'they understood'
/fihim-it_subj/	['fihimit]	'she understood'
/fihim-na_subj/	['fhimna]	'we understood'
/fihim-t_subj/	['fhimt]	'I understood'

(7) Transderivational similarity in Palestinian Arabic

Underlying	*Surface*	
/fihim-na$_{obj}$/	[fi'himna]	'he understood us'
/fihim-kum$_{obj}$/	[fi'himkum]	'he undersood you (plural)'
/fihim-ha$_{obj}$/	[fi'himha]	'he understood her'
/ma fihim-ʃ$_{neg}$/	[ma fi'himiʃ]	'he didn't understand'

Since Chomsky, Halle, and Lukoff (1956), facts like these have usually been attributed to the workings of the transformational cycle. The cycle requires rules to apply to inner constituents before they apply to outer ones. A further assumption is that the cycle is limited to constituents that are capable of standing alone as words. These assumptions account for the difference between (6) and (7) as follows (after Brame 1973):

(i)   In a word like /fihim$_{stem}$-na$_{subj}$/ 'we understood', the inner constituent /fihim/ isn't a cyclic domain because it's a bound stem rather than a free-standing word. Therefore, this form undergoes a single cycle of rule application. Stress is assigned to the penult, yielding [fi'himna], and then the unstressed [i] in the initial syllable is deleted, yielding ['fhimna].

(ii) In word like /fihim-Ø$_{subj}$-na$_{obj}$/ 'he understood us', the inner constituent is the free-standing word [fihim], meaning 'he understood'. On the first cycle, stress applies to the inner constituent, producing ['fihim]. On the second cycle, the object suffix /na$_{obj}$/ is added and the phonological rules are applied once again. Stress is assigned to the new penult, [him]. But the remnant of first-cycle stress prevents the vowel in the first syllable from deleting.

It is easy to imagine how cyclicity might be imported into OT. In a cyclic version of OT, cyclicity means applying GEN and EVAL to successively larger constituents, taking the output of the previous cycle as the input to the current cycle. For instance, /fihim/ 'he understood' is first submitted to GEN and EVAL, yielding ['fihim]. Then the enclitic /-na$_{obj}$/ is added, and this is submitted to GEN and EVAL once again. Because the syllable ['fi] is stressed in the input to the second cycle, a stress-sensitive positional faithfulness constraint can prevent it from deleting, yielding [fi'himna] 'he understood us'. Kenstowicz (1995), Kiparsky (2000, 2003), and Rubach (1997, 2000) are among the many works that develop cyclic or "stratal" versions of OT that work like this.

There is also a good deal of work pursuing an alternative theory of transderivational similarity. Known as transderivational or output–output faithfulness, this theory posits correspondence relations (§4.6) between the output forms of morphologically related words. A positional faithfulness constraint on the output–output correspondence relation between ['fihim] 'he understood' and [fi'himna] 'he understood us' protects the initial vowel of the latter from deleting. For further explanation and illustration of this idea, Kager (1999: chapter 6) is a good introduction to the topic. The theory is developed in Benua (1997), Crosswhite (1998), Pater (2000), and Steriade (1997, 1999, 2000), among others. Downing, Hall, and Raffelsiefen (2005) is an anthology focused on the related topic of paradigms and paradigmatic similarity.

The second argument in favor of derivations in OT is based on the phenomenon of phonological opacity. The concept of opacity comes from the *SPE* tradition: a rule is opaque if the fact that it applied or the context that determined whether it applied isn't visible in the surface form (Kiparsky 1973a). For instance, Bedouin Arabic has a process of palatalization before front vowels. This process applies even if the triggering front vowel deletes. In rule-based phonology, the interaction between these two processes is analyzed by ordering the palatalization rule before the syncope rule (8). This is a type of opaque rule order know as *counterbleeding*, since if the rules were applied in the opposite order, syncope would "bleed" palatalization by depriving it of some opportunities to apply.

(8) Opacity in rule-based phonology
    Underlying   /ħaːkim-iːn/
    Palatalization   ħaːkʲimiːn
    Syncope   ħaːkʲmiːn
    Surface   [ħaːkʲmiːn]

Opacity presents certain problems for classic OT. Because markedness constraints only see surface forms, the markedness constraint that favors palatalized [k] before a front vowel is irrelevant to evaluating the choice between [ħaːkʲmiːn] and *[ħaːkmiːn]. Since *[ħaːkmiːn] is more faithful, it should win. The problem with opacity is that conditions not visible in surface structure affect the evaluation of candidates, and here the /k/ is palatalized because it's followed by an underlying /i/ that isn't visible in surface structure. Classic OT has only one way of accessing a level of representation other than surface structure, and that is via faithfulness constraints. Faithfulness won't help here, however, since the intended winner [ħaːkʲmiːn] is less faithful than *[ħaːkmiːn].

Some approaches to opacity in OT stick rather close to classic OT's basic assumptions by enriching the surface representation. Other approaches incorporate something like derivations into the theory. The topic goes well beyond a textbook like this, but for further information see McCarthy (2007a), where the various proposals are reviewed and a new one is presented. Two older anthologies containing work on this topic are Hermans and van Oostendorp (1999) and Roca (1997).

6.5   How Is Ungrammaticality Accounted For?

We saw in chapters 1 and 2 that the basic OT theory of ungrammaticality is based on candidate competition: *[bnæg] and *What does Robin will eat? are ungrammatical in English because they aren't the most harmonic candidate for any input. This is the only possible theory of ungrammaticality in OT because of how EVAL is defined. Since EVAL looks for the candidate that is most favored by the constraint hierarchy, rather than insisting on a candidate that obeys all of the constraints, EVAL always chooses *some* candidate as optimal. The standard approach to ungrammaticality in many other theories – inviolable constraints and crashing derivations – is simply not an option in OT without some major revision to the theory.

Data challenging this view come from phonologically motivated gaps in the morphology. Rice's (2003, 2005) work on Norwegian imperatives supplies a nice example. The imperative is normally identical to the infinitive (see (9)), except that the imperative lacks the suffix spelled as -e and pronounced as [-ə]. But verb roots ending in a consonant cluster like [pn], [dl], or [kl] have no imperative (see (10)). The bare root *[åpn] is unpronounceable because of its final cluster, and obvious alternatives like epenthetic *[åpən] are ruled out for most speakers. Those speakers simply have no imperative form of the verb 'open', and so they must resort to circumlocution (typically, a modal plus the infinitive) when they wish to convey this meaning.

(9)   Norwegian imperatives

Infinitive	Imperative		
å spise	spis!	'eat'	
å snakke	snakk!	'talk'	
å løfte	loft!	'lift'	

(10)   Norwegian imperative gaps

Infinitive	Imperative	
å sykle	–	'bicycle'
å åpne	–	'open'
å paddle	–	'paddle'

What candidate wins when the input is /sykl+Imperative/? Presumably we do not want the phonological GEN to be so rich that it offers the phrasal circumlocution as a competing candidate. The alternative is to regard the gap itself is a candidate.

Prince and Smolensky (1993/2004: 57–61) hypothesize that every candidate set includes a member that is devoid of any structure whatsoever, the *null output*. The null output isn't just phonologically empty. Rather, it has no linguistic structure at all, no phonology or morphology or syntax or semantics. (The null output is therefore different from *pro*, which lacks only phonological structure.) The null output's advantage over other candidates is that, because it lacks all structure, it violates no markedness constraints. Markedness constraints either prohibit certain structures (e.g., phonological *COMPLEX-SYLLABLE, syntactic OPERATOR-IN-SPECIFIER or OBLIGATORY-HEADS) or they require structures, when present, to have certain properties (e.g., phonological ONSET, syntactic FULL-INTERPRETATION).[3] Because the null output has no structure at all, it vacuously satisfies all markedness constraints. Furthermore, for reasons given in Wolf and McCarthy (forthcoming), it also vacuously satisfies all faithfulness constraints. The null output, then, isn't the same as the phonologically empty output where all segments have been deleted (violating MAX) but the morphological and syntactic structures are preserved. The hypothesis is that the null output violates just one constraint, called MPARSE,[4] and no other candidate violates this constraint.

In Rice's analysis, the cover constraint SONORITY-SEQUENCING (SONSEQ) rules out faithful *[sykl] as the surface realization of the imperative verb 'bicycle!', and faithfulness constraints prohibit alternatives like epenthesis (*[sykəl]). These constraints must dominate MPARSE, as shown in (11). Because the null output is neither marked nor unfaithful, it beats these and any other candidates that violate constraints ranked above MPARSE. Since the null output is the winner in this tableau, speakers of Norwegian are forced to use circumlocution to express the meaning 'bicycle!' because they have literally no such word, not even a phonologically empty one.

(11) Ranking argument: SONORITY-SEQUENCING, DEP >> MPARSE

/sykl/	SONSEQ	DEP	MPARSE
a. → *null output*			*
b. sykl	*W		L
c. sykəl		*W	L

The null output is the closest that OT gets to the inviolable constraints and crashing derivations of other linguistic theories. Any constraint C that is ranked above MPARSE is effectively inviolable, since any candidate that violates C will lose to the null ouput. Legendre, Smolensky, and Wilson (1998: 257n.) call this effect of MPARSE a *harmony threshold*. In keeping with its basic premises, however, OT achieves this inviolability effect through candidate competition rather than through, say, a post-EVAL check on outputs.

The null output might seem like a good way to solve rich-base problems (§2.10.4). We know that /apak/ cannot map to [a.pak] in Yawelmani, since all syllables and all words are consonant-initial, but no evidence from alternations tells us what /apak/ maps to instead. Since any claim about what /apak/ maps to would be just a guess, why not map it to the null output?

Because of MPARSE's harmony-threshold property, the null output is unsuitable for this and many other rich-base problems. For the null output to be the most harmonic of /apak/'s candidates, as in (12), MPARSE has to be dominated by ONSET to rule out the faithful candidate. It also has to be dominated by MAX and DEP to rule out alternative ways of satisfying ONSET.

(12) Null output as winner for hypothetical /apak/ in Yawelmani

/apak/	*COMP-SYLL	ONSET	DEP	*V#	MAX	MPARSE	ID(long)
a. → *null output*						*	
b. a.pak		*W				L	
c. ʔa.pak			*W			L	
d. pak					*W	L	

But the ranking MAX >> MPARSE that (12) requires produces inconsistency when applied to examples like /taxaː-kʔa/ (see (13)). This is a case of the harmony-threshold property: if MAX dominates MPARSE, then no MAX-violating candidate should ever win. MAX should be effectively inviolable. Mappings like /taxaː-kʔa/ → [ta.xakʔ] show that this is incorrect.

(13) Inconsistent ranking with /taxaː-kʔa/ → [ta.xakʔ]

/taxaːkʔa/	*COMP-SYLL	ONSET	DEP	*V#	MAX	MPARSE	ID(long)
a. → ta.xakʔ					*		*
b. ta.xaː.kʔa				*W	L		L
c. ta.xaːkʔ	*W						L
d. ta.xaː.kʔaʔ			*W		L		L
e. *null output*					L	*W	L

On the other hand, in a language like Yawelmani but with no alernations involving deletion, there would be no objection to ranking MPARSE below MAX. So the null output can in principle yield a satisfactory solution to some but not all rich-base problems. The harmony-threshold property – no constraint that crucially dominates MPARSE can ever be violated by any nonnull output of the grammar – provides a simple test for whether a solution based on the null output is workable or not.

For more on the null output and related concepts, see the contributions to Rice (forthcoming) and references cited there.

EXERCISE

5 Can you reanalyze the Madurese system in (62) and (63) of chapter 2 using the null output? In the reanalysis, /bã/ and /ma/ should map to the null output, while /ba/ and /mã/ should map to [ba] and [mã], respectively. If the reanalysis is possible, present it. If it's not, explain why.

6.6 Is Faithfulness Enough?

Because OT is inherently typological, it focuses our attention on questions about what languages can and cannot do. Exploring factorial typology often reveals gaps – that is, phenomena that are unattested but might be expected to exist. This section is about gaps in how certain markedness constraints are satisfied: permuting the faithfulness constraints predicts behavior that is never observed. This is sometimes called the *too-many-solutions problem*.[5]

An example of this sort can be found in Lombardi (1995/2001). She starts from the assumption that there is a markedness constraint against voiced obstruents in coda position, No-Voiced-Coda. In German, Polish, Russian, and other languages with final devoicing, No-Voiced-Coda dominates Ident(voice): /bad/ → [bat]. But suppose the ranking of this and other faithfulness constraints is permuted, as shown in (14)–(16). The resulting typology has two significant gaps: languages that avoid voiced codas by deletion (15) and languages that avoid voiced codas by vowel epenthesis (16). There are languages that deal with codas in general by deletion or epenthesis, but no languages appear to target voiced codas specifically for this treatment.

(14) Ident(voice) at bottom (German)

/bad/	No-Voiced-Coda	Max	Dep	Id(voice)
a. → bat				*
b. bad	*W			L
c. ba		*W		L
d. badə			*W	L

(15) Max at bottom (unattested)

/bad/	No-Voiced-Coda	Id(voice)	Dep	Max
a. → ba				*
b. bad	*W			L
c. bat		*W		L
d. badə			*W	L

(16)   DEP at bottom (possibly unattested)[6]

/bad/	NO-VOICED-CODA	ID(voice)	MAX	DEP
a. → badə				*
b. bad	*W			L
c. bat		*W		L
d. ba			*W	L

When a factorial typology predicts unattested and presumably imposs-ible languages, the first solution to consider is removing some constraints from CON, so there will be fewer possible grammars. Taking away MAX and DEP isn't an option, however, since they are needed for other phe-nomena. That is why Lombardi undertakes a more thorough revision of the assumptions that underlie the flawed typology in (14)–(16).

One aspect of her proposal is connected with the discussion of featural faithfulness constraints in §4.6. When a voiced consonant deletes, IDENT(voice) is vacuously satisfied. This is how [ba] can win in (15). Suppose that CON is changed by replacing IDENT(voice) with MAX(voice). When a voiced consonant deletes, MAX(voice) is violated, as is segmental MAX. The effect of this change is that now [ba] is har-monically bounded by [bat] within this constraint set. (The constraints are shown as unranked in (17) because harmonic bounding is inde-pendent of ranking.) Both [ba] and [bat] violate MAX(voice), but [ba] also violates the MAX constraint that pertains to entire segments. Because of this change in the way featural faithfulness is viewed, deleting the whole coda is overkill, since deleting just its [voice] fea-ture is sufficient to satisfy NO-VOICED-CODA. (The other aspect of Lombardi's proposal is the topic of exercise 6.)

(17)   Harmonic bounding of [ba] with MAX(voice)

/bad/	NO-VOICED-CODA	MAX(voice)	DEP	MAX	
a. ba		*		*	*harmonically bounded*
b. bad	*				
c. bat		*			
d. badə			*		

The key idea in Lombardi's analysis is a revision of the theory of faithfulness so that deleting a voiced consonant is intrinsically less faithful than just devoicing it. This change solves the general typological problem of why there are plenty of languages that devoice voiced codas but there are no languages that delete them.

Steriade (2001b) takes an abstractly similar approach, but she provides it with a very different rationale. In her view, relative unfaithfulness is determined by perceptual similarity. Speakers prefer [bat] over [ba] because [bat] is more similar perceptually to faithful [bad]. Steriade's theory uses a universal scale of perceptual similarity called the P-Map to fix the rankings of certain faithfulness constraints. Because deleting a segment always causes a bigger perceptual change than devoicing it, MAX dominates IDENT(voice) universally. The ranking in (15) is therefore impossible in any language and the typological problem is again solved.

There are other instantiations of the too-many-solutions problem that aren't so tractable. The markedness constraint CODA-COND does not allow codas to license consonantal place features. This constraint can be satisfied by deleting a consonant: /patka/ → [pa.ka]. It can also be satisfied by place assimilation, so that the cluster shares a single place feature licensed by the onset: /pamka/ → [paŋ.ka]. In principle, this constraint could be satisfied by deleting or assimilating the second consonant in a cluster, but that almost never seems to happen: /patka/ → *[pa.ta], /pamka/ → *[pam.pa].[7] Why this asymmetry? Blumenfeld (2006) and Wilson (2000, 2001) address such questions by revising the theory of constraints to make them more rule-like; and in McCarthy (2007b) a derivational mechanism is developed.

Factorial typologies that offer too many solutions are sometimes described as "a problem for OT," but that's just a case of blaming the messenger for some bad news. Any linguistic theory needs to account for the ways in which inputs and outputs can and cannot differ from one another; this isn't some peculiar burden that only OT must bear. OT's inherently typological character is the reason why the problem was first discovered by Lombardi, Pater (1999), Steriade, and others. As we have seen, it may also be the place where the solution is to be found.

EXERCISE

6   Under the assumption that no language works like (16), Lombardi replaces No-VOICED-CODA with a context-free constraint against voiced obstruents that crucially interacts with a positional faithfulness constraint IDENT(voice)$_{\text{onset}}$

(see (39) in chapter 2). Based on these hints, fill in the details of her proposal and explain how it works.

Notes

1 Grimshaw (1997: 411) exploits the possibility of multiple optimal outputs to account for syntactic optionality. Hammond (2000) also contains discussion of this point.

2 For references to some of the many papers making and studying this claim, see McCarthy (2002: 231).

3 This is not a principled distinction between types of markedness constraints. Often, the same constraint could be defined either way.

4 The constraint name MParse is intended to recall the constraint name Parse, but limited to the morphology. In Prince and Smolensky's view, the null output's peculiarity is its failure to parse (= preserve) the morphological structure of the input. That is why they refer to the null output as the *null parse*. For more about Prince and Smolensky's approach to faithfulness, see §4.6.4.

5 The phrase "too many solutions" alludes to the idea that unfaithful mappings are "solutions" to the "problems" posed by markedness constraints. It is not ideal, but the alternative, "too many repairs," is even worse. Markedness constraints aren't problems, and unfaithful mappings aren't solutions or repairs. Unfortunately, no better name for this topic has been proposed.

6 Kwakwala may be an example of this pattern (Struijke 1998).

7 For documentation of the deletion asymmetry, see Steriade (2001b) and Wilson (2000, 2001). For the assimilation asymmetry, see Jun (1995), Ohala (1990), Steriade (2001a), and Webb (1982).

Afterword

When I was planning this book and writing it, I had several goals in mind. I wanted to spare readers the mistakes and confusions that I experienced while learning about OT. I also wanted to make explicit many of the techniques that experienced practitioners implicitly use when doing OT. I wanted to bring a wider audience to some ideas that I thought were useful and important, such as Prince's comparative tableaux. I wanted to proselytize for my views of how papers should be written. And I wanted to do all of this in a way that captures, as much as possible, the informal give-and-take of a classroom. I hope I have succeeded, at least partly, in achieving these goals.

If you have studied this book and done the exercises, then you are well positioned to go on to do research in OT. You are able to create sound analyses of your own and evaluate analyses that are presented to you. You can recognize when constraints need to be modified or eliminated, and you know how to define new constraints. You are able to assess and propose typologies. And you can recognize situations when OT's basic premises might prove to be insufficient. I wish you luck in your research, and I hope to hear from you about it! Feel free to write me at jmccarthy@linguist.umass.edu.

References

Items listed as ROA are available on the Rutgers Optimality Archive, http://roa.rutgers.edu.

Aissen, Judith (1999) Markedness and subject choice in Optimality Theory. *Natural Language and Linguistic Theory* **17**, 673–711.

Aissen, Judith (2003) Differential object marking: Iconicity vs economy. *Natural Language and Linguistic Theory* **21**, 435–483.

Al-Mozainy, Hamza Q. (1981) Vowel Alternations in a Bedouin Hijazi Arabic Dialect: Abstractness and Stress. Doctoral dissertation. University of Texas, Austin, Austin, TX.

Alderete, John (1997) Dissimilation as local conjunction. In: Kiyomi Kusumoto (ed.) *Proceedings of the North East Linguistic Society 27*. Amherst, MA: GLSA Publications, pp. 17–32.

Anttila, Arto (1997) Deriving variation from grammar. In: Frans Hinskens, Roeland van Hout, and W. Leo Wetzels (eds.) *Variation, Change, and Phonological Theory*. Amsterdam: John Benjamins, pp. 35–68.

Anttila, Arto (2006) Bibliography of variation and gradience in phonology. Handout from course presented at Phonology Fest 2006, Bloomington, IN. [Available at www.stanford.edu/~anttila/teaching/indiana/variation-biblio.pdf.]

Anttila, Arto (2007) Variation and optionality. In: Paul de Lacy (ed.) *The Cambridge Handbook of Phonology*. Cambridge: Cambridge University Press, pp. 519–536.

Archangeli, Diana (1997) Optimality Theory: An introduction to linguistics in the 1990's. In: Diana Archangeli and D. Terence Langendoen (eds.) *Optimality Theory: An Overview*. Oxford: Blackwell, pp. 1–32.

Archangeli, Diana and Pulleyblank, Douglas (1994) *Grounded Phonology*. Cambridge, MA: MIT Press.

Archangeli, Diana and Suzuki, Keiichiro (1997) The Yokuts challenge. In: Iggy Roca (ed.) *Derivations and Constraints in Phonology.* Oxford: Oxford University Press, pp. 197–226.

Aronoff, Mark, Arsyad, Azhar, Basri, Hassan, and Broselow, Ellen (1987) Tier configuration in Makassarese reduplication. In: Anna Bosch, Barbara Need, and Eric Schiller (eds.) *CLS 23: Parasession on Autosegmental and Metrical Phonology.* Chicago: Chicago Linguistic Society, pp. 1–15.

Asimov, Isaac (1950) *I, Robot.* New York: Signet.

Baertsch, Karen (1998) Onset sonority distance constraints through local conjunction. In: M. Catherine Gruber, Derrick Higgins, Kenneth S. Olson, and Tamra Wysocki (eds.) *CLS 34, Part 2: The Panels.* Chicago: Chicago Linguistic Society, pp. 1–15.

Baertsch, Karen (2002) An Optimality Theoretic Approach to Syllable Structure: The Split Margin Hierarchy. Doctoral dissertation. Indiana University, Bloomington, IN.

Baker, C. L. (1979) Syntactic theory and the projection problem. *Linguistic Inquiry* **10**, 533–581.

Bakovic, Eric (2000) Harmony, Dominance, and Control. Doctoral dissertation. Rutgers University, New Brunswick, NJ. [Available on Rutgers Optimality Archive, ROA-360.]

Bakovic, Eric and Keer, Edward (2001) Optionality and ineffability. In: Géraldine Legendre, Jane Grimshaw, and Sten Vikner (eds.) *Optimality-Theoretic Syntax.* Cambridge, MA: MIT Press, pp. 97–112. [Available on Rutgers Optimality Archive, ROA-384.]

Becker, Howard S. (1986) *Writing for Social Scientists: How to Start and Finish Your Thesis, Book, or Article.* Chicago: University of Chicago Press.

Becker, Howard S. (1998) *Tricks of the Trade: How to Think About Your Research While You're Doing It.* Chicago: University of Chicago Press.

Beckman, Jill (1997) Positional faithfulness, positional neutralization, and Shona vowel harmony. *Phonology* **14**, 1–46.

Beckman, Jill (1998) Positional Faithfulness. Doctoral dissertation. University of Massachusetts Amherst, Amherst, MA. [Available on Rutgers Optimality Archive, ROA-234. Published (1999) as *Positional Faithfulness: An Optimality Theoretic Treatment of Phonological Asymmetries,* New York: Garland.]

Benton, Richard (1971) *Pangasinan Reference Grammar.* Honolulu: University of Hawaii Press.

Benua, Laura (1997) Transderivational Identity: Phonological Relations Between Words. Doctoral dissertation. University of Massachusetts Amherst, Amherst, MA. [Available on Rutgers Optimality Archive, ROA-259. Published (2000) as *Phonological Relations Between Words,* New York: Garland.]

Berwick, Robert (1985) *The Acquisition of Syntactic Knowledge.* Cambridge, MA: MIT Press.

Blevins, Juliette (2004) *Evolutionary Phonology: The Emergence of Sound Patterns.* Cambridge: Cambridge University Press.

Blumenfeld, Lev (2006) Constraints on Phonological Interactions. Doctoral dissertation. Stanford University, Stanford, CA. [Available on Rutgers Optimality Archive, ROA-877.]

Blutner, Reinhard, de Hoop, Helen, and Hendricks, Petra (eds.) (2005) *Optimal Communication.* Stanford, CA: CSLI Publications.

Blutner, Reinhard and Zeevat, Henk (eds.) (2004) *Optimality Theory and Pragmatics.* Basingstoke, UK, & New York: Palgrave Macmillan.

Boersma, Paul (1998) *Functional Phonology: Formalizing the Interaction Between Articulatory and Perceptual Drives.* The Hague: Holland Academic Graphics. [Doctoral dissertation, University of Amsterdam.]

Boersma, Paul and Hayes, Bruce (2001) Empirical tests of the gradual learning algorithm. *Linguistic Inquiry* **32**, 45–86. [Available on Rutgers Optimality Archive, ROA-348.]

Boersma, Paul and Weenink, David (2007) Praat: Doing phonetics by computer (version 4.5.1.5). Computer program. [Available at www.praat.org.]

Borg, Alexander (1997) Maltese phonology. In: Alan S. Kaye (ed.) *Phonologies of Asia and Africa.* Winona Lake, IN: Eisenbrauns, pp. 245–285.

Brame, Michael (1973) On stress assignment in two Arabic dialects. In: Stephen R. Anderson and Paul Kiparsky (eds.) *A Festschrift for Morris Halle.* New York: Holt, Reinhart and Winston, pp. 14–25.

Brasoveanu, Adrian and Prince, Alan (2005) Ranking and necessity. Unpublished manuscript. Rutgers University, New Brunswick, NJ. [Available on Rutgers Optimality Archive, ROA-794.]

Bresnan, Joan and Aissen, Judith (2002) Optimality and functionality: Objections and refutations. *Natural Language and Linguistic Theory* **20**, 81–95.

Bresnan, Joan, Deo, Ashwini, and Sharma, Devyani (2007) Typology in variation: A probabilistic approach to *be* and *n't* in the survey of English dialects. *English Language and Linguistics* **11**, 301–346. [Available on Rutgers Optimality Archive, ROA-875.]

Burzio, Luigi (1994) *Principles of English Stress.* Cambridge: Cambridge University Press.

Casali, Roderic F. (1996) Resolving Hiatus. Doctoral dissertation. UCLA, Los Angeles. [Available on Rutgers Optimality Archive, ROA-215. Published (1998), New York: Garland.]

Casali, Roderic F. (1997) Vowel elision in hiatus contexts: Which vowel goes? *Language* **73**, 493–533.

Chomsky, Noam (1957) *Syntactic Structures.* The Hague: Mouton.

Chomsky, Noam (1965) *Aspects of the Theory of Syntax.* Cambridge, MA: MIT Press.

Chomsky, Noam (1968) *Language and Mind.* New York: Harcourt Brace Jovanovich.

Chomsky, Noam (1981) *Lectures on Government and Binding.* Dordrecht: Foris.

Chomsky, Noam (1991) Some notes on economy of derivation and representation. In: Robert Freidin (ed.) *Principles and Parameters in Comparative Grammar*. Cambridge, MA: MIT Press, pp. 417–454.

Chomsky, Noam (1995) *The Minimalist Program*. Cambridge, MA: MIT Press.

Chomsky, Noam and Halle, Morris (1968) *The Sound Pattern of English*. New York: Harper & Row.

Chomsky, Noam, Halle, Morris, and Lukoff, Fred (1956) On accent and juncture in English. In: Morris Halle, Horace Lunt, and Hugh Maclean (eds.) *For Roman Jakobson: Essays on the Occasion of His Sixtieth Birthday, 11 October, 1956*. The Hague: Mouton, pp. 65–80.

Chomsky, Noam and Lasnik, Howard (1977) Filters and control. *Linguistic Inquiry* **8**, 425–504.

Clayton, Mary L. (1976) The redundance of underlying morpheme-structure conditions. *Language* **52**, 295–313.

Coetzee, Andries (2004) What It Means to Be a Loser: Non-Optimal Candidates in Optimality Theory. Doctoral dissertation. University of Massachusetts Amherst, Amherst, MA. [Available on Rutgers Optimality Archive, ROA-687.]

Comrie, Bernard (1981) *The Languages of the Soviet Union*. Cambridge: Cambridge University Press.

Crosswhite, Katherine (1998) Segmental vs. prosodic correspondence in Chamorro. *Phonology* **15**, 281–316.

Crosswhite, Katherine (2004) Vowel reduction. In: Bruce Hayes, Robert Kirchner, and Donca Steriade (eds.) *Phonetically Based Phonology*. Cambridge: Cambridge University Press, pp. 191–231.

Davis, Stuart (1995) Emphasis spread in Arabic and Grounded Phonology. *Linguistic Inquiry* **26**, 465–498.

Davis, Stuart and Shin, Seung-Hoon (1999) The syllable contact constraint in Korean: An Optimality-Theoretic analysis. *Journal of East Asian Linguistics* **8**, 285–312.

de Hoop, Helen and de Swart, Henriette (eds.) (1999) *Papers on Optimality Theoretic Semantics*. Utrecht: Utrecht Institute of Linguistics/Onderzoeksinstituut voor Taal en Spraak.

de Lacy, Paul (2002) The Formal Expression of Markedness. Doctoral dissertation. University of Massachusetts, Amherst, Amherst, MA. [Available on Rutgers Optimality Archive, ROA-542.]

Dell, François and Elmedlaoui, Mohamed (1985) Syllabic consonants and syllabification in Imdlawn Tashlhiyt Berber. *Journal of African Languages and Linguistics* **7**, 105–130.

Dell, François and Elmedlaoui, Mohamed (1988) Syllabic consonants in Berber: Some new evidence. *Journal of African Languages and Linguistics* **10**, 1–17.

Dinnsen, Daniel A. and Gierut, Judith A. (eds.) (forthcoming) *Optimality Theory: Phonological Acquisition and Disorders*. London: Equinox Publishing.

Donegan, Patricia J. and Stampe, David (1979) The study of natural phonology. In: Daniel A. Dinnsen (ed.) *Current Approaches to Phonological Theory*. Bloomington, IN: Indiana University Press, pp. 126–173.

Downing, Laura J., Hall, T. Alan, and Raffelsiefen, Renate (eds.) (2005) *Paradigms in Phonological Theory*. Oxford: Oxford University Press.

Féry, Caroline and van de Vijver, Ruben (eds.) (2003) *The Syllable in Optimality Theory*. Cambridge & New York: Cambridge University Press.

Flack, Kathryn (2007) The Sources of Phonological Markedness. Doctoral dissertation. University of Massachusetts Amherst, Amherst, MA.

Fodor, Jerry A. and Lepore, Ernest (1998) The emptiness of the lexicon: Reflections on James Pustejovsky's *The Generative Lexicon*. *Linguistic Inquiry* **29**, 269–288.

Fukazawa, Haruka (1999) Theoretical Implications of OCP Effects on Features in Optimality Theory. Doctoral dissertation. University of Maryland, College Park, MD. [Available on Rutgers Optimality Archive, ROA-307.]

Fukazawa, Haruka and Miglio, Viola (1998) Restricting conjunction to constraint families. In: Vida Samiian (ed.) *Proceedings of the Western Conference on Linguistics 9 (WECOL 96)*. Fresno, CA: Department of Linguistics, California State University, Fresno, pp. 102–117.

Furby, Christine (1974) Garawa Phonology. *Papers in Australian Linguistics* **7**, 1–11. [Pacific Linguistics, Series A, no. 37. Australian National University, Canberra.]

Gafos, Adamantios (1998) Eliminating long-distance consonantal spreading. *Natural Language and Linguistic Theory* **16**, 223–278.

Gnanadesikan, Amalia (1995/2004) Markedness and faithfulness constraints in child phonology. In: René Kager, Joe Pater, and Wim Zonneveld (eds.) *Constraints in Phonological Acquisition*. Cambridge: Cambridge University Press, pp. 73–108. [Originally circulated in 1995. Available on Rutgers Optimality Archive, ROA-67.]

Gold, E. Mark (1967) Language identification in the limit. *Information and Control* **10**, 447–474.

Goldsmith, John (1976a) Autosegmental Phonology. Doctoral dissertation. MIT, Cambridge, MA. [Published (1979), New York: Garland Press.]

Goldsmith, John (1976b) An overview of autosegmental phonology. *Linguistic Analysis* **2**, 23–68.

Goldsmith, John (1990) Autosegmental and Metrical Phonology. Malden, MA and Oxford: Blackwell.

Gouskova, Maria (2003) Deriving Economy: Syncope in Optimality Theory. Doctoral dissertation. University of Massachusetts Amherst, Amherst, MA. [Available on Rutgers Optimality Archive, ROA-610.]

Gouskova, Maria (2004) Relational hierarchies in Optimality Theory: The case of syllable contact. *Phonology* **21**, 201–250.

Gouskova, Maria (2007) DEP: Beyond epenthesis. *Linguistic Inquiry* **38**, 759–770.

Greenberg, Joseph (1978) Some generalizations concerning initial and final consonant clusters. In: Joseph Greenberg (ed.) *Universals of Human Language*. Stanford: Stanford University Press, pp. 243–280.

Grimshaw, Jane (1997) Projection, heads, and optimality. *Linguistic Inquiry* **28**, 373–422. [Available on Rutgers Optimality Archive, ROA-68.]

Grimshaw, Jane (2002) Economy of structure in OT. In: Angela Carpenter, Andries Coetzee, and Paul de Lacy (eds.) *University of Massachusetts Occasional Papers in Linguistics 26: Papers in Optimality Theory II.* Amherst, MA: GLSA Publications, pp. 81–120. [Available on Rutgers Optimality Archive, ROA-434.]

Guy, Gregory (1991) Explanation in variable phonology. *Language Variation and Change* **3**, 1–22.

Hale, Kenneth (1973) Deep-surface canonical disparities in relation to analysis and change: An Australian example. In: Thomas Sebeok (ed.) *Current Trends in Linguistics.* The Hague: Mouton, pp. 401–458.

Hale, Mark and Reiss, Charles (2000) 'Substance abuse' and 'dysfunctionalism': Current trends in phonology. *Linguistic Inquiry* **31**, 157–169.

Halle, Morris and Clements, George N. (1983) *Problem Book in Phonology: A Workbook for Introductory Courses in Linguistics and in Modern Phonology.* Cambridge, MA: MIT Press.

Hammond, Michael (2000) The logic of Optimality Theory. Unpublished manuscript. University of Arizona, Tucson, AZ. [Available on Rutgers Optimality Archive, ROA-390.]

Harris, Zellig (1946) From morpheme to utterance. *Language* **22**, 161–183.

Haspelmath, Martin (1999) Optimality and diachronic adaptation. *Zeitschrift für Sprachwissenschaft* **18**, 180–205. [Available on Rutgers Optimality Archive, ROA-302.]

Hayes, Bruce (1995) *Metrical Stress Theory: Principles and Case Studies.* Chicago: University of Chicago Press.

Hayes, Bruce (1999) Phonetically driven phonology: The role of Optimality Theory and inductive grounding. In: Michael Darnell, Frederick J. Newmeyer, Michael Noonan, Edith Moravcsik, and Kathleen Wheatley (eds.) *Functionalism and Formalism in Linguistics, Volume I: General Papers.* Amsterdam: John Benjamins, pp. 243–285.

Hayes, Bruce, Kirchner, Robert, and Steriade, Donca (eds.) (2004) *Phonetically Based Phonology.* Cambridge: Cambridge University Press.

Hayes, Bruce, Tesar, Bruce, and Zuraw, Kie (2003) OTSoft 2.1. Computer program. [Available at www.linguistics.ucla.edu/people/hayes/otsoft.]

Healey, Alan, Isoroembo, Ambrose, and Chittleborough, Martin (1969) Preliminary notes on Orokaiva grammar. *Papers in New Guinea Linguistics* **9**, 33–64.

Hermans, Ben and van Oostendorp, Marc (eds.) (1999) *The Derivational Residue in Phonological Optimality Theory.* Amsterdam: John Benjamins.

Hohepa, Patrick (1967) *A Profile Generative Grammar of Maori.* Baltimore: Indiana University at the Waverly Press. [Supplement to *International Journal of American Linguistics*, v. 33, no. 2. pt. 3, April 1967.]

Holt, D. Eric (ed.) (2003) *Optimality Theory and Language Change.* Dordrecht & Boston: Kluwer Academic.

Hrafnbjargarson, Gunnar Hrafn (2004) Person meets case: Restrictions on nominative objects in Icelandic. Unpublished manuscript. University of Aarhus, Aarhus. [Available at www.hum.uit.no/a/hrafnbjargarson/handout/20040917_synsem.pdf.]

Hughes, Everett C. (1984) *The Sociological Eye*. New Brunswick, NJ: Transaction Books.

Inkelas, Sharon (1989) Prosodic Constituency in the Lexicon. Doctoral dissertation. Stanford University. [Published 1990, New York: Garland Press.]

Ito, Junko (1989) A prosodic theory of epenthesis. *Natural Language and Linguistic Theory* 7, 217–259.

Ito, Junko and Mester, Armin (1992/2003) Weak layering and word binarity. In: Takeru Honma, Masao Okazaki, Toshiyuki Tabata, and Shin-ichi Tanaka (eds.) *A New Century of Phonology and Phonological Theory: A Festschrift for Professor Shosuke Haraguchi on the Occasion of His Sixtieth Birthday*. Tokyo: Kaitakusha, pp. 26–65. [Revision of UC Santa Cruz Linguistics Research Center report published in 1992.]

Ito, Junko and Mester, Armin. (1996) Rendaku I: Constraint conjunction and the OCP. Handout of talk presented at Kobe Phonology Forum 1996, Kobe University. [Available on Rutgers Optimality Archive, ROA-144.]

Ito, Junko and Mester, Armin (1998) Markedness and word structure: OCP effects in Japanese. Unpublished manuscript. University of California at Santa Cruz. [Available on Rutgers Optimality Archive, ROA-255.]

Ito, Junko and Mester, Armin (1999) The structure of the phonological lexicon. In: Natsuko Tsujimura (ed.) *The Handbook of Japanese Linguistics*. Oxford: Blackwell, pp. 62–100.

Ito, Junko and Mester, Armin (2003a) *Japanese Morphophonemics: Markedness and Word Structure*. Cambridge, MA: MIT Press.

Ito, Junko and Mester, Armin (2003b) On the sources of opacity in OT: Coda processes in German. In: Caroline Féry and Ruben van de Vijver (eds.) *The Syllable in Optimality Theory*. Cambridge: Cambridge University Press, pp. 271–303. [Available on Rutgers Optimality Archive, ROA-347.]

Jakobson, Roman (1941) *Kindersprache, Aphasie, und allgemeine Lautgesetze*. Uppsala: Almqvist & Wiksell.

Jakobson, Roman (1962) *Selected Writings I: Phonological Studies*. The Hague: Mouton.

Janda, Richard and Joseph, Brian (1986) One rule or many? Sanskrit reduplication as fragmented affixation. *Ohio State University Working Papers in Linguistics* 34, 84–107.

Johnston, Raymond Leslie (1980) *Nakanai of New Britain: The Grammar of an Oceanic Language*. Canberra: Australian National University.

Joos, Martin (1967) Bernard Bloch. *Language* 41, 3–19.

Joshi, S. D. and Kiparsky, Paul (1970) *Siddha* and *asiddha* in Paninian phonology. In: Daniel A. Dinnsen (ed.) *Current Approaches to Phonological Theory*. Indiana University Press, Bloomington, IN, pp. 223–250.

Jun, Jongho (1995) Perceptual and Articulatory Factors in Place Assimilation: An Optimality Theoretic Approach. Doctoral dissertation. UCLA, Los Angeles.

Kager, René (1999) *Optimality Theory*. Cambridge: Cambridge University Press.

Kager, René (2001) Rhythmic directionality by positional licensing. Handout of talk presented at Fifth HIL Phonology Conference (HILP 5), University of Potsdam. [Available on Rutgers Optimality Archive, ROA-514.]

Kager, René, Pater, Joe, and Zonneveld, Wim (eds.) (2004) *Constraints in Phonological Acquisition*. Cambridge: Cambridge University Press.

Karttunen, Lauri (1998) The proper treatment of optimality in computational phonology. In: *FSMNLP '98: Proceedings of the International Workshop on Finite State Methods in Natural Language Processing*. Ankara: Bilkent University, pp. 1–12. [Available on Rutgers Optimality Archive, ROA-258.]

Karttunen, Lauri (2006) The insufficiency of paper-and-pencil linguistics: The case of Finnish prosody. In: Miriam Butt, Mary Dalrymple, and Tracy Holloway King (eds.) *Intelligent Linguistic Architectures: Variations on Themes by Ronald M. Kaplan*. Stanford, CA: CSLI Publications, pp. 287–300. [Available on Rutgers Optimality Archive, ROA-818.]

Kaun, Abigail (1995) The Typology of Rounding Harmony: An Optimality Theoretic Approach. Doctoral dissertation. UCLA, Los Angeles. [Available on Rutgers Optimality Archive, ROA-227.]

Kawahara, Shigeto (2006) A faithfulness scale projected from a perceptibility scale: The case of [+voice] in Japanese. *Language* **82**, 536–574.

Kenstowicz, Michael (1994) Syllabification in Chukchee: A constraints-based analysis. In: Alice Davison, Nicole Maier, Glaucia Silva, and Wan Su Yan (eds.) *Proceedings of the Formal Linguistics Society of Mid-America 4*. Iowa City: Department of Linguistics, University of Iowa, pp. 160–181. [Available on Rutgers Optimality Archive, ROA-30.]

Kenstowicz, Michael (1995) Cyclic vs. non-cyclic constraint evaluation. *Phonology* **12**, 397–436. [Available on Rutgers Optimality Archive, ROA-31.]

Kenstowicz, Michael and Kisseberth, Charles (1977) *Topics in Phonological Theory*. New York: Academic Press.

Kenstowicz, Michael and Kisseberth, Charles (1979) *Generative Phonology: Description and Theory*. New York: Academic Press.

Kiparsky, Paul (1973a) Abstractness, opacity and global rules. In: Osamu Fujimura (ed.) *Three Dimensions of Linguistic Theory*. Tokyo: TEC, pp. 57–86.

Kiparsky, Paul (1973b) Phonological representations. In: Osamu Fujimura (ed.) *Three Dimensions of Linguistic Theory*. Tokyo: TEC, pp. 3–136.

Kiparsky, Paul (1986) The phonology of reduplication. Unpublished manuscript. Stanford University, Stanford, CA.

Kiparsky, Paul. (1993) Variable rules. Handout of talk presented at Rutgers Optimality Workshop I, Rutgers University, New Brunswick, NJ. [Available at www.stanford.edu/~kiparsky/nwave94.pdf.]

Kiparsky, Paul (2000) Opacity and cyclicity. *The Linguistic Review* **17**, 351–367.

Kiparsky, Paul (2003) Syllables and moras in Arabic. In: Caroline Féry and Ruben van de Vijver (eds.) *The Syllable in Optimality Theory*. Cambridge: Cambridge University Press, pp. 147–182. [Available at www.stanford.edu/~kiparsky/Papers/syll.pdf.]

Kisseberth, Charles (1970) On the functional unity of phonological rules. *Linguistic Inquiry* **1**, 291–306.

Kitagawa, Yoshihisa (1986) Subjects in Japanese and English. Doctoral dissertation. University of Massachusetts Amherst, Amherst, MA.

Koopman, Hilda and Sportiche, Dominique (1991) The position of subjects. *Lingua* **85**, 211–258.

Korn, David (1969) Types of labial vowel harmony in the Turkic languages. *Anthropological Linguistics* **11**, 98–106.

Kurisu, Kazutaka (2001) The Phonology of Morpheme Realization. Doctoral dissertation. University of California, Santa Cruz, Santa Cruz, CA. [Available on Rutgers Optimality Archive, ROA-490.]

Lamontagne, Greg (1996) Relativized contiguity, part I: Contiguity and syllable prosody. Unpublished manuscript. University of British Columbia, Vancouver, BC. [Available on Rutgers Optimality Archive, ROA-150.]

Legendre, Géraldine (2001) An introduction to Optimality Theory in syntax. In: Géraldine Legendre, Jane Grimshaw, and Sten Vikner (eds.) *Optimality-Theoretic Syntax*. Cambridge, MA: MIT Press, pp. 1–28.

Legendre, Géraldine, Grimshaw, Jane, and Vikner, Sten (eds.) (2001) *Optimality-Theoretic Syntax*. Cambridge, MA: MIT Press.

Legendre, Géraldine, Smolensky, Paul, and Wilson, Colin (1998) When is less more? Faithfulness and minimal links in *wh*-chains. In: Pilar Barbosa, Danny Fox, Paul Hagstrom, Martha McGinnis, and David Pesetsky (eds.) *Is the Best Good Enough? Optimality and Competition in Syntax*. Cambridge, MA: MIT Press, pp. 249–289. [Available on Rutgers Optimality Archive, ROA-117.]

Levelt, Clara C. and van de Vijver, Ruben (2004) Syllable types in cross-linguistic and developmental grammars. In: René Kager, Joe Pater, and Wim Zonneveld (eds.) *Constraints in Phonological Acquisition*. Cambridge: Cambridge University Press, pp. 204–218. [Available on Rutgers Optimality Archive, ROA-265.]

Liberman, Mark and Prince, Alan (1977) On stress and linguistic rhythm. *Linguistic Inquiry* **8**, 249–336.

Lombardi, Linda (1995/2001) Why Place and Voice are different: Constraint-specific alternations in Optimality Theory. In: Linda Lombardi (ed.) *Segmental Phonology in Optimality Theory: Constraints and Representations*. Cambridge: Cambridge University Press, pp. 13–45. [First circulated in 1995. Available on Rutgers Optimality Archive, ROA-105.]

Lombardi, Linda (1997/2002) Coronal epenthesis and markedness. *Phonology* **19**, 219–251. [Earlier version appears in *University of Maryland Working Papers in Linguistics 5*, pp. 156–175 (1997). Available on Rutgers Optimality Archive, ROA-245.]

Lombardi, Linda (1999) Positional faithfulness and voicing assimilation in Optimality Theory. *Natural Language and Linguistic Theory* **17**, 267–302. [Excerpted in John J. McCarthy (ed.) *Optimality Theory in Phonology: A Reader*, Malden, MA & Oxford: Blackwell (2004).]

Lombardi, Linda (ed.) (2001) *Segmental Phonology in Optimality Theory: Constraints and Representations*. Cambridge & New York: Cambridge University Press.

Lombardi, Linda (2003) Markedness and the typology of epenthetic vowels. Unpublished manuscript. University of Maryland, College Park, MD. [Available on Rutgers Optimality Archive, ROA-578.]

Łubowicz, Anna (2002) Derived environment effects in Optimality Theory. *Lingua* **112**, 243–280. [Available on Rutgers Optimality Archive, ROA-103. Excerpted in *Optimality Theory in Phonology: A Reader*, ed. by John J. McCarthy, Malden, MA and Oxford, Blackwell (2004).]

Łubowicz, Anna. (2005) Restricting local conjunction. Handout of talk presented at Old World Conference in Phonology 2, Tromsø, Norway. [Available at www-rcf.usc.edu/~lubowicz/docs/ocp-2-handoutwebpage.pdf.]

Łubowicz, Anna (2006) Locality of conjunction. In: John Alderete, Chung-hye Han, and Alexei Kochetov (eds.) *Proceedings of the 24th West Coast Conference on Formal Linguistics*. Somerville, MA: Cascadilla Press, pp. 254–262.

Marlett, Stephen A. and Stemberger, Joseph P. (1983) Empty consonants in Seri. *Linguistic Inquiry* **14**, 617–639.

McCarthy, John J. (1993) A case of surface constraint violation. *Canadian Journal of Linguistics* **38**, 169–195.

McCarthy, John J. (1997) Process-specific constraints in Optimality Theory. *Linguistic Inquiry* **28**, 231–251.

McCarthy, John J. (1999) *Introductory OT on CD-ROM*. CD-ROM. Amherst, MA: GLSA Publications.

McCarthy, John J. (2000) Faithfulness and prosodic circumscription. In: Joost Dekkers, Frank van der Leeuw, and Jeroen van de Weijer (eds.) *Optimality Theory: Phonology, Syntax, and Acquisition*. Oxford: Oxford University Press, pp. 151–189.

McCarthy, John J. (2002) *A Thematic Guide to Optimality Theory*. Cambridge: Cambridge University Press.

McCarthy, John J. (ed.) (2003a) *Optimality Theory in Phonology: A Reader*. Malden, MA, & Oxford: Blackwell.

McCarthy, John J. (2003b) Optimality Theory: An overview. In: William Frawley (ed.) *Oxford International Encyclopedia of Linguistics* (2nd edition). Oxford: Oxford University Press.

McCarthy, John J. (2003c) OT constraints are categorical. *Phonology* **20**, 75–138. [Available at http://people.umass.edu/jjmccart/categorical.pdf.]

McCarthy, John J. (2004) Headed spans and autosegmental spreading. Unpublished manuscript. University of Massachusetts Amherst, Amherst, MA. [Available on Rutgers Optimality Archive, ROA-685.]

McCarthy, John J. (2005) The length of stem-final vowels in Colloquial Arabic. In: Mohammad T. Alhawary and Elabbas Benmamoun (eds.) *Perspectives on Arabic Linguistics XVII–XVIII: Papers from the Seventeenth and Eighteenth Annual Symposia on Arabic Linguistics*. Amsterdam: John Benjamins, pp. 1–26. [Available on Rutgers Optimality Archive, ROA-616.]

McCarthy, John J. (2007a) *Hidden Generalizations: Phonological Opacity in Optimality Theory*. London: Equinox Publishing.

McCarthy, John J. (2007b) Slouching towards optimality: Coda reduction in OT-CC. In: Phonological Society of Japan (ed.) *Phonological Studies 10*. Tokyo: Kaitakusha. [Available on Rutgers Optimality Archive, ROA-878.]

McCarthy, John J. (2007c) What is Optimality Theory? *Language and Linguistics Compass* 1, 260–291.

McCarthy, John J. and Prince, Alan (1986/1996) Prosodic Morphology 1986. Technical Report. Rutgers University Center for Cognitive Science, New Brunswick, NJ. [Available at http://ruccs.rutgers.edu/pub/papers/ pm86all.pdf. Excerpts appear in John Goldsmith (ed.) *Essential Readings in Phonology*. Oxford: Blackwell, pp. 102–136 (1999).]

McCarthy, John J. and Prince, Alan (1993a) Generalized Alignment. In: Geert Booij and Jaap van Marle (eds.) *Yearbook of Morphology*. Dordrecht: Kluwer, pp. 79–153. [Available on Rutgers Optimality Archive, ROA-7.]

McCarthy, John J. and Prince, Alan (1993b) Prosodic Morphology: Constraint Interaction and Satisfaction. Technical Report. Rutgers University Center for Cognitive Science, New Brunswick, NJ. [Available on Rutgers Optimality Archive, ROA-482.]

McCarthy, John J. and Prince, Alan (1994a) The emergence of the unmarked: Optimality in prosodic morphology. In: Mercè Gonzàlez (ed.) *Proceedings of the North East Linguistic Society 24*. Amherst, MA: GLSA Publications, pp. 333–379. [Available on Rutgers Optimality Archive, ROA-13. Excerpted in John J. McCarthy (ed.) *Optimality Theory in Phonology: A Reader*, Malden, MA & Oxford: Blackwell (2004).]

McCarthy, John J. and Prince, Alan (1994b) Two lectures on Prosodic Morphology (Utrecht, 1994). Part I: Template form in Prosodic Morphology. Part II: Faithfulness and reduplicative identity. Unpublished manuscript. University of Massachusetts Amherst and Rutgers University, Amherst, MA and New Brunswick, NJ. [Available on Rutgers Optimality Archive, ROA-59.]

McCarthy, John J. and Prince, Alan (1995) Faithfulness and reduplicative identity. In: Jill Beckman, Laura Walsh Dickey, and Suzanne Urbanczyk (eds.) *University of Massachusetts Occasional Papers in Linguistics 18*. Amherst, MA: GLSA Publications, pp. 249–384. [Available on Rutgers Optimality Archive, ROA-103.]

McCarthy, John J. and Prince, Alan (1999) Faithfulness and identity in Prosodic Morphology. In: René Kager, Harry van der Hulst, and Wim Zonneveld (eds.) *The Prosody–Morphology Interface*. Cambridge: Cambridge University

Press, pp. 218–309. [Excerpted in John J. McCarthy (ed.) *Optimality Theory in Phonology: A Reader*, Malden, MA & Oxford: Blackwell (2004).]

Morén, Bruce (1999) Distinctiveness, Coercion and Sonority: A Unified Theory of Weight. Doctoral dissertation. University of Maryland, College Park, MD. [Available on Rutgers Optimality Archive, ROA-346.]

Moreton, Elliott (2003) Non-computable functions in Optimality Theory. In: John J. McCarthy (ed.) *Optimality Theory in Phonology: A Reader*. Malden, MA, & Oxford: Blackwell, pp. 141–163. [Available on Rutgers Optimality Archive, ROA-364.]

Morris, Richard E. (2000) Constraint interaction in Spanish /s/-aspiration: Three peninsular varieties. In: Héctor Campos, Elena Herburger, Alfonso Morales-Front, and Thomas J. Walsh (eds.) *Hispanic Linguistics at the Turn of the Millennium: Papers from the 3rd Hispanic Linguistics Symposium*. Somerville, MA: Cascadilla Press. [Available on Rutgers Optimality Archive, ROA-391.]

Myers, Scott (1991) Persistent rules. *Linguistic Inquiry* **22**, 315–344.

Myers, Scott and Hansen, Benjamin B. (2005) The origin of vowel-length neutralization in vocoid sequences: Evidence from Finnish speakers. *Phonology* **22**, 317–344.

Nash, David (1979) Warlpiri vowel assimilations. *MIT Working Papers in Linguistics* **1**, 12–24.

Nash, David (1980) Topics in Warlpiri Grammar. Doctoral dissertation. MIT, Cambridge, MA. [Published (1986), New York: Garland Press.]

Nespor, Marina and Vogel, Irene (1986) *Prosodic Phonology*. Dordrecht: Foris.

Newman, Stanley (1944) *Yokuts Language of California*. New York: Viking Fund.

Newmeyer, Frederick J. (2002) Optimality and functionality: A critique of functionally-based Optimality-Theoretic syntax. *Natural Language and Linguistic Theory* **20**, 43–80.

Ohala, John (1983) The origin of sound patterns in vocal tract constraints. In: Peter MacNeilage (ed.) *The Production of Speech*. New York: Springer-Verlag, pp. 189–216.

Ohala, John (1990) The phonetics and phonology of aspects of assimilation. In: John Kingston and Mary Beckman (eds.) *Papers in Laboratory Phonology*. Cambridge: Cambridge University Press, pp. 258–275.

Oller, D. Kimbrough (2000) *The Emergence of the Speech Capacity*. Mahwah, NJ: Erlbaum.

Orie, Olanike Ola and Bricker, Victoria R. (2000) Placeless and historical laryngeals in Yucatec Maya. *International Journal of American Linguistics* **66**, 283–317.

Osborn, Henry (1966) Warao I: Phonology and morphophonemics. *International Journal of American Linguistics* **32**, 108–123.

Paradis, Carole (1988a) On constraints and repair strategies. *The Linguistic Review* **6**, 71–97.

Paradis, Carole (1988b) Towards a theory of constraint violations. *McGill Working Papers in Linguistics* **5**, 1–43.

Paradis, Carole and LaCharité, Darlene (1997) Preservation and minimality in loanword adaptation. *Journal of Linguistics* **33**, 379–430.

Parker, Stephen G. (2002) Quantifying the Sonority Hierarchy. Doctoral dissertation. University of Massachusetts Amherst, Amherst, MA. [Available at http://scholarworks.umass.edu/dissertations/AAI3056268/.]

Parker, Steve (1997) An OT account of laryngealization in Cuzco Quechua. In: Stephen A. Marlett (ed.) *Work Papers of the Summer Institute of Linguistics, University of North Dakota Session.* Grand Forks, ND: Summer Institute of Linguistics. [Available at www.und.nodak.edu/dept/linguistics/wp/1997Parker.PDF.]

Parker, Steve and Weber, David (1996) Glottalized and aspirated stops in Cuzco Quechua. *International Journal of American Linguistics* **62**, 70–85.

Pater, Joe (1999) Austronesian nasal substitution and other NC effects. In: René Kager, Harry van der Hulst, and Wim Zonneveld (eds.) *The Prosody–Morphology Interface.* Cambridge: Cambridge University Press, pp. 310–343. [Available on Rutgers Optimality Archive, ROA-160. Reprinted in John J. McCarthy (ed.) *Optimality Theory in Phonology: A Reader*, Malden, MA, & Oxford: Blackwell (2004).]

Pater, Joe (2000) Nonuniformity in English secondary stress: The role of ranked and lexically specific constraints. *Phonology* **17**, 237–274. [Available on Rutgers Optimality Archive, ROA-107.]

Pater, Joe and Paradis, Johanne (1996) Truncation without templates in child phonology. In: Andy Stringfellow, Dalia Cahana-Amitay, Elizabeth Hughes, and Andrea Zukowski (eds.) *Proceedings of the 20th Annual Boston University Conference on Language Development.* Somerville, MA: Cascadilla Press, pp. 540–552.

Payne, David L. (1981) *The Phonology and Morphology of Axininca Campa.* Arlington, TX: The Summer Institute of Linguistics and University of Texas at Arlington.

Perlmutter, David (1971) *Deep and Surface Structure Constraints in Syntax.* New York: Holt, Rinehart, and Winston.

Pesetsky, David (1998) Some optimality principles of sentence pronunciation. In: Pilar Barbosa, Danny Fox, Paul Hagstrom, Martha McGinnis, and David Pesetsky (eds.) *Is the Best Good Enough? Optimality and Competition in Syntax.* Cambridge, MA: MIT Press, pp. 337–383.

Prentice, D. J. (1971) *The Murut Languages of Sabah.* Canberra: Australian National University.

Prince, Alan (1983) Relating to the grid. *Linguistic Inquiry* **14**, 19–100.

Prince, Alan (1990) Quantitative consequences of rhythmic organization. In: Michael Ziolkowski, Manuela Noske, and Karen Deaton (eds.) *Parasession on the Syllable in Phonetics and Phonology.* Chicago: Chicago Linguistic Society, pp. 355–398.

Prince, Alan (1997a) Endogenous constraints on Optimality Theory. Course handout from Summer Institute of the Linguistic Society of America, Cornell

University, Ithaca, NY. [Available at http://ling.rutgers.edu/gamma/talks/insthdt1.pdf.]

Prince, Alan (1997b) Paninian relations. Handout of talk presented at University of Massachusetts Amherst, Amherst, MA. [Available at http://ling.rutgers.edu/gamma/talks/umass1997.pdf.]

Prince, Alan (1997c) Stringency and anti-Paninian hierarchies. Course handout from Summer Institute of the Linguistic Society of America, Cornell University, Ithaca, NY. [Available at http://ling.rutgers.edu/gamma/talks/insthdt2.pdf.]

Prince, Alan (2002a) Arguing optimality. In: Angela Carpenter, Andries Coetzee, and Paul de Lacy (eds.) *University of Massachusetts Occasional Papers in Linguistics 26: Papers in Optimality Theory II.* Amherst, MA: GLSA Publications, pp. 269–304. [Available on Rutgers Optimality Archive, ROA-562.]

Prince, Alan (2002b) Entailed ranking arguments. Unpublished manuscript. Rutgers University, New Brunswick, NJ. [Available on Rutgers Optimality Archive, ROA-500.]

Prince, Alan (2006a) Implication and impossibility in grammatical systems: What it is and how to find it. Unpublished manuscript. Rutgers Optimality Archive, New Brunswick, NJ. [Available on Rutgers Optimality Archive, ROA-880.]

Prince, Alan (2006b) No more than necessary: Beyond the 'four rules', and a bug report. Unpublished manuscript. Rutgers University, New Brunswick, NJ. [Available on Rutgers Optimality Archive, ROA-882.]

Prince, Alan and Smolensky, Paul (1993/2004) *Optimality Theory: Constraint Interaction in Generative Grammar.* Malden, MA, & Oxford: Blackwell. [Revision of 1993 technical report, Rutgers University Center for Cognitive Science. Available on Rutgers Optimality Archive, ROA-537.]

Prince, Alan and Smolensky, Paul (1997) Optimality: From neural networks to universal grammar. *Science* **275**, 1604–1610.

Prince, Alan and Smolensky, Paul (2003) Optimality Theory in phonology. In: William Frawley (ed.) *Oxford International Encyclopedia of Linguistics* (2nd edition). Oxford: Oxford University Press, vol. 3, pp. 212–222. [Available at http://ling.rutgers.edu/gamma/oiel.pdf.]

Prince, Alan and Tesar, Bruce (2004) Learning phonotactic distributions. In: René Kager, Joe Pater, and Wim Zonneveld (eds.) *Constraints in Phonological Acquisition.* Cambridge: Cambridge University Press, pp. 245–291. [Available on Rutgers Optimality Archive, ROA-353.]

Pulleyblank, Douglas (1986) *Tone in Lexical Phonology.* Dordrecht: D. Reidel.

Pulleyblank, Douglas (1988) Vocalic underspecification in Yoruba. *Linguistic Inquiry* **19**, 233–270.

Radhakrishnan, R. (1981) *The Nancowry Word: Phonology, Affixal Morphology and Roots of a Nicobarese Language.* Edmonton: Linguistic Research.

Rice, Curt (2003) Syllabic well-formedness in Norwegian imperatives. *Nordlyd* **31**, 372–384. [Available on Rutgers Optimality Archive, ROA-642.]

Rice, Curt (2005) Optimal gaps in optimal paradigms. *Catalan Journal of Linguistics* **4**, 155–170. [Available at LingBuzz, http://ling.auf.net/buzzdocs/.]

Rice, Curt (ed.) (forthcoming) *Modeling Ungrammaticality in Optimality Theory*. London: Equinox Publishing.

Roca, Iggy (ed.) (1997) *Derivations and Constraints in Phonology*. Oxford: Oxford University Press.

Rosenthall, Sam (1994) Vowel/Glide Alternation in a Theory of Constraint Interaction. Doctoral dissertation. University of Massachusetts Amherst, Amherst, MA. [Available on Rutgers Optimality Archive, ROA-126.]

Rubach, Jerzy (1993) *The Lexical Phonology of Slovak*. Oxford: Oxford University Press.

Rubach, Jerzy (1997) Extrasyllabic consonants in Polish: Derivational Optimality Theory. In: Iggy Roca (ed.) *Derivations and Constraints in Phonology*. Oxford: Oxford University Press, pp. 551–582.

Rubach, Jerzy (2000) Glide and glottal stop insertion in Slavic languages: A DOT analysis. *Linguistic Inquiry* **31**, 271–317.

Salzmann, Zdenek (2001) Book notice on *The Emergence of the Speech Capacity* by D. Kimbrough Oller. *Language* **77**, 604–605.

Samek-Lodovici, Vieri (1992) Universal constraints and morphological gemination: A crosslinguistic study. Unpublished manuscript. Brandeis University, Waltham, MA.

Samek-Lodovici, Vieri and Prince, Alan (1999) Optima. Unpublished manuscript. University of London and Rutgers University, London and New Brunswick, NJ. [Available on Rutgers Optimality Archive, ROA-363.]

Sapir, Edward (1921) *Language*. New York: Harcourt, Brace & World.

Sapir, J. David (1965) *A Grammar of Diola-Fogny*. Cambridge: Cambridge University Press.

Schaefer, Ronald P. (1987) *An Initial Orthography and Lexicon for Emai*. Bloomington, IN: Indiana University Linguistics Club Publications.

Schane, Sanford and Bendixen, Birgitte (1978) *Workbook in Generative Phonology*. Englewood Cliffs, NJ: Prentice-Hall.

Selkirk, Elisabeth (1980) Prosodic domains in phonology: Sanskrit revisited. In: Mark Aronoff and Mary-Louise Kean (eds.) *Juncture*. Saratoga, CA: Anma Libri, pp. 107–129.

Selkirk, Elisabeth (1981) Epenthesis and degenerate syllables in Cairene Arabic. In: Hagit Borer and Joseph Aoun (eds.) *Theoretical Issues in the Grammar of the Semitic Languages (MIT Working Papers in Linguistics 3)*. Cambridge, MA: Department of Linguistics and Philosophy, MIT, pp. 111–140.

Selkirk, Elisabeth (1995) The prosodic structure of function words. In: Jill Beckman, Laura Walsh Dickey, and Suzanne Urbanczyk (eds.) *University of Massachusetts Occasional Papers in Linguistics 18: Papers in Optimality Theory*. Amherst, MA: GLSA Publications, pp. 439–470.

Sells, Peter, Bresnan, Joan, Butt, Miriam, and King, Tracy Holloway (2001) *Formal and Empirical Issues in Optimality Theoretic Syntax*. Stanford, CA: CSLI Publications.

Sherer, Tim (1994) Prosodic Phonotactics. Doctoral dissertation. University of Massachusetts Amherst, Amherst, MA.

Silverstein, Michael (1976) Hierarchy of features and ergativity. In: Robert M. W. Dixon (ed.) *Grammatical Categories in Australian Languages*. Canberra: Australian Institute of Aboriginal Studies, pp. 112–171.

Smith, Jennifer L. (2006) Loan phonology is not all perception: Evidence from Japanese loan doublets. In: Timothy J. Vance and Kimberly A. Jones (eds.) *Japanese/Korean Linguistics 14*. Stanford, CA: CSLI Publications, pp. 63–74.

Smolensky, Paul (1995) On the structure of the constraint component Con of UG. Handout of talk presented at UCLA, Los Angeles, CA. [Available on Rutgers Optimality Archive, ROA-86.]

Smolensky, Paul (1997) Constraint interaction in generative grammar II: Local conjunction, or random rules in Universal Grammar. Handout from Hopkins Optimality Theory Workshop/Maryland Mayfest '97, Baltimore, MD.

Smolensky, Paul (2006) Optimality in phonology II: Harmonic completeness, local constraint conjunction, and feature-domain markedness. In: Paul Smolensky and Géraldine Legendre (eds.) *The Harmonic Mind: From Neural Computation to Optimality-Theoretic Grammar, Volume 2*. Cambridge, MA: MIT Press/Bradford Books, pp. 27–160.

Smolensky, Paul and Legendre, Géraldine (2006) *The Harmonic Mind: From Neural Computation to Optimality-Theoretic Grammar*. Cambridge, MA: MIT Press/Bradford Books.

Smolensky, Paul, Legendre, Géraldine, and Tesar, Bruce (2006) Optimality Theory: The structure, use, and acquisition of grammatical knowledge. In: Paul Smolensky and Géraldine Legendre (eds.) *The Harmonic Mind: From Neural Computation to Optimality-Theoretic Grammar, Volume 1: Cognitive Architecture*. Cambridge, MA: MIT Press/Bradford Books, pp. 453–535.

Spencer, Andrew (1993) The optimal way to syllabify Chukchee. Handout from Rutgers Optimality Workshop I, Rutgers University, New Brunswick, NJ.

Stampe, David (1973) A Dissertation on Natural Phonology. Doctoral dissertation. University of Chicago, Chicago. [Published 1979, New York: Garland.]

Stemberger, Joseph P. and Bernhardt, Barbara H. (1999) Contiguity, metathesis, and infixation. In: Kimary N. Shahin, Susan J. Blake, and Eun-Sook Kim (eds.) *The Proceedings of the West Coast Conference on Formal Linguistics 17*. Stanford, CA: CSLI Publications, pp. 610–624.

Steriade, Donca (1997) Lexical conservatism and its analysis. Unpublished manuscript. UCLA, Los Angeles. [Available at www.linguistics.ucla.edu/people/steriade/papers/Korea_lexical_conservatism.pdf.]

Steriade, Donca (1999) Lexical conservatism in French adjectival liaison. In: J.-Marc Authier, Barbara Bullock, and Lisa Reid (eds.) *Formal Perspectives on Romance Linguistics*. Amsterdam: John Benjamins, pp. 243–270.

Steriade, Donca (2000) Paradigm uniformity and the phonetics-phonology boundary. In: Janet Pierrehumbert and Michael Broe (eds.) *Acquisition and the Lexicon* (Papers in Laboratory Phonology 5). Cambridge: Cambridge University Press, pp. 313–334.

Steriade, Donca (2001a) Directional asymmetries in place assimilation. In: Elizabeth Hume and Keith Johnson (eds.) *The Role of Speech Perception in Phonology*. San Diego: Academic Press, pp. 219–250. [Available at www.linguistics.ucla.edu/people/steriade/papers/ICPHS2000.pdf.]

Steriade, Donca (2001b) The phonology of perceptibility effects: The P-map and its consequences for constraint organization. Unpublished manuscript. UCLA, Los Angeles. [Available at www.linguistics.ucla.edu/people/steriade/papers/P-map_for_phonology.doc.]

Stevens, Alan M. (1968) *Madurese Phonology and Morphology* (American Oriental Series 52). New Haven, CT: American Oriental Society.

Struijke, Caroline (1998) Reduplicant and output TETU in Kwakwala. In: Haruka Fukazawa, Frida Morelli, Caroline Struijke, and Yi-ching Su (eds.) *University of Maryland Working Papers, vol. 7 (Papers in Phonology)*. College Park, MD: Department of Linguistics, University of Maryland, pp. 150–178. [Available on Rutgers Optimality Archive, ROA-261.]

Suzuki, Keiichiro (1998) A Typological Investigation of Dissimilation. Doctoral dissertation. University of Arizona, Tucson, AZ. [Available on Rutgers Optimality Archive, ROA-281.]

Tesar, Bruce, Grimshaw, Jane, and Prince, Alan (1999) Linguistic and cognitive explanation in Optimality Theory. In: Ernest Lepore and Zenon Pylyshyn (eds.) *What is Cognitive Science?* Oxford: Blackwell, pp. 295–326.

Tesar, Bruce and Smolensky, Paul (1998) Learnability in Optimality Theory. *Linguistic Inquiry* **29**, 229–268. [Available on Rutgers Optimality Archive, ROA-155. Reprinted in John J. McCarthy (ed.) *Optimality Theory in Phonology: A Reader*, Malden, MA, & Oxford: Blackwell (2004).]

Tesar, Bruce and Smolensky, Paul (2000) *Learnability in Optimality Theory*. Cambridge, MA: MIT Press.

Tessier, Anne-Michelle (2006) Biases and Stages in OT Phonological Acquisition. Doctoral dissertation. University of Massachusetts Amherst, Amherst, MA.

Truckenbrodt, Hubert (1995) Phonological Phrases: Their Relation to Syntax, Focus, and Prominence. Doctoral dissertation. Massachusetts Institute of Technology.

Urbanczyk, Suzanne (2006) Reduplicative form and the root-affix asymmetry. *Natural Language and Linguistic Theory* **24**, 179–240.

van Eijk, Jan P. (1997) *The Lillooet Language: Phonology, Morphology, and Syntax*. Vancouver, BC: University of British Columbia Press.

Vihman, Marilyn M. (1996) *Phonological Development*. Cambridge, MA & Oxford: Blackwell.

Voorhoeve, Clemens Lambertus (1965) *The Flamingo Bay Dialect of the Asmat Language.* The Hague: M. Nijhoff. [Verhandelingen van het Koninklijk Instituut voor Taal-, Land- en Volkenkunde, 46.]

Webb, Charlotte (1982) A constraint on progressive consonantal assimilation. *Linguistics* **20**, 309–321.

Weimer, Harry and Weimer, Natalia (1970) Reduplication in Yareba. *Papers in New Guinea Linguistics* **11**, 37–43.

Weimer, Harry and Weimer, Natalia (1975) A short sketch of Yareba Grammar. In: Tom E. Dutton (ed.) *Studies in Languages of Central and South-Eastern Papua.* Canberra: Australian National University. [Pacific Linguistics, Series C, no. 29.]

Whitney, William Dwight (1889) *A Sanskrit Grammar.* Cambridge, MA: Harvard University Press.

Wiese, Richard (2001) The structure of the German vocabulary: Edge marking of categories and functional considerations. *Linguistics* **39**, 95–115.

Wilson, Colin (2000) Targeted Constraints: An Approach to Contextual Neutralization in Optimality Theory. Doctoral dissertation. Johns Hopkins University, Baltimore, MD.

Wilson, Colin (2001) Consonant cluster neutralization and targeted constraints. *Phonology* **18**, 147–197.

Wilson, Colin (2003) Unbounded spreading in OT (or, Unbounded spreading is local spreading iterated unboundedly). Handout from SWOT 8, Tucson, AZ.

Wilson, Colin (2004) Analyzing unbounded spreading with constraints: Marks, targets, and derivations. Unpublished manuscript. UCLA, Los Angeles.

Wilson, Colin (2006) Unbounded spreading is myopic. Handout of talk presented at Phonology Fest 2006, Bloomington, IN. [Available at www.linguistics.ucla.edu/people/wilson/Myopia2006.pdf.]

Wolf, Matthew and McCarthy, John J. (forthcoming) Less than zero: Correspondence and the null output. In: Curt Rice (ed.) *Modeling Ungrammaticality in Optimality Theory.* London: Equinox Publishing. [Earlier version available on Rutgers Optimality Archive, ROA-722.]

Wright, William (1971) *A Grammar of the Arabic Language.* Cambridge University Press, Cambridge. [Third edition revised by William Robertson Smith and Michael Jan de Goeje, originally published 1896.]

Yip, Moira (2002) *Tone.* Cambridge Cambridge: University Press.

Zagona, Karen (1982) Government and Proper Government of Verbal Projections. Doctoral dissertation. University of Washington, Seattle.

Constraint Index

Constraints that appear only in the classified list of phonological markedness constraints (pp. 224–9) are not included in this index. Warning: Some of the constraints listed below are ad hoc or even illegitimate (e.g., No-Onset). Therefore, do not use any of them in an analysis without first consulting the text.

Language Index

Subject Index

Major discussion of a topic is indicated by boldface.

CPSIA information can be obtained
at www.ICGtesting.com
Printed in the USA
BVHW090028231218
535923BV00021BA/308/P

9 781405 151368